The Nature of HISTORY
in Ancient Greece and Rome

EIDOS | Studies in Classical Kinds

Thomas G. Rosenmeyer, General Editor

THE NATURE OF
HISTORY
IN ANCIENT
GREECE AND ROME

CHARLES WILLIAM FORNARA

University of California Press

Berkeley • Los Angeles • London

University of California Press
Berkeley and Los Angeles, California
University of California Press, Ltd.
London, England
© 1983 by
The Regents of the University of California

Library of Congress Cataloging in Publication Data

Fornara, Charles W.
    The nature of history in ancient Greece and Rome.

    (Eidos)
    Includes index.
    1. Greece—Historiography.   2. Rome—Historiography.
3. Historiography—Greece.   4. Historiography—Rome.
I. Title.   II. Series: Eidos (University of California
Press)
DE8.F67   1983   949.5'0072   82-21888
ISBN 0-520-04910-1

Printed in the United States of America

1 2 3 4 5 6 7 8 9

For Michael Putnam

Contents

Preface

This book has had a long history, not least because it proved difficult to reconcile the discussion of necessarily recondite material and abstruse theoretics with the requirement of the University of California Press that the work be intelligible to the general reader. Primarily, the problem arose because I felt the need to write an analytical study of ancient historiography, not a set of essays based on well-known historians. The continuous development of historical writing over the course of seven hundred years is *not* illustrated by the works of Herodotus, Thucydides, Polybius, Sallust, Livy, and Tacitus; important innovations (for good or ill) were made by other writers who were not the less significant because their works have not survived and they are obscure to us. Secondly, a host of scholars have explored, from one vantage point or another, every aspect of this development, leading to the warm debate of almost all subjects treated here.

My first attempts to take into account this massive secondary literature led to manuscripts that only a specialist, if even he, would have considered "readable." Under the firm but gentle suasion of the editor of this series, Professor Thomas Rosenmeyer, I therefore pruned and revised successive versions. The abundance of citations remaining will nevertheless permit the reader to test the conclusions presented.

From what has been said, it seems superfluous to add that this volume is not a "handbook" providing a quick rundown of major or minor figures. The reader will therefore not be surprised at the absence of brief biographical sketches. What really matters, in any case, are the *dates* of the figures under discussion, and this has been provided. For the chronology is vital if we are to determine the relative order (and likely nexus) of progressive developments in historiographical technique and theory. Further information can easily be gained from either edition of the *Oxford Classical Dictionary* or, for readers of German, the much superior *Kleine Pauly*. Both works provide sound basic bibliographies, often supplementing the material cited by me, for my own citation of authorities is limited to those works I regard as fundamental. Here I depart from the current trend, where the modernity of the scholarship or the pseudo-scientific impulse towards systematic and indiscriminate citation are the ruling criteria governing bibliographical reference. Beyond the works mentioned, readers of German will discover that Felix Jacoby's commentary in *Die Fragmente der griechischen Historiker* (= *FGrHist*) to author numbers 1–607 is absolutely indispensable. (His commentary to numbers 323ᵃ–334, on the Athenian local historians, is written in English.)

Having mentioned Jacoby, I cannot begin the enumeration of my debts except by giving this unrivaled scholar pride of place. Jacoby's works have been my constant companion for over twenty years. However I may have misapplied his learning and method, I have tried to train myself and learn about historiography from their close and repeated study. That it is apparently fashionable to ignore his work today is not an auspicious sign of the direction present and future studies will take, and it is heart-breaking to see a falling away from the method he established with such painstaking care, knowledge, and skill. Naturally, Jacoby is often mentioned in this book, primarily, I am sorry to say, in polemic. But an honest confrontation with his views, surely, is precisely what he would have wished. In any case, it was necessary: no fresh work can be undertaken in this field unless one stands on Jacoby's shoulders.

My more immediate obligations are to good friends. Professor W. F. Wyatt, Jr., my colleague at Brown, read an early version of this book with a gimlet eye; that he put aside his own work to devote his careful and critical attention to mine is typical of his generous nature. Thomas Rosenmeyer, the editor of this series, has been as kindly and helpful as he has been firm. His was a difficult task; that he accomplished it with the augmentation of my respect and friendship gives a fair measure of his humane sense of responsibility. To Mrs. Frances Eisenhauer I owe deep thanks for the kindly, willing, and motivated assistance she provided by typing more than one version of the manuscript. Her help came at critical points, when I badly needed the respite. Mrs. Ruth-Ann Whitten, the secretary of the Department of Classics at Brown, though she had no direct involvement with the manuscript, also deserves my warm thanks and gratitude for the countless instances in which she smoothed day-to-day difficulties connected with administrative and teaching duties, making it all the easier for me to devote myself tranquilly to my writing and teaching. Finally, I would also like to express my appreciation for the unfailingly courteous and deft assistance of the readers and staff of the University of California Press.

Abbreviations

AHR	*American Historical Review*
BICS	*Bulletin of the Institute of Classical Studies*
CP	*Classical Philology*
CQ	*Classical Quarterly*
FGrHist	F. Jacoby, *Die Fragmente der griechischen Historiker* (Berlin and Leiden, 1923–)
Gomme, HCT	A. W. Gomme, A. Andrewes, and K. J. Dover, *A Historical Commentary on Thucydides*, 4 vols. (Oxford, 1945–81)
HistZeit	*Historische Zeitschrift*
JHS	*Journal of Hellenic Studies*
JRS	*Journal of Roman Studies*
Kleine Pauly	*Der Kleine Pauly, Lexicon der Antike*, edited by K. Ziegler and W. Sontheimer (Munich, 1975–79)
Peter, or HRR	Hermannus Peter, *Historicorum Romanorum Reliquiae*, 2 vols. (Stuttgart, 1906)
RE	Pauly's *Real-Encyclopädie der klassischen Altertumswissenschaft*

Walbank,   F. W. Walbank, *A Historical Commentary on*
Commen-   *Polybius*, 3 vols. (Oxford, 1957–79)
tary

Bold italics appearing in quoted material indicate the author's emphasis.

I

History and Related Genres

When we speak of the "historical writing" of the Greeks and Latins, we refer in a general and imprecise way to a variety of works principally devoted to the establishment or the preservation of some part of the record of the past. On closer inspection, this literature proves to divide into a small number of distinct genres, each with its own rules, often unstated conventions, and particular focus.[1] Five basic types of historical writing (here listed in their probable order of development) can be isolated: genealogy or mythography, ethnography, history, horography or local history, and chronography. *Genealogy* records heroic tradition and seeks to bring coherence to the sometimes contradictory data of legend, myth, and aetiology. *Ethnography* attempts the description of foreign lands and peoples; the focus is large, the aim to present a general picture of a people's mode of life within the setting of its natural and historical environment. *History*, as the ancients elementally defined it, provides the description of men's "deeds," or *praxeis* (Aristotle *Rhet.* 1. 1360A35); it is

---

[1] The fundamental discussion remains that of Felix Jacoby, "Über die Entwicklung der griechischen Historiographie . . . ," in *Abhandlungen zur griechischen Geschichtsschreibung*, ed. H. Bloch (Leiden, 1956), pp. 16–64 (= *Klio* 9 [1909], 8–123). My profound admiration of that magisterial study is in no way diminished by the inevitable disagreements.

the *expositio rerum gestarum*, "the narration of deeds" (Quintilian 2. 4. 2).[2] *Horography* sets down the year-by-year record of a city-state from the time of its foundation, while *chronography* provides a system of time-reckoning, international in scope, permitting the calibration of events taking place in different parts of the civilized world. All five genres had come into existence by the end of the fifth century B.C. and generally retained their formal integrity thereafter. For although numerous instances can be found where the kind of writing peculiar to any one of these genres appears in a work of another type, such mutual influence provided variety and richness without destroying the inherent logic and structure of the debtor genre.

The types of historical writing identified here conform in definition and nomenclature to ancient conceptions (although a certain imprecision of language can be found in every era) and these categories have therefore not unnaturally been accepted as fundamental by modern scholars—with one all-important exception. Felix Jacoby was unwilling to grant to the ancients the practice of "history" as a genre, and he substituted in place of "history" the term *Zeitgeschichte*, "contemporary history."[3] Consequently, all five genres became forms of "historical writing," but no one of them was "history" itself.[4] Jacoby's decision was undoubtedly based on the conviction that "history" (as the moderns defined it) never properly developed as a genre in Greco-Roman antiquity. It "did not exist in the ancient world" as "an independent science" "specifically devoted to the investigation and the description of historical events of the far or near past."[5] But although the ancients would have agreed that history was not a science,[6] this is not a valid reason to deprive them of the genre they named history and regarded as the quintessential historical form.

---

[2] See P. Scheller, *De hellenistica historiae conscribendae arte* (Diss., Leipzig, 1911), pp. 9f., and chapter 3 below.

[3] Jacoby, "Über die Entwicklung," pp. 34ff.

[4] On this view, therefore, ethnography and *Zeitgeschichte* were equally "historical" genres. But ethnography is no more a different kind of "historical writing" than it is a different kind of geography, another close relative. See Jacoby, "Über die Entwicklung," p. 27, and M. Ninck, *Die Entdeckung von Europa durch die Griechen* (Basel, 1945), p. 34. The difference in orientation was well emphasized by Ed. Schwartz, "Über das Verhältnis der Hellenen zur Geschichte," *Logos* 9 (1920), reprinted in *Gesammelte Schriften* (Berlin, 1938), vol. 1, pp. 58f.

[5] Jacoby, "Über die Entwicklung," p. 20. Here he followed U. von Wilamowitz-Moellendorff, *Greek Historical Writing* (Oxford, 1908), p. 15.

[6] They classified history as a branch of rhetoric: see, e.g., Cicero *De orat.* 2. 62, 3. 211, Sextus Empiricus *Adv. gramm.* 268 Mau, Marcellinus *Vita Thuc.* 41. Cf. Wilamo-

It is something more than interesting to observe how Jacoby's reluctance to confer this accolade placed him between the horns of a dilemma. Is it really the case that the only historical writing of the ancients (we exclude biography because it is an ethical, not historical, form) was mythography, ethnography, horography, chronography, and *contemporary* history? However much Jacoby sought to minimize the difficulty by defining as writers of *Zeitgeschichte* "all authors who, without restricting themselves to localities [the horographers], portrayed the history of the community of the Hellenes in their own times or [from some earlier point] down to their own times,"[7] the term is inapplicable to the greater number of Greco-Roman historians. For although on the strength of this definition Jacoby could maintain that the authors of monographs, universal histories, Greek histories (*Hellenica*), and other works were united as writers of *Zeitgeschichte*, the truth of the matter is that the presence of contemporary history in their works defines them less essentially than their common subject, purpose, and methodology. That is why the term "history" was adopted by the ancients (when they were not speaking loosely, just as we do when we speak of "historical writing") to describe works of precisely these categories: monographs, contemporary histories, universal histories, and so on.[8] The defining quality shared by all of them was their direct concern with the description of *res gestae*, man's actions in politics, diplomacy, and war, in the far and near past.

The ancients must therefore be conceded their practice of history as a theoretically independent endeavor, science or no. For them it became the form of historical writing par excellence, though the other genres were naturally honored as well. To discover their nature and to learn how they relate to one another, let us consider each in

witz, *Greek Historical Writing*, p. 16. Nineteenth-century scientism prompted some very peculiar judgments. The basis for the ancient view can be inferred from *De orat.* 2. 145.

[7] Jacoby, "Über die Entwicklung," p. 34.

[8] The fact was recognized by Jacoby, "Über die Entwicklung," p. 34. The ancient nomenclature was very imprecise; a "historian" or "historiographer" can be any non-fiction prose writer, grammarians included, who dealt with some aspect (dates, individuals, places, deeds) of human and heroic activity in past time. But history itself, it must be emphasized, retained its quite specific definition as the *expositio rerum gestarum* or "description of the deeds of men" ("great events and struggles," says Plutarch in *Alex.* 1. 3). The contradiction arises naturally from the inherent ambiguity (modern as well as ancient) of the adjective "historical."

turn, remembering always that all these literary forms developed within the same creative matrix within a comparatively short span of time.

Genealogy

Genealogy, the study of the family relationships of the heroes of mythical times, is a clear-cut *genos* in form, substance, and style. The nature of the subject makes it plausible that the genre was the earliest form of literary prose attempted by the Greeks. Signs of heroic genealogy are already present in Homer (*Od.* 11. 235ff.), but it is Hesiod in the *Theogony* who epitomizes the impulse to bring order to the genealogical confusion that must have confounded poets and audience alike. It is therefore a straightforward development that a number of writers who flourished in the early fifth century or shortly before—as soon as prose replaced poetry for expository discourse— continued Hesiod's work of recording heroic tradition (and cosmogonical theory).[9] The affiliation was recognized in antiquity. Clement of Alexandria (ca. 200 A.D.) charged (*FGrHist* 2 T 5) that "Eumelus [of Corinth] and Acusilaus [of Argos], the historiographers, turned Hesiod's poetry into prose and published it as if it were their own." The process was understood more correctly by Josephus, the Jewish historian of the first century A.D., who wrote (*FGrHist* 2 T 6) that Hellanicus of Lesbos had *corrected* Acusilaus in the same way that Acusilaus had *corrected* Hesiod. Of this fragments 5–6 of Acusilaus give good examples.

Acusilaus's work embraced cosmogony, theogony, and genealogy. Comparable work was undertaken ca. 450 by Pherecydes of Athens (*FGrHist* 3). We may infer that a number of sages dispersed throughout Hellas, in Ionia as well as in Greece, particularly in locations (like Argos and Athens) redolent of heroic myth, wrote down local saga and attempted to incorporate it into the larger body of the mythic history of the Greeks. In this context, Hecataeus of Miletus (ca. 500) proved epoch-making. His *Genealogiai* were not only decisive in validating the genealogical tradition by establishing a satisfactory system of generational relationships, it was Hecataeus (apparently) who simultaneously dictated the limits of "mythical,"

[9] For a good general discussion, see H. Fränkel, *Early Greek Poetry and Philosophy* (Oxford, 1975), pp. 96ff.

"genealogical," and "historical" times. For it is a reasonable inference that Hecataeus drew a boundary between "heroic times" and "historical times"—the point at which the genealogical approach could be replaced by the exercise of historical memory. Hence the formulation of the *spatium historicum*, "the age of history."

To fathom Greek attitudes toward the preceding period, their Age of Heroes, one must begin with the recognition that the Greeks of Hecataeus's day, like those who followed, firmly believed that their heroic traditions preserved the memory of real individuals (e.g., Heracles) and actual events (the sacks of Thebes and Troy). By an irrefutable historical principle, Isocrates could assert (*Paneg.* 69) that "tradition" could not have recorded the events of the far past unless these deeds were mighty enough to withstand the assault of Time; their historicity followed a fortiori. All the ancients conceded the principle: something does not come out of nothing; Troy must have fallen because the Poet remembered it. But the Greeks were equally aware that their tradition was burdened with flagrant violations of probability, or worse. Hecataeus became the authoritative writer in the field by dealing with this question satisfactorily.

Unfortunately, the opening words of the preface of Hecataeus's *Genealogiai* (*FGrHist* 1 F 1) do not make his position entirely clear. Hecataeus here ridicules the accounts, the *logoi*, of others because they are contradictory and absurd.[10] His exact words are that "the tales of the Greeks are many and absurd." The usual interpretation[11] holds that Hecataeus proposed rational explanations of the miracles and other absurdities disfiguring the saga. He intended, in other words, to reduce the world of myth to the prosaic world of history. Certainly, Hecataeus's denunciation of the *logoi* as absurd favors this view. What does not, however, is the incontestable presence of fabulous elements in his own work, e.g., a vine springing from the blood of a dog (F 15) and a talking ram (F 17). It would be arbitrary to deprive Hecataeus of the responsibility for these tales—as if, for example, he were reporting a story to which he himself took excep-

---

[10]"Contradictory" or "diverse" is the proper explication of the word *polloi* ("the accounts [*logoi*] are *many* and absurd"). Hecataeus seems primarily to object to a variety of different accounts of the same subjects. So also G. Nenci, *Hecataei Milesii fragmenta* (Florence, 1954), p. xxv.

[11]E.g., J. B. Bury, *The Ancient Greek Historians* (New York, 1909), pp. 13ff., K. von Fritz, *Die Griechische Geschichtsschreibung* (Berlin, 1967), vol. 1, p. 71. Nenci (n. 10) takes the view that Hecataeus wished to unify, not rationalize, the traditions.

tion. It would also be improper to smooth over the difficulty by assuming that Hecataeus was some sort of embryonic rationalist incapable of consistency, the possessor of an "Ionian rationalistic spirit" insufficiently developed to be applied with rigor. The principle of immutable regularity, once grasped, is readily and universally applicable, and if it were Hecataeus's intent to rationalize heroic times he must have operated with consistency.

It follows that Hecataeus was not *primarily* concerned to ridicule and correct the fabulous, but was seeking to obviate some other "absurdity." His reference to the plurality as well as the absurdity of mythical accounts therefore deserves attention. The preface may be explained as a criticism of the inconsequence of the genealogical tradition in the strict sense of the word. There existed a profusion of imputed relationships making a mockery of the real genealogical possibilities. Genealogies were askew and mutually contradictory. A given *Stammvater*, for example, would have been credited with children and grandchildren coexisting in mutually exclusive generations, and relationships would have been formed simultaneously in far-flung parts of Greece. We may assume, therefore, that traditions given out in various parts of Hellas were based on mutually incompatible combinations. Hecataeus regarded it necessary to correct this confusion on the "scientific" basis of generational chronology, the ostensible purpose of a book entitled *Genealogies* (though its name is sometimes given as *Historiai*, "Investigations"). Thus, although it was certainly a part of Hecataeus's intent to set forth the details of the heroic tradition in order to clarify family relationships, the main piece of business was the genealogies themselves.

Hecataeus viewed the world ambivalently, for his presentation of an account at once fabulous and rationalized implies an essentially conservative skepticism. We may assume that he was content to report purely mythical elements of the heroic tradition when no palmary explanation of the distortion occurred to him. What would not be mended, he refused to tear down. On the other hand, to this laudable but agnostic reverence for tradition, Hecataeus united faith in the soundness of the chronological system based on that very tradition: genealogical data and the chronological information it provided were securely based and verifiable even though the traditions informing these relationships were in some degree contaminated by myth and their exact measure of truth was conjectural. Now what it is important to note here is that Hecataeus must therefore, explicitly or implicitly, have set a terminus, a boundary line, between heroic and historical times. He must have believed that at some point the quality of tradition altered from the conjectural to the knowable, from the mythical to the prosaic. In Hecataeus, in other words, the concept of a dividing line separating the heroic age from the *spatium historicum* was either latent or explicit.

In either case, the concept was already taken for granted by the historical writers of the fifth century. Herodotus's insistence on the separation of the age of myth from the age of history is well known. Thus, in 3. 122, he emphatically asserts that "Polycrates is the first Hellene of whom we know who conceived the idea of controlling the sea—except Minos . . . and whoever else there may have been before him who ruled the sea. But Polycrates was the first of the so-called human generation." Herodotus's reluctance to connect "heroic history" with the activities of the "human generation," where "knowledge" is possible, first appears in the programmatic statement of 1. 5, where he was simply content to stress the problematical nature of the various reports attaching guilt to Asians or Europeans of heroic times: "But I am not going to say about these matters that they took place either this way or in some other way; [I will begin with] the man whom I myself *know* to have been the first to begin unjust actions against the Hellenes."

Curiously, Jacoby held that Herodotus expressed "an unconscious and very weak feeling that historical recollections and epic traditions are incommensurable quantities." [12] In fact, Herodotus's statements are self-confident; if anything, they reflect a conventional and accepted polarity. He is explicit and definite—"human generation," "men of whom we know" [13]—and the assumption is untenable that he would have announced peremptorily so important a theoretical and methodological decision (the exclusion of heroic antecedents) at the beginning of his work unless he knew that it was in principle acceptable to the public. If Hecataeus had taken another view or if Herodotus were a pioneer, polemic and self-defense would have been mandatory. The heroic antecedents of the conflict between East and West figured too large in the consciousness of the Hellenes,

[12] Jacoby, "Über die Entwicklung," p. 37 n. 63.
[13] Hippias of Elis, the late fifth-century sophist, drew the same dichotomy in Plato *Hippias Major* 285D.

educated as they were by Homer, to have been ignored in this fashion. In short, Herodotus's alleged "unconscious feeling" derived
from the implications (at least) of Hecataeus's genealogical work.

Thucydides sheds little light on the question. His discussion of
the House of Atreus (1. 9) merely confirms that the genealogical relationships of the heroic families had been set in order by Hecataeus
and his successors and were regarded as solidly based in the main.
The *tradition* about heroic events Thucydides seems to have regarded
in the same light as Hecataeus and Herodotus: the material was susceptible to rationalistic explanation, but "likelihood" was the best
criterion available for assessing even the latest and best-attested
events of heroic times. It should be admitted, however, that Thucydides' objections to Homer's account of the Trojan War seem primarily based on the fact that Homer was a poet and, as such, prone
to exaggerate the truth (1. 10. 3; cf. Pindar *Ol*. 1. 29). In other
words, the main problem for Thucydides apparently did not arise
from the heroic date of the war. But Hecataeus and those who followed probably concluded willingly enough that events closest to the
spatium historicum became reliable proportionately.

Plato's terminology in *Timaeus* 22A, if it can be trusted, helps us
to see more clearly how the Greeks may have conceptualized their
distant past. Solon of Athens is presented in this dialogue as lec-
turing the Saites of Egypt about the earliest Greek times. Having
commenced with the Greeks' most ancient figures, Phoroneus and
Niobe, he passes to the time of the Flood and then gives an account
of the myths (*mythologein*) of Deucalion and Pyrrha. After that he
relates the genealogies (*genealogein*) of their descendants. The inference seems solid that these were now the standard terms, accurately applied. Since these definitions of narrative method are also
evaluations of content, Plato-Solon appears to have categorized the
levels of knowledge appropriate to prehistorical times. One "re-
counts the myths" of Deucalion's era and "supplies the genealogies"
of subsequent generations. It would be inappropriate to speak of the
"history" of either period.

By the late fourth century, if not before, the exact date of the
opening of the "historical age" was fixed and apparently uncon-
troversial. For Ephorus of Cyme (*FGrHist* 70), perhaps the most authoritative and certainly the most conventionally minded historian
of the fourth century, undoubtedly followed the guidelines of an es-

tablished tradition when he began his Universal History with the Return of the Heracleidae (the Greek equivalent of the Dorian conquest, which they dated to 1069 B.C.). It cannot be coincidence that Hellanicus of Lesbos, a strong influence on Ephorus,[14] had terminated his many mythographical works precisely at this point. The date, which may already have been conventional in Herodotus's time (9. 26), remained epochal thereafter.[15]

Thus the belief crystallized that the heroic tradition was authentic, in the sense that the great heroes were real figures and their deeds actually accomplished, but the details were contaminated by myth. Time had obfuscated a tradition also distorted by the exaggeration of poets and the accretion of dubious allegations. As Ephorus wrote even of historical times (*FGrHist* 70 F 9),

> We consider most trustworthy those who give most detail about contemporary events. But we believe that those who write in this fashion about ancient events are completely unpersuasive. We postulate that it is not probable that all of the deeds or the greater part of the speeches were kept in [exact] memory for so great a span of time.

The mythical period was not, of course, thereby expelled from the Greek historical universe. No law went forth that mythical stories about the prehistorical Greeks could not be told; it was inevitable that historians, e.g., Thucydides and Ephorus,[16] would occasionally backtrack. Some writers like the late-fourth-century rhetorical historians Zoilus and Anaximenes (*FGrHist* 71–72) found the prospect of describing heroic times an irresistible occasion for oratorical display; others such as the first-century writer Diodorus Siculus not illogically concluded that a universal history of the known world should contain the earliest traditions of civilized peoples. It does not follow that any of these writers confounded the mythical and historical record in principle, although the desire to believe must fre-

---

[14] See Jacoby, *RE* s.v. "Hellanikos," cols. 149ff.

[15] Cf. P. Pédech, *Polybe Histoires XII* (Paris, 1961), p. 18 n. 1. Varro, the great Roman scholar of Cicero's time, made 776 the epochal date (F 3 Peter); he perhaps desired to make the beginning of the *spatium historicum* coincide as closely as possible with the foundation of Rome. From his perspective (totally different from that of fifth-century Greeks) 776 (when the system of Olympiad dating began) will also have seemed an intrinsically sensible dividing-line.

[16] Thuc. 2. 29. 3, 102. 5–6; Ephorus, *FGrHist* 70 F 31.

quently have secured the result. In the absence of any criterion but the general and rather useless skepticism of the historiographical confraternity, individual writers assessed the intrinsic properties of particular episodes for themselves.

Nor was rhetorical theory, which dealt with this subject in the larger context of the classification of types of material, of the slightest assistance. Rhetorical theory divided stories (*diegemata, fabulae*) into the "mythical," the "historical," and the "lifelike." These theoreticians were not, however, interested in the actual veracity even of the "historical" story. Quite simply, a story was "mythical" if it was "contrary to nature," while a "historical" narrative possessed verisimilitude and concerned actual events and people (including heroes recognized by the literary tradition).[17] Some grammarians, however, whose business it was to expound literary texts, and who accordingly assumed the burden of historical exegesis as well as higher criticism and semantic and dialectical analysis,[18] apparently claimed the ability to discriminate truth from falsity and fictions (*plasmata*) whatever the period of the stories. Thus Asclepiades of Myrlea, a grammarian of the first century B.C. and the author of a treatise on the *Art* or *Science of Grammar*, held (if I understand him aright)[19] that material relating to gods, heroes, and famous men, to chronology and places, and (thirdly) to deeds, was susceptible of verification. The only category of falsity recognized by Asclepiades was the "genealogical story"—here apparently the metamorphosis of

---

[17] For the details see E. Barwick, "Die Gliederung der narratio in der rhetorischen Theorie . . . ," *Hermes* 63 (1928): 261–87, and O. Schlissel von Fleschenberg, "Die Einteilung der HISTORIA bei Asklepiades Myrleianus," *Hermes* 48 (1913): 623–28.

[18] According to Dionysius of Thrace *On Grammar* 1 (*Grammatici Graeci* 1. 1, pp. 5f.), "the ready explication of stories (*historiai*)" comprised one of the six parts of *grammatike empeiria*, the "practice of the grammarian." Cf. Sextus Empiricus *Adv. gramm.* 43 Mau.

[19] By the law that renders ancient writers, especially theoreticians, vulnerable to analysis in inverse proportion to our knowledge of their opinions and their apparent influence on the intellectual history of antiquity, Asclepiades has been much discussed. The recent literature is cited by F. W. Walbank, *A Historical Commentary on Polybius* (Oxford, 1979), vol. 3, pp. 584f. The fact that Asclepiades was a grammarian is generally ignored even though it must bear vitally on the interpretation of his views. Apparently he wished to elevate the grammatical "practice" of Dionysius of Thrace to the level of science (*techne*). To that end, he proposed to explain why stories (*historiai*) about events in historical and mythical times were true or false. He was not attempting to establish criteria for the historian.

creatures from one kind into another.[20] How the theory worked is unknown; Asclepiades was apparently discreet enough to avoid promulgating specific criteria (*Adv. gramm.* 267 Mau), and it is entirely possible that the determination of "truth" and "falsity" rested on nothing more than the application of general probability. In any case, it is clear that neither rhetoric nor grammar functioned as an ancilla to history or as a guide to the historicity of the events of the heroic age.

Meanwhile, in contrast to the details, the genealogical framework, once validated by Hecataeus, was judged to be unassailably secure. On the basis of this generational chronology, the Greeks proceeded to connect systematically to themselves the prehistory of the barbarian nations lying on the ever-receding periphery of the outside world.[21] Rome is an obvious case in point. Consistent with their inventive explanations for the establishment of the other important communities in barbarian Italy, the Greeks assimilated Roman origins into their generational chronology by providing Trojan founders and "scientific" dates. It could for example confidently be inferred that the destroyer of Cacus (Livy 1. 7. 3ff.) was Heracles. The obvious chronological implications were duly registered, as was the date of Aeneas's arrival in Italy. The Romans were thus denied the pleasure or the labor of reconstructing their own prehistory; the only real question left for them was to determine the proper generational interval between Aeneas and Romulus. After that, it was merely a matter of supplementing the jejune record of admittedly historical times.

Although the importance of the work in genealogy initiated by Hecataeus[22] can hardly be overestimated, in one respect it may have

[20]The term "genealogical story" is a well-known crux. My interpretation derives from Sextus's running commentary on Asclepiades (*Adv. gramm.* 264 Mau). It is possible that he also had in mind the children of the gods: see Cicero *ND* 3. 60 with A. S. Pease. Observe that the *genealogike historia* of Asclepiades bears no relation to the genre of genealogy, in spite of the phraseology. For all but one of Asclepiades' categories of "true stories" were essential components of genealogy as it was generally understood (Polyb. 9.1. 3f.).

[21]B. Niese, "Die Sagen von der Gründung Roms," *HistZeit* 59, n.s. 23 (1888): 485; and E. Bickerman, "Origines Gentium," *CP* 47 (1952): 65–81.

[22]No implication is intended that Hecataeus was the first of the genealogists. No sound basis exists for dating Acusilaus and others of the first generation of prose writers. In any case, Hecataeus's introductory remark presupposes the existence of ge-

been exaggerated. Nothing in the nature of genealogy suggests that Jacoby was correct in declaring the work seminal of history as we know it from Herodotus.[23] The skepticism that limited Hecataeus to the adumbration of a genealogical chronology preserving the main lines of heroic tradition without seeking to historicize the legendary material, though it may well reflect a "critical historical spirit," hardly leads in inspiration or in method to the *expositio rerum gestarum*, the "setting-forth of deeds done." If anything, the influence of genealogy was salubriously negative: it helped to define the "historical age" by marking it off from heroic times in respect to its quality as well as its date. After Hecataeus, the work of collection and correction continued throughout the fifth century. The mine, however, was soon spent, and genealogy ended as a serious study with the works of Hellanicus and Damastes (*FGrHist* 5), ca. 400 B.C.

Ethnography

The ancient form of literature now described as ethnography possessed no specific categorical name in ancient times. The Greeks designated particular works of this class by an adjective naming the people and locality under discussion, e.g., *Lydiaka, Babyloniaka, Romaika*. This genre, unlike genealogy, enjoyed a full life extending from the early fifth century to the late Roman Empire.[24] The form was invigorated whenever the Greeks, and later the Romans, established contact with a new and independent foreign people. Early ethnography is marked by a scientific objectivity and unprejudiced characterization of alien modes of life that are a pleasure to behold.[25] It has been asserted that a precondition of such detachment was the relative amity of Greek and barbarian in Ionia until the time of Croesus.[26] But ethnography originated after Croesus's fall; as we know from Herodotus and the roughly contemporaneous author of

nealogical literature; he marks a new stage in its evolution, one of reflection and criticism.

[23] Jacoby, "Über die Entwicklung," pp. 22f., 34ff.

[24] See, in general, K. Trüdinger, *Studien zur Geschichte der griechisch-römischen Ethnographie* (Diss., Basel, 1918).

[25] See, for example, Jacoby, *RE* s.v. "Hekataios," col. 2682 for discussion of Hecataeus's comparative treatment of foreign customs.

[26] H. Schwable, "Bild der fremden Welt bei den frühen Griechen," *Entretiens Hardt* 8 (1961): 23.

Airs Waters Places, the scientific perspective was maintained in spite of the Ionian Revolt and the Persian Wars. No special explanation of this impressive Hellenic mental trait is required.

Just as genealogical writing was inspired by Hesiodic poetry reflecting a natural interest in what the Greeks conceived to be their heroic past, so the poetry of Homer reveals a natural curiosity about foreign lands, partly real and partly imaginary, that ultimately helped to inspire the development of ethnography. Some of the post-Homeric stages can be inferred from the existence of travel epics like Aristeas's *Arimaspeia*, though he and his work are but shadows to us, and the voyage-reports of Scylax and Euthymenes,[27] the former an explorer for Darius (Hdt. 4. 44), the latter from Marseilles and an investigator of the coast of Africa. A final stage is indicated by the publication of Hecataeus's other great work, the *Periodos Ges*, or "Circuit of the Earth."

Hecataeus's work was by any standard a stupendous achievement. Consisting of two books, one dealing with Europe, the other with Asia, Egypt, and Libya, the *Periodos Ges* (also entitled *Periegesis*) was a narrative geography with map attached. Unlike the writers of utilitarian voyage-accounts, which seem to have been common, and which provided information about the distances from one emporium to the next along the coastlines travelled by the Greeks, Hecataeus attempted a comprehensive description of the entire known (and unknown) world.[28] Naturally, it incorporated the results of the author's travels and the reports of others, published and oral; it also contained the heavy admixture of theory proper to an essentially scientific work.

In Hecataeus's vision, the continents balanced each other and the landscape consisted of geophysical symmetries. Though we may smile, we should also remember that logic seemed to dictate cosmic regularity and order, while personal observation could all too easily be beguiled into sympathetic corroboration. Hecataeus described

---

[27] For Aristeas, see Ed. Schwartz, *Fünf Vorträge über den griechischen Roman* (Berlin, 1896), p. 29, and von Fritz, *Griechische Geschichtsschreibung*, pp. 34f. The latter interpolates "historical thought" into Aristeas. For Scylax and Euthymenes, see von Fritz, pp. 28f., 52f.

[28] For the connection of Hecataeus's work with Anaximander and Milesian philosophy, see Jacoby, *RE* s.v. "Hekataios," col. 2690, and von Fritz, *Griechische Geschichtsschreibung*, pp. 39ff.

the Mediterranean seacoast clockwise from Spain, listing the names of individual peoples dwelling along the coast and as far into the interior as possible. He gave the characteristics of each land: the flora and fauna and interesting properties of the inhabitants, especially their attire (F 284, 287) and mode of subsistence (F 154, 322). From quotations in other authors and unmistakable vestiges in Herodotus,[29] it is clear that Hecataeus's schema contained four basic rubrics: the description of the land, the dynastic succession of its rulers, the "wonders" of the locality, and the customs of the inhabitants.

Although Hecataeus's work was not "ethnography" but a geography containing subordinate ethnographies, most of them inevitably brief and perfunctory, it is generally assumed that he invented the genre. Though it seems idle to contest a pure assumption, it is perhaps more reasonable to suppose that he integrated an already established methodology into the new literary form of the *Periodos Ges*. The fact that Dionysius of Miletus (*FGrHist* 687) wrote his *Persika* at approximately the same time also suggests that the genre had already taken root. But one can only speculate.

The evolution of ethnography, after its employment by Xanthus of Lydia (*FGrHist* 765), who seems to have written around the time of Herodotus, was determined by two concurrent developments. On the one hand, ethnographies became increasingly "historical." The section originally containing an encapsulation of the dynastic succession of a people's rulers developed into an extensive historical narrative. For example, Ctesias (*FGrHist* 688), the contemporary of Xenophon and Court Physician of Artaxerxes, includes within his *Persika* the detailed dynastic history of all the realms of Asia, beginning with Assyria. When he reached the events of his own time, he gave an account of the Ten Thousand and Artaxerxes indistinguishable from history. Yet the work formally remains an ethnography, the description of a foreign land including, but not wholly consisting of, an account of the history of its rulers.[30]

The other development, already manifest in Herodotus, was the interpolation of ethnography into a history. Ethnographical tracts appear as digressions from the exposition of *res gestae*. With increasing frequency, historians introduced ethnographical segments into

[29] See Trüdinger, *Griechisch-römischen Ethnographie*, pp. 10ff.
[30] See, e.g., F 1 (4), (7)–(8), (15), (17), F 5, 10–12, 34–35.

their work to round the picture, refresh the reader, or add interesting information that the rules of history would have excluded from the narrative. The Alexander-historians freely availed themselves of this tactic. One of them, Onesicritus (*FGrHist* 134 F 17) gave an account of India and its wise men in the context of Alexander's progress; another, Aristobulus (*FGrHist* 139 F 19, 20, 23, 35, 39, 42), provided extensive ethnographical-geographical notes; Nearchus (*FGrHist* 133) described India (F 11, 22, 23), the so-called Ichthyophagoi (F 29), natural phenomena such as whales (F 30), and the "Island of the Sun" (F 31). Later writers, most notably Polybius, Posidonius, Sallust, Trogus, and Ammianus Marcellinus, do the same. In all such cases, the writer was guided by the conventions of ethnography (as if he were, in fact, an ethnographer); once finished with the ethnographical digression, he resumes his allegiance to the rules of history.

The point deserves emphasis, because the conventions of ethnography vitally differed from those of history. The laws of evidence and obedience to truth were at least in theory mandatory in history. Ethnography permitted the publication of the unconfirmed report of even the improbable. The *physis*, the nature, of ethnography was *historia* in the original sense: "inquiry" into what was "worthy of relation," "marvelous," "deserving to be heard." Whether something was true or likely to be true was secondary to the fact that it was a *logos* told by an informant.[31] Perfectly just men living on the periphery of the world (Herodotus), man-eating ants (Onesicritus), fish living underground (Polybius)—all were grist for the mill. These were *logoi* deserving of preservation in an ethnographical work or in the ethnographical part of a historical work. Naturally, this convention gave a free hand to the writer; it is no wonder that we come upon exaggerated reports more often than we would like. But it would be wrong to suppose that the custom was shaped by some deficiency in the historical sense of the ancients. It was part of the genre of ethnography, even when wedded to history.

It is evident from what has been said that ethnography and history were genres of unusual compatibility. That they also stood in direct

---

[31] See, for example, Hdt. 3. 9: "The more persuasive account has been narrated; but the less persuasive must also be stated since in fact it is related." See 2. 123, 125 and 7. 152 with Jacoby, *RE* s.v. "Herodotos," coll. 472f.

"genetic" relation to each other, as Jacoby alleged,[32] is another matter entirely. It is quite true that Herodotus progressed from the ethnographic stage to the historical,[33] and in the process he carried over a number of traits native to ethnography—chiefly *historia* (investigative work), the concept of relating things "memorable" or "amazing," and the use of ethnographical description in its own right. But Herodotus's work is history in spite of his inclusion of ethnographical material, not because of it. He wrote history when he decided to describe and explain a sequential development and not merely to report it. The work would be equally a history, if less great, were book 2 and the other extensive ethnographical sections excised from the text. But were we to strip away the connecting threads and the descriptions of events, the work would present a different character and be history no more.

Horography: Greek

Local history, or horography (so named from *horos*, "year"),[34] gave the record of a city's life year by year. As in a chronological table, information of all kinds—antiquarian, religious, public—was appended to a list of those annual magistrates in each city-state who gave their name to the civil year. The principle of arrangement dictated that all occurrences of a given year be listed in series even if mutually unrelated; the organizing principle was chronological, not thematic.

The origin of the form in Greece is problematic. Writers before Jacoby assumed that it was one of the oldest historical genres.[35] This was also the ancient opinion, and analogy with the primitive Roman *annales maximi*, an indubitable form of horography and incontestably ancient, gave it support. Jacoby argued, however, that the evidence from the fifth-century literary scene contradicts these assumptions.

[32] Jacoby, "Über die Entwicklung," p. 40.

[33] C. W. Fornara, *Herodotus, An Interpretative Essay* (Oxford, 1971), pp. 17ff.

[34] For the nomenclature, see Jacoby, "Über die Entwicklung," p. 49 n. 89, and *Atthis* (Oxford, 1949), pp. 1f.

[35] E.g., F. Creuzer, *Die historische Kunst der Griechen in ihrer Entstehung und Fortbildung* (Leipzig, 1845), 2nd ed., pp. 265ff., Wilamowitz, *Aristoteles und Athen* (Berlin, 1893), vol. 2, pp. 17ff.

He noted the singular fact that local histories were unknown to Herodotus, who must have used them had they existed. Furthermore, as Jacoby pointed out, we are reliably informed that the *first* local history of Athens was written by a *foreigner*, Hellanicus of Lesbos (*FGrHist* 323ᵃ), at the *close* of the fifth century (F 26). Nothing could more powerfully militate against the assumption that horography was early and, as it were, a "natural" product of the city-state itself. Hence Jacoby's view that the form did not develop until late in the fifth century.

A statement of Dionysius of Halicarnassus in *De Thuc.* 5, however, unquestionably contradicts Jacoby's adoption of a relatively late date. Since it is the only serious obstacle in the way of Jacoby's view, it behooves us to consider it closely. The first-century author here speaks of the great number of ancient writers (*syngrapheis*) who flourished before the Peloponnesian War,

> including Euagon of Samos, Deiochus [of Cyzicus, Bion] of Proconnesus, Eudemus of Paros, Democles of Phygela, Hecataeus of Miletus, Acusilaus of Argos, Charon of Lampsacus, and Amelesagoras of Chalcedon. Those who were a little before the Peloponnesian War and extended down to the time of Thucydides are Hellenicus of Lesbos, Damastes of Sigeum, Xenomedes of Ceos, Xanthus of Lydia, and many others. All of these showed a like bent in the choice of their subjects and there was little difference in their ability. Some wrote treatises dealing with Greek history, the others dealt with non-Greek history. And they did not blend together these histories [into] one work, but subdivided them by nations and cities and gave a separate account of each, keeping in view one single and unvarying object, that of bringing to the common knowledge of all whatever records or traditions were to be found among the natives of the individual nationalities or states, whether recorded in places sacred or profane, and to deliver these just as they received them without adding thereto or subtracting therefrom, rejecting not even the legends which had been believed for many generations nor dramatic tales which seem to men of the present time to have a large measure of silliness. For the most part they used the same style—which was characterized by per-

spicuity, the use of current words, purity, conciseness, adaptation to subject matter, and the absence of any display of technical elaboration.[36]

Now since Dionysius's analysis includes (without discrimination) local historians as well as ethnographers and mythographers, it is evident that horography (like the other genres) has been set by him in the period before Thucydides and Herodotus, i.e., the mid-fifth century or earlier.

The question is whether Dionysius can be trusted. Many of the individuals named by him are unknown to us, while the dates he attributes to these people, whether at first or second hand, are in all probability conjectural and theoretical. Biographical data were not contained in their writings, least of all in those of the horographers, and the close analysis of what material there was did not antedate the Callimachean scholarship of the third century. It is a large assumption that Callimachus was able to docket these obscure works for the Alexandrian library and that Dionysius derived his information therefrom.[37]

The alternative approach, much more concordant with ancient methods, was based on the theory of style. Authors and groups of authors were dated with reference to the relative complexity of their style and elaboration of their technique. This was the yardstick developed and expounded by students of rhetoric and is, in fact, unmistakable in Dionysius. The all-important observation is that the "historians" are grouped by style and "mentality"—not by genre. Prose writers, in other words, are here collected in accordance with their stylistic and methodological characteristics, which were then equated and measured off against the corresponding traits of Herodotus and Thucydides, universally regarded as the more perfect writers because of the complexity of their works and the mature brilliance of their style.

The inference that Dionysius's arrangement is solely the result of

---

[36] The translation is by W. K. Pritchett in *Dionysius of Halicarnassus: On Thucydides* (Berkeley and Los Angeles, 1975), p. 3. He expresses skepticism about Jacoby's position in his commentary, pp. 50ff.

[37] For Callimachus and the author-catalogues containing biographical information (*pinakes*), see F. Leo, *Die griechisch-römische Biographie nach ihrer literarischen Form* (Leipzig, 1901), pp. 130f., and F. Schmidt, *Die Pinakes des Kallimachos* (Berlin, 1922), pp. 46ff.

rhetorical doctrine is strongly supported by his misdating of Hellanicus, for although Dionysius regarded the latter as a predecessor of
Thucydides, F 26 of his local history of Athens proves that the work
extended at least to 406 B.C. Another solid indication that Dionysius's chronological arrangement indeed derives from rhetorical
doctrine is provided by a parallel and similarly derivative discussion
in Cicero:

> Many writers have emulated this type of writing [i.e., that prac-
> ticed in the priestly annals of Rome, the *annales maximi*]. They
> have set down, without any elaboration, merely the chronicle
> of times, men, places and deeds. Therefore, our Cato and Pic-
> tor and Piso were writers of the same type as were Pherecydes,
> Hellanicus, Acusilaus and very many others among the Greeks.
> They neither understood the means by which prose was to be
> adorned . . . and they believed that brevity was the sole virtue
> of composition. [*De oratore* 2. 53]

Theophrastus was perhaps the ultimate authority for this view (as it
applied to the Greeks),[38] and it is in any case pre-Callimachean.

It appears, therefore, that although Dionysius first gave the dates
of these men and then characterized their method and style, it was
the identification of their style and method that was used to determine their dates. In sum, the most that can legitimately be deduced
from Dionysius is that the horographers possessed, or affected, a style
that in comparison with historical prose seemed as primitive as the
stark simplicity of the format they had adopted. The inference that
these writers were therefore early arrivals is not, however, cogent.
Style is a function of genre, and the prose of the local historians—
even fourth-century Athenian horographers—continues bare and
unembellished. Therefore, though to later theorists this characteristic appeared an infallible sign of immaturity, we must seek a different

[38] So, with minor variations, M. Gelzer, "Der Anfang römischer Geschichtsschreibung," in *Kleine Schriften* (Wiesbaden, 1964), vol. 3, p. 101 (reprinted from *Hermes*
69 [1934]), Jacoby, *Atthis*, p. 178, and F. Wehrli, "Die Geschichtsschreibung im Lichte
der antiken Theorie," in *Eumusia: Festgabe für Ernst Howald* (Erlenbach, 1947), pp.
60f. T. S. Brown, "Herodotus and his Profession," *AHR* 59 (1954): 834ff., like Pritchett (see n. 36), considers Dionysius's testimony a valuable guide. In this context, it
is significant that Dionysius considered Antiochus of Syracuse (*FGrHist* 555) "ex-
tremely ancient" (T 2): we know that Antiochus ended his work in the year 424/3
(T 3).

explanation consistent with Jacoby's date for the origination of the genre. For Jacoby's inference from Herodotus is sound; we also know that comparatively late writers like Phaeneas of Eresos, Ephorus of Cyme, and Theopompus of Chios wrote the local histories of their native cities, and although we do not know the situation at Eresos and Cyme, Theopompus was in fact the *first* writer to provide Chios with a local history (*FGrHist* 115 F 305).

If, however, Jacoby's date for the development of horography is acceptable, his explanation of its genesis is not. He initially believed, with Eduard Schwartz,[39] that local history arose out of a romantic nostalgia for the golden past. Warmth of sentiment seemed to explain the antiquarian orientation of these writers. Without disavowing this view, Jacoby later emphasized the stimulating influence of Hecataeus, Herodotus, and Hellanicus. They,

> each in his own time and with different success, roused the historical sense and the interest in the history of the writer's native town. . . . [This] upspringing historical interest and the wish to provide for their native town a place in the Great History of the Greek people, both for the mythical time and for the recent national contest against Persia [gave birth to the genre].[40]

It is hard to doubt that Jacoby's wish to tie together all the various forms of historical writing into one vast "genetic" complex built out of challenges and responses dulled his perception of the outright inconsequence of his hypothetical relationship. Local historians, if they were incited as Jacoby supposed, would scarcely have adopted *this* literary form in order to propagate the claims of their cities in the international arena of "Great History." The salient characteristic of horography is its parochiality. Although events of national importance would naturally be listed in the record when they impinged on the affairs of the city-state, horography was not *designed* to exploit them. That the form and compass of a literary work correspond to the intent of the writer is an obvious truth. The purpose of horography was, therefore, not patriotic in the broad sense argued by Jacoby—the patriotism of competing claims by natives of one city or another, of cities that desire the Hellenic world to know of their ne-

[39] Jacoby, "Über die Entwicklung," p. 49, and Ed. Schwartz, "Timaios' Geschichtswerk," *Hermes* 34 (1899): 491.
[40] Jacoby, *Atthis*, p. 289 n. 111.

glected exploits—but at most a love of city prompting the desire to set out its records and to provide a chronological sequence of developments important to it.[41] It is, above all, significant that these writers made no attempt to write explanatory or descriptive history, the kind of writing necessary for the purposes envisioned by Jacoby. Thus not only is there no reciprocation in alleged intent, but the format and style of history and horography almost calculatedly face in opposite directions. If, in fact, history evoked something of the response Jacoby imputed to the local historians, it is to be sought in rhetorical circles, in declamations comparable to the *Areopagiticus* of Isocrates. Declamatory rhetoric, not local history, was the proper medium for the display of civic virtue and the contributions of one's ancestors to Hellenism.

If we look for another explanation, we may take the involvement of Hellanicus as the illuminating sign. The chroniclelike form of the local histories, the nature of the material they provide, and their plain unvanished prose style (which misled the ancient critics) make it apparent that in horography we are witnessing the antiquarian expansion of state records begun in the scientific spirit already attested to in Hellanicus by his other works. The similarity in form of his *Priestesses of Hera at Argos* (*FGrHist* 4 F 74–84), a work of international scope arranged annalistically, and the (annalistic) *Atthides*, or *Local Histories of Athens* (*FGrHist* 323 ª–328), is not coincidental. In each case, we observe the provision of a chronological table: the same method has been applied to different subjects. In the chronographical work, the *Priestesses*, the data were culled from the entire known world; in the local history they were of course limited to what was strictly relevant to the city-state. What Hellanicus attempted for Hellas, he sought also to accomplish for individual cities. It is the same organizational principle externally and internally applied—applied, that is, in large and in small.[42]

Hellanicus's work in local history belongs in the context of sci-

---

[41] Not that these writers were mere impersonal chroniclers without interest in the political implications of their work. Indeed, as the local histories of Athens unmistakably show, tradition was manipulated in support of one contemporary position or another. But these were local matters keyed to the internal life of the individual city-state.

[42] Jacoby, "Über die Entwicklung," p. 25 n. 6, oddly maintained that this "similarity is purely external." The method and structure are identical; it is only the standpoint that changes.

ence, not patriotism, precisely as we should expect from the fact that this scholar from Lesbos wrote the first Athenian local history. Horography was the Hellenic side of ethnography, a product of the same urge to codify the collective lives of disparate groups. It owed its distinctive form to the fact that an annalistic system of recording events already functioned in each Greek city-state, while sufficient historical and antiquarian material was preserved to allow the writers to flesh out at least a considerable portion of the history of the city year by year—something impossible for Greeks to do with Persia or Egypt, where the analysis naturally became less minute. It is, therefore, part of the movement we associate with the "sophistic" generation, when antiquities were studied and arranged for their own sake—that is, because of the belief, impossible to justify in specific utilitarian terms, that systematizing of this kind possessed obvious scientific value. The same impulse induced Hippias of Elis (FGrHist 6) to collect and arrange chronologically the names of the victors in the Olympic Games. Indeed, whether or not we identify a "movement" including specific scholars like Hellanicus, Charon of Lampsacus, Damastes of Sigeum, and Hippias,[43] their simultaneous pursuit of the same kind of research speaks for itself. Local history was an offshoot of the scientific impulse driving the Greeks to collect, arrange, and correct their poetry, their language, and their antiquities. It is a movement reflected even by the Athenian leadership, which commissioned the publication in marble of its archon-list ca. 425.[44]

By an independent route, we therefore find ourselves in general agreement with Theophrastus and Dionysius with regard to their *explanation* of horography's purpose: the old local historians kept in view "one single and unvarying object, that of bringing to the common knowledge of all whatever records or traditions were to be found." However, the local historians suited their style to their sub-

[43] See Jacoby, *RE* s.v. "Hellanikos, cols. 107ff., *FGrHist* III a Komm. p. 1, and A. Momigliano, *Studies in Historiography* (London, 1966), p. 4.

[44] R. Meiggs and D. Lewis, *Greek Historical Inscriptions* (Oxford, 1969), no. 6, pp. 9–12. It is perhaps worth adding here that the first horographers may well have been influenced by Oriental models. Contact with Egypt and Persia, if not Babylonia, will have familiarized them with the form. The fact that Charon (*FGrHist* 262) appears to have been one of the earlier local historians, while his city, Lampsacus, possessed old Persian connections, is intriguing. Of all Greek forms, horography is closest to Oriental historiography.

ject and adopted the persona of the antiquarian, impersonal reporter. Since these works were written without rhetorical adornment or descriptive intent, Theophrastus and Dionysius were misled
as to their date, thereby considering them primitive. In fact, the
association of Hellanicus with horography and of horography with
the intellectual currents of the last third of the fifth century are our
safest guides.

Horography: Roman

Unlike Greek local history, where the collection of public records
proceeded from private individuals in response to no official man-
date, the antecedent or model of the Latin local historians, or, as
they are generally known, annalists, was the chronicle of the *pon-
tifices maximi* (the heads of the college presiding over state cult),
published around 120 B.C. by P. Mucius Scaevola, but available before that time to interested individuals.[45] This chronicle, called the
annales maximi, was already familiar enough in the time of Ennius
(236–169) for him to use it as the title of his historical epic (the
Annales). Cicero described the pontifical *annales* as follows:

> From the beginning of Rome to the time when P. Mucius was
> *pontifex maximus*, the *pontifex maximus* had every occurrence of
> each year written down in order to safeguard the memory of the
> public record. He recorded this onto a white notice-board and
> displayed the tablet at his house so that the people would be
> able to know it. Even now they are called the *annales maximi*.
> [*De or.* 2. 12, 52]

According to Servius Danielis, the Latin commentator on Virgil
(*Aeneid* 1. 373),

> the *annales* were drawn up as follows: every year the *pontifex
> maximus* kept a white tablet. After writing down the names of
> the consuls and other magistrates, he would make indication of
> events that were worthy of remembrance at home and on cam-
> paign by land and sea from day to day. Our ancestors transferred

[45] J. P. V. D. Balsdon, "Some Questions about Historical Writing in the Second
Century B.C.," *CQ* 47 (1953): 162, and E. Badian, "The Early Historians," in *The
Latin Historians*, ed. T. A. Dorey (London, 1966), p. 15.

the annual records comprising such diligence into eighty vol-
umes, and they named them the *annales maximi* from the *pon-
tifices maximi* by whom they had been composed.

The amount and type of material this annual record preserved is,
like the date of its commencement, a matter of dispute and uncertainty.[46] Cato censured the record for its historical inadequacy (F 77
Peter): "It is disagreeable to write what stands in the tablet at the
house of the *pontifex maximus*—how often grain was costly, how
often darkness or something else blocked the light of the moon or
the sun." But Cato's complaint should not be taken at face value: he
would not have criticized the *annales maximi* unless they were worth
criticizing and possessed some measure of historical utility. His criticism, in other words, proceeds from the comparative and selective
standpoint of the historian of deeds, *res gestae*, who would inevitably
have found them improperly oriented. Horography was not written
from history's point of view; dearth and abundance are important
from the historical viewpoint only if they precipitate events. In the
annals, they are important in themselves. Cicero, likewise, when he
called the *annales* banal and jejune (*De legg.* 1. 2, 6), was mentally
contrasting them with Greek history, not stigmatizing them in any
absolute sense. We may be sure, therefore, that if Cato found mention of the price of grain and lunar eclipses, he also found material
that was useful for a historical account, even if it were spotty and
frustrating. It is salutary to recall and apply the analogous criticism
by Thucydides of Hellanicus's local history of Athens as "skimpy and
chronologically imprecise" (1. 97. 2). That Hellanicus's *Atthis* contained important historical information no one would deny.

The generic separation of Roman horography from history is less
clear-cut than that which obtained for Hellas, where each genre retained its clear demarcation from the other. In Rome, the annalistic
form, once popularized, imposed itself even on writers of history,

---

[46] F. Altheim, *Rom und der Hellenismus* (Amsterdam, n.d.), pp. 34–39, infers that
the tradition reaches back beyond 390 B.C.; Balsdon, "Some Questions," 162–64,
and Badian, "Early Historians," pp. 1f., set the date at 390. T. P. Wiseman, *Clio's
Cosmetics* (Leicester, 1979), p. 17, following E. Rawson, "Prodigy Lists and the Use of
the Annales Maximi," *CQ* 21 (1971): 158–69, denies the presence of historical material (lists of magistrates) by a source-criticism that subverts the basic testimonia. For
an optimistic view, see F. Klingner, *Römische Geisteswelt*[5] (Munich, 1965), pp. 70f.;
A. M. McDonald, "The Style of Livy, *JRS* 47 (1957): 156, is more skeptical.

who found the structure convenient to their own ends. This does not apply, however, to the earliest Roman historians—Fabius Pictor, Cincius Alimentus, Gaius Acilius, Postumius Albinus, and Cato the Elder, writers who date from the Second Punic War to ca. 150 B.C. This group composed not "historical annals," but histories on the Greek pattern, for the popularization of the annal came as a later development after the close of their epoch. The fragments of Cassius Hemina (Peter, pp. 98–111), who wrote in the last half of the second century, are the first to preserve the unmistakable signs of horography. In all probability, Hemina begins the series of the annalists.

The character of Hemina's work shows a clear differentiation of his interests and method from that of his historian predecessors. To be sure, his treatment of what is conventionally termed the *archaeologia* or "account of earliest times" is probably similar to what the historians provided. But his record of the republic shows the standard content of local history. F 18 (Peter) registers the intercalation of the calendar in 450 B.C.; F 23 demolition work ordered by the censors; F 26 the arrival of the first Greek doctor at Rome; F 27 a musical exhibition probably connected with the arrival at Rome of the cult of the Great Mother; F 32 the corruption of vestal virgins; F 37 the fourth presentation of the *ludi saeculares* (a ceremony of expiation held at the end of every hundred years) in 146 B.C. Pliny the Elder (*NH* 13. 84) was right to call Hemina "the oldest annalist." The defining characteristic of local history is that its annalistic structure dictates the arrangement and suitability of its contents. The year, not a thematic criterion, determines the selection of material; that which is relevant to the city demands inclusion without regard to category or even intrinsic memorability. On the other hand, the record of the celebrated deeds of men self-evidently does not include calendric change, public building, or religious practices.

One difference from Greek practice is striking. As stated, the Greeks, with a fine sense of genre, maintained the separation of history and horography. If essentially historical material (e.g., the progress of a war) needed mention, horographers provided selective notices, leaving history to the historians. By the end of the fifth century, both genres were practiced simultaneously; any local historian of any *polis* could safely presuppose continuous writing of the history of Greek affairs. This is not to deny that in Hellenistic times some local historians, notably from Rhodes, came to write extensively about events in which their cities were playing prominent parts; but they were exceptions to the general rule.

Such compartmentalization did not obtain at Rome: for whatever reason, the Roman annalists *supplanted* the historians; Greek-style historiography ceased. Thus the annalists perforce came to serve two masters. In addition to material that was by nature appropriate to horography—the kind of detail making the *annales maximi* seem to Cato to lack serious purpose—the annalists inherited the duty of incorporating the deeds of men, *res gestae*, in large scale, and not as mere notices, into their work. For this, unfortunately, the annalistic pattern became a complicating factor. Historians could use an annalistic system to provide a chronology of the events they traced—as, for example, did Thucydides; it was no impediment to their pursuit of a linear progression of events, e.g., a war. On the other hand, the nature of the genre compelled the annalists to deal again and again, as they progressed from consular year to consular year, with a multiplicity of categories, of which only one was *res gestae*. Thus, although they continued to narrate the subjects their historian predecessors had treated in "pragmatic" fashion (Polybius 39. 1. 4, of A. Postumius Albinus),[47] they were compelled to chop them up into annual segments, depriving them of continuity and topical coherence because of the obligatory and multifarious interruptions entailed by the genre.

To attempt an explanation for the origin of the annalistic movement—Hemina is associated with a cluster of other writers, notably Piso Frugi and Gn. Gellius—is hazardous. We neither know the dates of publication of these writers nor their relative order, though Hemina and Piso appear to have written before the publication of the *annales maximi* by Scaevola, and Gellius thereafter. Even so, there is no mistaking the sudden burst of activity in the sphere of

---

[47]M. Gelzer, "Nochmals über den Anfang der römischen Geschichtsschreibung," *Kleine Schriften* (Wiesbaden, 1964), vol. 3, p. 110 n. 44 (= *Hermes* 82 [1954]) rightly objects to Balsdon's explanation of "pragmatic history" (Polybius's term for his own work) merely as "serious history" ("Some Questions," p. 161 n. 2) because it is too vague and "colorless." Polybius is referring to what he regards as an obligatory standard for the writing of narrative and explanatory political and military history, precisely as he explains in his attack against Phylarchus in 2. 56. The category of local history can therefore be dismissed from consideration, since it pursues essentially divergent aims. At the very least, by classing Postumius's work with his own, Polybius implies the comparability of both works in formal terms.

local history, and this in turn suggests that the phenomenon arose from some special inducement. Although the *annales* were hardly modeled on atthidography, as some suggest, Greek influence seems undeniable. What Jacoby urged for Greek horography may well apply to the Latins. The general familiarity of the Romans with Greece and Greek horography, which was prolific, may not unnaturally have suggested that Roman local history required commensurate attention. By the last half of the second century B.C., the evolution of Rome had invested the city with commanding importance. It behooved the Romans to set forth the record of their local history precisely as was done by Greek communities important and unimportant. That the Romans possessed an endemic horography (the *annales maximi*) rendered the adoption of this form all the more desirable.

Annalistic history proved congenial at Rome. Its structure, though not its contents, was retained even by those writers, like Fannius and Asellio, the historians of the Gracchan Revolution, who replaced antiquarian interest with political historiography.[48] Though they wrote up *res gestae* and did not seek, as horography required, to list all types of material relevant to the city under the appropriate year, they nevertheless cast their history in annalistic form.[49] Similarly, though Claudius Quadrigarius, Valerius Antias, and Licinius Macer wrote horography in the strict sense in the first century, those writers who acknowledged the primacy of history—for example, Sisenna, Sallust, Livy, Pollio, Tacitus, and Ammianus—continued to apply the selective annalistic technique developed by Fannius and Asellio. Thus they retained (though not with absolute rigidity) the structure imposed by horography (see, e.g., *Annales* 4. 71). It is a notable and curious development. The pontifical annals existed side by side with the early products of Greek-style historiography written by Fabius

[48] The historical writers automatically rejected the cultural, phenomenological, and antiquarian material properly at home in annals. If some part of it were included (e.g., Sisenna F 5 Peter), it subserved rhetorical purposes. Livy, however, whose scope was wider, could include more of this material. The idea that something must be said about the city of Rome (the central annalistic bias) proved so tenacious that Ammianus Marcellinus (e.g., 17. 11. 5) continued to regard it as de rigueur even at his late date.

[49] Asellio (F 1 Peter) objected to horography in the strict sense as mere diaries, the unconnected listing of events. His criticism comprehends Gellius, Piso, and perhaps the *annales maximi* published by Scaevola. But he does not reject the annalistic pattern of year-by-year *history*. For the irrelevant distinctions of the rhetoricians, who equated annals and history with the treatment of past or present times, see Scheller, *De hellenistica arte*, pp. 11ff.; cf. Gelzer, "Anfang," passim.

Pictor et al.; annals then crowded out the latter genre and became the orthodox mode of historical writing; the emergent breed of historians subsequently found it impractical to break completely with the form, while for Livy, especially, the modified annal proved the perfect vehicle for his multifaceted approach to the Roman past.

Chronography

The invention of chronography, history's backbone, can be associated with the simultaneous development of local history in Greece. As has already been observed, the form is analogous with horography; indeed, Cicero (*De republica* 2. 10, 18) actually described chronography as *annales*. Hellanicus's great work, *The Priestesses of Hera at Argos* (*FGrHist* 4 F 74–84), gave in order the names of the priestesses of Hera and dated events according to the sequence of their years of tenure. Hellanicus adopted a universal perspective. We possess fragments or quotations from his work that allude to events in Macedonia (F 74), Greece (F 75), Phrygia (F 76), Corcyra (F 77), Ambracia (F 83), Sicily (F 79), and Italy (F 84).

Hellanicus was in his way as ambitious a writer as Hecataeus. That he created a chronological record reaching from heroic times to the present is but one aspect of his achievement. Hellanicus needed to collect the events deserving inclusion as well as to authenticate the tradition of the actual events to be assigned, though here, it is true, he was able to stand on the shoulders of Hecataeus and to benefit from the work of some of his contemporaries who were investigating the same traditions. To be sure, it is disconcerting to find that he gave exact dates to events in heroic times (though the practice was not inconsistent with Hecataean generational chronology). In F 79b, for example, we learn that the Sicels left Italy for Sicily "in the third generation before the Trojan War when Alcyone was priestess at Argos for the twenty-sixth year." But it is unnecessary to believe that the chronological indications are capricious, even though we cannot determine their basis. In any case, this work of pure scholarship laid the foundation for later attempts, by Timaeus (died 260), Eratosthenes (ca. 275–194), and others, to provide the Greeks and barbarians with a secure chronology with fixed and easily comprehensible points of reference. For the historical period, Timaeus's probable system of reckoning by Olympiad, which commenced in 776 and were counted every four years, won out for the Greeks and remained the major chronological system in antiquity, with competition only from the Roman eponymous magistrates, the consuls whose names served to date the year in which they held office. Naturally, in imperial times, the consular year universally became the orthodox dating system for all peoples, not entirely to the satisfaction of some Greeks (see Libanius *Orat.* 12. 15ff.). Needless to state, Latin historians, through Ammianus (end of the fourth century A.D.), used consular dates.

If ancient definitions are our guide, chronography is assuredly not, as Jacoby maintained,[50] a form of history, but belongs in a category of its own. The end of chronography is the arrangement of events in a mechanically sequential pattern. That pattern is determined without regard for the interrelation of events; by the same token, it condones the juxtaposition of incommensurables. The nature of chronography is to articulate disparate material by fixed intervals; history depicts the actions of men as they occur in time. The genres are connected only in their common utilization of some of the data of the past.

History

THE GENESIS OF THE WAR MONOGRAPH

The nature of the genre of history as it originates with Herodotus is indeed centered in the depiction of the actions of men as they occur in time, and it is this character that makes history unique among the types with which it is associated. In theory, if not always in fact, mythography, ethnography, local history, and chronography collect data and report them; only history is mimetic. Ethnography, for example, may note that a certain war occurred and inform the reader of its result. History alone is concerned to depict *how* it was carried through.[51] The propensity, shared by Jacoby with many others, to regard Herodotus as the lineal successor of Hecataeus, just as, in a

---

[50] Jacoby, "Über die Entwicklung," pp. 24f.

[51] Naturally, once historical description became a standard mode of narration, any writer in any genre could adopt it. Thus Ctesias provided a "history" of the war between Semiramis and the Indians (*FGrHist* 688 F 16), just as Quadrigarius (F 12 Peter) presented a picture of single combat along the lines of Callisthenes and other writers heavily influenced by Homer.

truer sense, we view him as the predecessor of Thucydides, has been over-indulged. The fact has been obscured that the debt to Hecataeus, though real enough, is *accidental* to Herodotus's major advance. The final decision to write the history of a major war including an exhaustive account of its origins owes nothing in spirit to Hecataeus, and accordingly produced a work categorically dissimilar to the conventional historical writing of his day. To state (with Jacoby) that Herodotus united "historical thought" to Hecataeus's "descriptive element" [52] is to infer that his *Histories* mechanically derive from the subordination of "Hecataean" material to an inquiry after causes. This synthetic concept is misleading. Herodotus's account of the Persian War in books 7–9, which is the heart of his *expositio rerum gestarum* and the epitome of his historical technique, is on its most fundamental level not an inquiry after causes but the verisimilitudinous and self-explanatory description of a two-year-long war. In contrast, the Hecataean "descriptive element," which Herodotus allegedly inherited, involved not the portrayal of men's actions but merely, when relevant, a statement about their occurrence and an explanation of why they were taken.

The debt of Herodotus to Hecataeus was twofold. In the first place, Herodotus gives every sign of having once proceeded as did Hecataeus in the *Periodos Ges*. Ethnography, geography, even climatology are Ionian historiographical interests reflected in substantial portions of the *Histories*. Their importance in Herodotus's account cannot be minimized. But none of these components are historical in the sense of the ancient use of the word. They are embedded, like fossils, in a work that is history for notably different reasons. Secondly, Herodotus owes a method of inquiry to Hecataeus and to Ionian historiography. The investigation of oral tradition remained the essential method of the historian from Herodotus through Polybius to Ammianus Marcellinus. The primary importance of this need not be belabored. Yet it was not the ingredient we are seeking either: Hecataeus possessed it and wrote no history. Both debts, therefore, though heavy, mark stages of Herodotus's intellectual evolution, rather than contributing to his creation of a new kind of work. But when we separate the record of Herodotus's development

[52] Jacoby, "Über die Entwicklung," p. 40.

from our judgment of his work *qua* history, no doubt is possible as to the real model or catalyzing influence: it was Homer.

The connection between the two writers cuts deeper than is indicated by Herodotus's use of Homeric language, his introduction of direct speech, his application of Homeric motifs, and his similar construction of episodes, though these influences were in themselves enough to make it a truism among the ancients that Herodotus was the "most Homeric" of writers (Pseudo-Dionysius *On The Sublime* 13. 3). For, as Friedrich Creuzer long ago observed, important correspondences exist in spirit, causal system, and narrative plan.[53] Creuzer made a profound observation when he stated that it was entirely "natural that the *Iliad* and the *Odyssey* hovered in Herodotus's imagination from the time he conceived the idea [of writing about the Persian War] to the time of its implementation." Indeed, the categorical similarity of subject (cf. Hdt. 7. 20) made it inevitable that Herodotus would draw inspiration from its acknowledged master. The most fundamental similarity linking the two works, however, concerns the *means* of description employed, for Herodotus accommodated Homer's instruments of poetic representation to his prose work.

Nothing in the tradition of Ionian *historia* suggested to Herodotus that he turn the results of his inquiries into narrative pictures of events that he had never seen, thus cutting himself free from his sources, especially in books 7–9, to create the illusion that he *was* the observer of the deeds under description. Our habituation to books and to the quotation of speeches they contain dulls our appreciation of this remarkable artistic innovation. The book-reader spoke the words aloud and to that extent *heard* the author himself (cf. Hdt. 1. 125. 1). Consider, then, the dramatic effect of the direct oration, when the reader "listened" to the actual words of Xerxes or Miltiades and was "present" at the very scene Herodotus described. Imagine the force of descriptive passages in which the illusion was created of the author's actual presence. It was precisely as if the reader were reciting the text of the *Iliad*; mutatis mutandis, this relationship to heroic events was reproduced by Herodotus for the Per-

---

[53] *Historische Kunst*, pp. 114–17; the quotation appears on p. 115. Cf. A. W. Gomme, *The Greek Attitude to Poetry and History* (Berkeley and Los Angeles, 1954), p. 92.

sian Wars by means of the same mimetic techniques isolated in Homer by Plato (*Republic* 3. 392Cff.).

Herodotus's *Histories* represent a fusion of prose and poetry, of the Homeric epic and a now utterly transformed Ionian historiography. History thereafter remained a mimetic genre, devoted to the description of the memorable actions of men. Herodotus set these actions into a context that was radically different from Homer's, however, though also related to it. What Achilles' anger was to Homer, the Persian War represented to Herodotus. Instead of commencing *in medias res* like Homer, in order to chart the devastating repercussions of heroic passion, Herodotus made the Great War his subject and also attempted to trace the sequence of unjust actions ultimately provoking it by reaching back to the time of Croesus in the midsixth century. The massive treatment of this prehistory—of Oriental as well as Hellenic affairs—was as epochal as the establishment of war as the theme of history. By embroidering into a causative structure the basic history of the main actors—Sparta, Athens, Corinth on the one side, Persia and her more illustrious subjects on the other—Herodotus's *archaeologia*, his account of the furthest antecedents of the Persian Wars, swelled into universal history.[54]

The line of development from Herodotus to Thucydides is direct and straightforward. The war monograph implicit in Herodotus emerged perfected at Thucydides' hands. This historian accepted Herodotus's mimetic techniques but eschewed ethnography (though there were occasions for him to include it, had he been so minded) and virtually eliminated digressions, except when severely functional purposes were served. Subsequent writers of monographs, such as Callisthenes, Philinus, Silenus (*FGrHist* 124, 174, 175), Coelius Antipater (Peter, pp. 158–77), and Sallust in the *Jugurthine War*, were less austere.

HELLENIKA, OR HISTORIES OF GREECE

Thucydides' decision to write about the course of an incipient war (1. 1. 1) was utterly extraordinary; the choice of a contemporary subject, however, was momentous. Potential historians learned from his

---

[54]Jacoby, "Über die Entwicklung," p. 33 n. 49, takes too restricted a view of Herodotus's work by limiting its subject to "the deeds of the Hellenic people." Dionysius of Halicarnassus, *De Thuc.* 5, gave an assessment closer to the truth.

example that history belonged to the present as well as to the past. And, indeed, now begins the series of sequential histories by the historians of their own times—*Zeitgeschichte* in the true sense of the word. These works, *Hellenika* so-called, written after Thucydides and devoted to Greek affairs, as their name implies, represent a species distinct from the monograph. For although at least three writers continued the history Thucydides left as a torso broken off at the year 411, all of them, Xenophon, Theopompus, and the "Oxyrhynchus historian" (otherwise unknown, and named from the Egyptian site from which a small portion of his work was recovered), departed from Thucydides' plan. Instead of terminating their histories at the end of the Peloponnesian War, they continued beyond. Theopompus broke off at 394 and the battle of Cnidus; Xenophon continued until the battle of Mantinea in 362; at what point after 404 the Oxyrhynchus historian ended his work is a matter of conjecture.

The decision by all of these writers to provide a history of Greek affairs (and not merely to carry out Thucydides' intention of providing a self-contained account of the Peloponnesian War) evidently came naturally. They apparently considered it axiomatic that a continuous record of Hellenic warfare and its consequences should be provided for present and future generations. As Xenophon remarked at the very end of his *Hellenika*, "Let my account extend to this point; perhaps someone else will have a care for the events that followed after these."[55] In so doing, however, these writers insensibly created a new form of history that lacked the clear-cut boundaries and thematic unity of the Thucydidean war monograph.

Taken as a historical subject, Greek affairs after the Peloponnesian War, when the old fifth-century polarity of Athenians and Spartans with their respective allies was finished, raised new problems. The natural subject of historical description increased in complexity and altered in perspective. The narration of the course of a war, originally the essence of history, was subordinated to a grand conception of the course of Greece's collective development. To be sure, that conception was already implicit in Herodotus and Thucydides: both writers leave no doubt about what they regarded as the mighty historical developments that culminated in their respective wars. In the *Hellenika*, however, the emphasis is reversed. Diplomatic his-

---

[55] There is a poignant echo in Ammianus Marcellinus, *ad fin.*

tory, the shift in political relationships among the Greek powers, and the loss or gain of hegemony are superior in interest to the conflicts that resulted in such changes. History is not the account of a war and its causes; that narrow teleology is henceforth reserved for the monograph alone. The *Hellenika*, children of the monograph, are the comprehensive contemporary histories of the political and military life of Greece [56]—a character they retained in spite of subsequent shifts of emphasis within the genre.

THE CENTRALITY OF LEADING INDIVIDUALS

The most notable of the shifts of emphasis alluded to above attaches closely to the name of Alexander the Great, who exemplifies the cult of personality that developed in the fourth century. Heralded by the popularity of Alcibiades and Lysander, it is reflected, as well, in the realistic detail of portrait statuary. Literary examples of the new concentration on the individual are numerous—for example, the apologetic Socratic literature, Xenophon's *Agesilaus*, and the encomiastic speeches of the rhetorician Isocrates. More strictly relevant here, because of its historical context, is Xenophon's reference to the rise of Jason of Pherae as "the deeds of Jason" (*Hell.* 6.i.19), a conceptualization that clearly anticipates the organization of "memorable deeds" around the activities of a single individual. Thus Theopompus (*FGrHist* 115) entitled his major work the *Philippika* because of Philip's centrality, stating in his preface (F 27) that he was writing it because never before had Europe brought forth such a man. This tendency became flagrant, however, in the history of Alexander's campaign against Persia written by Aristotle's grandnephew, Callisthenes (*FGrHist* 124 F 28ff.). It may well be that the combination of Alexander's personality and the tremendous expectations raised by the Asian campaign were necessary to bring about the radical alteration we detect in Callisthenes' perspective, just as the fulfillment of those expectations explains the same phenomenon in later writers. For although this unfinished work was probably cast in the form of a *Hellenika*, with its nominal subject the conquest of Asia by the Hellenes, led by Alexander, in fact the primary object of

---

[56] It is but a short step to the philosophical-historical concept of the "Life of Hellas" of Dicaearchus (Wehrli F 47ff.).

interest was Alexander himself. The deeds of an individual are described as if he were a Homeric hero (though in proper historical context), while the actions of men or the successes and failures of collective entities are of secondary importance. The lens has turned from the events to the leader. The *Hellenika* widened the historical narrative to embrace Greek affairs in general and not merely war, but at the same time sharply reduced the perspective by anchoring the story to the deeds of a single person.

A deep interest in individuals persisted; its effect is evident in many subsequent histories, whether *Hellenika* by Duris of Samos and Phylarchus of Athens (*FGrHist* 76, 81), "universal histories" by Polybius and the first-century writer Timagenes (*FGrHist* 88), or "imperial histories" by Tacitus and Ammianus. The change of focus naturally engendered a new preoccupation with personal description. Personality traits, emotions, attire, virtues, vices, dreams, and portents became routine subjects of narration. But the cult of personality deriving from the "deeds" of Alexander, besides putting its stamp on the contents of *Hellenika* and the numerous histories of the Hellenistic kings who succeeded to portions of Alexander's great empire, spawned a type of history strictly coterminous with the deeds of a single individual.

What was implicit in Callisthenes, in other words, became explicit with the other writers of Alexander's train and their successors. They attempt a sort of biographical history. Thus Chares of Mytilene (*FGrHist* 125) wrote an undisguisedly personal account of Alexander and his deeds—that is to say, not even a nominal *Hellenika*. Similarly, the title of Onesicritus's work (*FGrHist* 134) was *How Alexander Became Educated*. The title of the work by Ptolemy I (*FGrHist* 138), written in his old age, is unfortunately unknown, but the logic of his position as the king of Egypt supports the evidence of the fragments to indicate that it, too, was a history of Alexander's deeds (and of Ptolemy's affiliation with the great man). Most important of all was Clitarchus's work (*FGrHist* 137), also written in this tradition, though in the next generation, for it became a famous book much read in subsequent times (T 3, 6–8, etc.). It began with Alexander's accession to power and ended with his burial. The type of history taking the deeds of an individual as its explicit subject was now fully developed, and important figures such as Agathocles of

Syracuse, Attalus of Pergamum, Ptolemy IV Philopator, Antiochus the Great, Hannibal, Tigranes of Armenia, and the great Pompey all were celebrated in this fashion by notable historians.

That history of this type tended to the encomiastic will easily be conceived. Callisthenes was himself accused of deifying Alexander (*FGrHist* 124 T 20–21), and some of the fragments (F 14, 31, 36) sustain the charge. Cleitarchus availed himself of the opportunity to glorify both Alexander and Ptolemy, now king of Egypt (*FGrHist* 137 F 24). Onesicritus made Alexander a Cynic philosopher. Since exaggeration of the facts marches with stylistic excess, these prose epics led by a natural progression to the rhetorical fireworks of Hegesias of Magnesia (*FGrHist* 142), a writer who managed to overstep the generous limits of the endurable.[57]

SIKELIKA, OR HISTORIES OF SICILY

Another species of history harder to classify than the *Hellenika* and its offshoots came into existence in Sicily during the last half of the fifth century B.C. The relatively early date of the first writer of the series, Antiochus of Syracuse (*FGrHist* 555), precludes direct influence by Herodotus and Thucydides, though the effect of Thucydides on Antiochus's successor, Philistus (*FGrHist* 556), is evident from his mildly contemptuous nickname—"the little Thucydides." But it is idle to attempt a mechanical explanation of the origin of Sicilian historiography. In Sicily flowed intellectual currents now quite untraceable. Intellectual society was cosmopolitan, of course, and Ionian historiography no doubt contributed to the interest of the Sicilians in their own past. The results, in any case, are visible in the *Sikelika* of Antiochus, Philistus, and their successors, especially Timaeus of Tauromenium (*FGrHist* 566), the great third-century historian.

The name of the species, *Sikelika*, suggests an affiliation with ethnography (cf. *Persika*, *Aigyptiaka*), and Jacoby indeed so classified it.[58] He rejected the possibility that *Sikelika* were analogous with *Hellenika* (and were thereby history and not ethnography) because of

[57] See E. Norden, *Die antike Kunstprosa* (Leipzig, 1898), pp. 134ff.
[58] Jacoby, "Über die Entwicklung," pp. 30, 39, and especially p. 44 n. 76. Neither here nor in *FGrHist* IIIb I, pp. 479–82, did Jacoby deny the decidedly historical emphasis of these works.

what he regarded as an "essential distinction"—namely, that the starting-point of the *Hellenika* is the recent past, while the *Sikelika*, like the ethnographies, commence with a prehistory of Sicily, or *archaeologia*. But the matter is not quite so simple: several "essential distinctions" seem to be in competition with one another. As Jacoby also observed, *Hellenika* were the opposites or complements of ethnography because their subject was Hellas. Precisely on that ground, it would seem proper to exclude any Hellenic history from the category *ethnographica*, even if it contains an *archaeologia*.

The decisive point, as Jacoby more than any other scholar has made clear, is that ethnography is a definable genre because its essential characteristics, taken as a whole, differentiate it from other literary forms. If a writer is an ethnographer, he proceeds with unmistakable method, whether he be Hellanicus, Ctesias, or Tacitus (in the *Germania*). The genre dictates the presentation of a balanced picture of a locality that includes discussion of geography, dynastic history, customs, and marvels. The inflation of any portion of the totality is not accompanied by the rejection of all the others, though special circumstances might dictate the omission of one or another of the usual rubrics. Most essential is the Ionian tradition of reporting hearsay, the local traditions, or *logoi*, of the natives of the country.

None of this is present, or would be appropriate, in the *Sikelika*. They possess one feature only that also appears in the ethnographies: *archaeologiae*, or accounts of earliest times. Antiochus wrote the history of Sicily from Cocalus (allegedly of Minoan times) to 424 B.C. (T 3); Philistus began his in the year 1205. These *archaeologiae* were, however, indispensable preliminaries to the subject of the Greek settlement of Italy (Antiochus F 2) and Sicily (Philistus F 1–2)—the logically prior theme. Thus Antiochus discussed the naming and the extent of Italy (F 3, 5), the migration to Sicily by the Sikeloi (F 4), and, finally, the Greek colonization of Italy and Sicily (F 8–13). In this context, it is significant that Antiochus's successor, Philistus, compressed both *archaeologia* and colonization into his first book alone. The emphasis placed on the early fifth-century (Greek) tyrants shows the actual orientation of the writer and the nature of the genre, and lends full support to the ancient definition of *Sikelika* as generic history that we find in the Suda, s.v. "Philiskos or Philistos"

(= 556 T 1): "They are [the account of] hostile activities of Greek against Greek." Like the *Hellenika*, they recorded the political and military life of the Hellenic community, in this instance in Sicily.

Jacoby has, therefore, allowed the presence of one element of substance common to ethnography and *Sikelika* to dictate the identity of the latter, as if the presentation of "origins" were the salient characteristic of the form and incompatible with history into the bargain. It is a curious logical process. Even ethnographies were not identified as such by Jacoby because of the *archaeologiae* within them; they are merely a predictable component of the description of a foreign land on the historical plane. It would seem to follow that they can also be an appropriate component of the historical description of a Hellenic land wrested from the barbarians. We must judge the function of any segment of a narrative from the nature of the entire work—and not identify the genre, instead, from isolated judgment of the probable character of one of its least weighty components. *Hellenika*, moreover, lacked an *archaeologia* and began at a starting point recent in time for a special reason: they formed part of a chain reaching back through Thucydides to Herodotus and his discussion of archaic Greek history, while the heroic origins of the Greeks had already been fully covered by Hecataeus and his followers. In Sicily, history of necessity began for Antiochus with the arrival of the Greeks. But the subject mandated discussion of earlier migrations and the prehistory of Sicily. Thus, though the procedure here is similar to that followed in ethnography, any formal relationship is adventitious. *Sikelika* are the West Greek counterparts of the *Hellenika*.

THE FIRST ROMAN HISTORIANS

The *Sikelika*, though important in their own right, gain added interest from the likelihood that they served as models for the first Roman historians (late third century) who, not incidentally, wrote in Greek rather than Latin. Since one consequence of Rome's development into an Italian and then Mediterranean power was her exposure to the culture of the Greeks, first in Italy, then in Sicily, and finally (after 200) in Greece, nothing seems more natural than the propagation of Greek historiography in Rome itself. Since the *Sikelika* must of all types have been the most familiar to the Romans, a connection of some sort would seem probable on purely general grounds.

However, the work of the first Roman historian, Fabius Pictor, who wrote a history of Rome from its foundations (the *archaeologia*) to his own times, is usually affiliated with a special group of Greek-inspired ethnographies written in the East by learned and Hellenized natives, usually priests, after the conquest of the East by Alexander.[59] The group had access to special information and its members were motivated to write corrective and patriotic accounts of their homelands in order to compensate for inaccurate or otherwise objectionable versions of their history published by the Greeks. The common assumption is that Fabius's work was of a similar type: he was a priest writing in Greek, intending (in part) to correct Greek misconceptions. In form his work was therefore an ethnography owing whatever distinctive character and superiority to Greek versions that it possessed to his access to pontifical annals, funeral eulogies, family archives, and the like.

The analogy is grossly inexact. Although Fabius has typically been compared with and "explained" by the non-Greek ethnographers Manetho of Egypt and Berossus of Babylonia (*FGrHist* 609, 680), who most suit the picture sketched above, these writers were in a totally different milieu from that of Fabius, and their psychology had been shaped and affected by conditions not even remotely obtaining at Rome. Egypt and Babylonia were extinct as culturally and politically autonomous powers. Manetho and Berossus were moved to write in order to correct a simplistic and erroneous literature on their homeland written by the Greeks. It was their aim to establish a veracious *ancient* record (609 F 1) from the native sources testifying to the earlier greatness of their motherlands (680 F 1b [1]). The antiquarian orientation is unmistakable; indeed, it is notable that Josephus (*Ant. Jud.* 1. 107) described these writers primarily as the authors of *archaeologiae*, "ancient histories." Self-evidently, neither Fabius's work nor the *Sikelika* can be so described. Furthermore, far from combating the (hitherto modest) Greek historical writing about Rome, Fabius actually relied upon a Greek author, probably Diocles of Peparethos (*FGrHist* 820), for a substantial portion of Rome's earliest history (Plutarch *Romulus* 3). Instead of showing signs of special knowledge deriving from his research into the native

---

[59] Jacoby, "Über die Entwicklung," pp. 28f., Badian, "Early Historians," p. 3, and A. Momigliano, *Alien Wisdom* (London, 1975), pp. 18, 92.

traditions, the texture of Fabius's account (F 5[b] Peter) is artfully Hellenistic and the substance palpably Greco-Roman. It is not written in the spirit of Berossus. Secondly, one vital area in which Fabius might have bettered Greek accounts, the early Roman Republic, the section separating his accounts of Rome's origins and the two Punic Wars, was the sketchiest part of the work. The main substance was in fact Fabius's lengthy and detailed account of the first two Punic Wars. The emphasis of his work, therefore, was contemporary, and it shows a character radically different from the ethnographies to which it has been compared. It is history (with prolegomena) in the usual sense, written along the lines of the *Sikelika*, though adapted to the special needs of its subject—Rome, a single city-state, not a plurality of communities as in Sicily or Greece.[60]

The form is the same as that of the *Sikelika* and so are the omissions. The geography of Italy, its climate, and the customs of the Romans are ignored. (That aspect of the record, a true element of ethnography, awaited Cato, whose remarkable work, the *Origines*, constituted a generic departure.)[61] Fabius wrote the continuous history of the Romans from their beginnings to his own day; in comparison ethnography is a frozen form. The significance of the past derives from the achievements of the present; the reverse obtained for Berossus and Manetho. The important fact about Fabius's identity is not that he was a priest, but that he was a Roman, a senator, and, above all, a member of one of the greatest and most powerful of the patrician families of the day, the Fabii.

Rejection of the analogy between Fabius's work and "native ethnographies" excludes the related inference that his purpose was primarily "diplomatic," "apologetic," or "corrective." Naturally, Fabius

---

[60] It follows a fortiori that Fabius did not write "annals" as some have held in spite of Gelzer, e.g., P. Bung, *Q. Fabius Pictor, der erste römische Annalist* (Diss., Cologne, 1951). This is not to dispute that Fabius probably dated events by the consular year. But Thucydides, too, wrote "annalistically"; as we have seen, the distinction between history and horography cuts deeper than the use of sequential dating, and horography was of all forms the least suitable for a Hellenized Roman who wished to direct himself to an international audience expecting conventional history. There is paradox in the notion that Fabius wrote in Greek but simultaneously adopted a genre disassociated from the exposition of men's deeds.

[61] Cato's treatment not only of the origins of Italian communities but of the nature of the land and the character of its peoples marks the work, certainly the first two books, as ethnographic in type. In this respect, Cato was the first Latin (though he was anticipated by the Greeks Hieronymus and Timaeus) firmly to set Rome and Italy in the larger context of the known civilized world.

could not have been indifferent to the impression his history would produce, and he was hardly "undiplomatic." But the most straight-forward explanation of his primary intent seems the best: Fabius was proud of his people and desired to parade its greatness before the international community. To understand the Second Punic War and the Roman victory, one needed to know about Rome's origins and development. Certainly, Fabius's account of the wars was a patriotic history of a "pious and just set of engagements."[62] But they were "pious and just" because this was the Romans' view of their world. The concept was not manufactured for foreign consumption.

From what has been said, it is evident that Fabius's history differs from the *Sikelika* and *Hellenika* in one crucial aspect. The Greek historians wrote from an ecumenical viewpoint; the native city of the writer was irrelevant, at least in principle, to the work's perspective. History centered on the evolving relationships of a group of city-states categorically identical. For Fabius (and for the Romans), history was the *res gestae populi Romani*, "the deeds of the Roman people"; to the Greeks this notion of the *history* of a city-state (except as annals) was a contradiction in terms. Roman history, from Fabius, remains sharply ethnocentric; the Latins viewed the world from within the *pomerium*, Rome's city limits, whether the author was Cato, Sallust, Livy, or Tacitus. However, to impute the disfiguring subjectivity of Roman historical writing to Fabius may be excessive: a uniquely fortunate development permitting the Roman to view the world as a simple polarity, Rome and all else, is perhaps explanation enough. But we should not underrate the formative importance of the type of history Fabius adopted. The narrow and confined structure containing the *archaeologia* of Rome and detailing the progress of a city-state connected with others simply by the dynamic of conquest (so that "history" did not exist except when Rome was involved) remained standard thereafter and entailed egocentricity by its form alone. Only that mattered which was directly relevant to

[62] To designate the work an instrument of public policy designed to illuminate the Roman national character (*proairesis*) in order to combat hostile Greek attitudes— e.g., M. Gelzer, "Römische Politik bei Fabius Pictor," *Kleine Schriften* (Wiesbaden, 1964), vol. 3, pp. 51ff. (= *Hermes* 68 [1933]); cf. Badian, "Early Historians," p. 5—is to elevate a normal and latent expectation on the part of (the naturally partisan) Fabius into an overriding purpose. Fabius wished the world to know that Rome was a great power morally. If the level of generality seems banal, it was likewise banal for Aeschylus to write the *Persae*, informed as he was by quite comparable feelings of patriotism and a vaulting sense of "manifest destiny."

Roman foreign policy or "impinges on Roman affairs" (Livy 29. 48. 6). Livy spoke for his predecessors as well as for himself when he wrote: "But it is not worthwhile to discuss the manner in which the mutual wars of foreign peoples were fought. I carry more than enough of a burden in giving a thorough account of the deeds done by the Roman people" (41. 25. 8). That the form suited the national spirit we need not doubt; it seems equally reasonable to infer that the prestige it acquired impeded the development of other historical approaches, such as universal history.

UNIVERSAL HISTORY

Although no historical innovation can properly be regarded as inevitable, the appearance of universal history in fourth-century Greece is readily comprehensible. An extensive historical literature had by then come into existence; apart from history itself, the practice of horography and ethnography, literary-historical criticism, philosophical research, and the collection of antiquarian data had immensely augmented the sum of written knowledge about the history of the Hellenes and their barbarian neighbors. But the record consisted of fragments in need of synthesis and unification. Precisely this was attempted by the historian Ephorus (*FGrHist* 70): he compiled a vast and unified history beginning with the Dorian conquest of the Peloponnesus in 1069/8 (T 8, 10) and ending at the year 341/40. The contents of the work were described by the ancients as "all the deeds in Hellas and barbarian lands" (T 7), "universal [history]" (T 7), "the deeds of the Hellenes and the barbarians" (T 8, 11). It gave a history of the Hellenes, both in Greece and in the colonies, and of the barbarians who anywhere impinged upon them. The work, obviously, was a tremendous undertaking; it is a pity that the connection, real or imagined, between Ephorus and the rhetorician Isocrates has made it a matter of course for moderns to despise both Ephorus and his work.[63]

[63] No ancient writer could withstand the combined assaults of Wilamowitz, Schwartz, and Jacoby, who made Ephorus the incarnation of all that was objectionable in Greek historiography. Wilamowitz, *Greek Historical Writing*, pp. 10f., descended to caricature: "Ephorus, an utterly thoughtless writer, has at best the doubtful merit of having been the first to compose a universal history. . . . He mastered a great mass of material, and, inasmuch as he made it trivial, succeeded the better in making it homogenous. He 'pragmatized' history, as they call it; that is, he took care that everything should run on such lines as an enlightened Philistine can at a pinch imagine. He also took care that the moral and patriotic feelings of the public should in the end receive the satisfaction which they expect in the fifth act of a bad tragedy."

The reasons prompting Ephorus to undertake this work must be deduced from purely general considerations, for nothing of his own survives that bears on the question, and apart from the tradition linking him to Isocrates, and anecdotes spun from that dubious combination, nothing is known of him. It seems reasonable, however, to seek Ephorus's inspiration in the needs of the educated circles of his day. The concept and requirements of "mental culture," *paedeia*, undoubtedly made felt the absence of any systematic treatment of Hellenic history as a whole. Certainly the increasing kinship among Hellenes, already emphasized by the numerous works describing their common history in the East and West and by the pronouncements of the fourth-century sophists and rhetors who urged a union of hearts and common war against the barbarian, gave special propriety and intrinsic justification to a universal history. Above all, this was the age of rhetoric, and the prospect was open to apply the precepts of the new art in a field eminently suitable to their display. The opportunity was at hand to parade philosophy, describe deeds, and combine the whole in a seamless work that would modernize the archaic authors and replace their separate products with one comprehensive work. We may infer that Ephorus envisioned a history greater than the sum of its parts because of the unity of vision, treatment, and style he would provide.[64]

The difficulties confronting Ephorus in the organization of a work of unprecedented scope and complexity must have been considerable. From Diodorus Siculus (5. 1. 4) we learn that Ephorus wrote "history by category," apparently in individual books, or groups of books, devoted to a unitary concept such as a "topic" or geographical area.[65] Thus Ephorus's book 6 contained the history of the Peloponnesus, book 7 of the West Greeks, and books 8 and 9 of Lydia and Persia, all in archaic times. Furthermore, within individual books as we also learn from Diodorus (e.g., book 11, passim), Ephorus adopted a comparable system of topical arrangement for dealing

---

[64] Jacoby, "Über die Entwicklung," p. 43 n. 75.

[65] Polybius's classification of "historical fields" in 9. 1. 3f. includes (after genealogy and before "the deeds of nations, cities, and dynasts") "colonies, foundations, and relationships," i.e., the great period of colonization commencing with the return of the Heracleidai. Research into the foundations of cities (*ktiseis*) became popular by the end of the fifth century (Plato *Hipp. Major* 285E). Individual *ktiseis* were published, although inclusive monographs on the general subject do not seem to have been written. The topic certainly was treated by Ephorus, and after him became a common historical subject.

with simultaneous occurrences within a given category. In this matter, Ephorus broke formally with the practice of Thucydides, which had also been followed (less and less willingly) by the authors of *Hellenika*. For Thucydides had been rigorous in his devotion to strict chronological order. To be sure, Thucydides also provided some absolute dates (2. 2. 1) and regarded the end of his war as a definite point from which to calculate the time of prior events (1. 13. 3, 18. 1–2). But for the war itself, he followed an undeviating annalistic pattern, dividing the year by seasons (e.g., 2. 31. 1; cf. 5. 26) and with reference to astronomical points (2. 78. 2). By dating events in strict relative order within the seasons, he was able to provide a secure chronology, though without absolute dates, for all the events of the war. Ephorus now completely abandoned this chronological system, though he really had no choice: Thucydides' system was (of course) incompatible with topical arrangement, while topical arrangement was in fact necessitated by the plurality of subjects with which Ephorus was required to deal. Not only did he trace independent historical lines of development that coincided in time; working within a larger historical field than was a war, he was compelled to treat of simultaneous but unrelated events within the same area.

Ephorus has been castigated by modern scholars for adopting a topical arrangement because it must have militated against chronological precision. How he dated events is, in fact, unknown; we should not on that account assume that he was indifferent to the problem. Presumably events were tied together synchronistically and dated in relation to well-known epochs such as the reign of Croesus, the era of the Persian War, and the outbreak of the Peloponnesian War, by generations in archaic times, and by intervals of years thereafter. There is no reason to doubt that Ephorus's readers could calculate any event's date by information presented somewhere in the work. His history must have presented on a huge scale something like Thucydides' own system of relative dates attached to a few fixed points. Only within each of his separate categories would the topical arrangement have caused difficulty. As we can see, for example, from Diodorus's compression of the adventures of Themistocles into the year 471 (11. 54ff.),[66] Ephorus would discuss one subject from its beginning to its end and then *revert back* to begin another that was already in progress. But it seems unjust to blame Ephorus for Dio-

---

[66] For Diodorus's use of Ephorus, see Schwartz, *RE*, s.v. "Diodoros," col. 679ff.

dorus's epitome or abbreviated utilization of Ephorus; it may well be that the latter made the temporal connections clearer than we can tell from Diodorus. Indeed, a possible model may perhaps be found in Ammianus 26. 5. It is important to observe, in any case, that the testimonia accuse him of material errors (*FGrHist* 70 T 14b, 16) but not of chronological inadequacy; and Timaeus's criticism (70 T 30), of which the point is unknown, is more than balanced by Polybius's praise, which, in fact, embraces Ephorus's organization of his history.

For good or ill, Ephorus's system of topical organization within narrow chronological limits became the norm for Greek writers thereafter. Polybius himself (perhaps following Timaeus) divided the world into distinct theatres and proceeded to discuss each locality (the Roman West, Greece, Egypt, etc.) within the framework of Olympiads, which provided four-year-long intervals for the description of events in each locality.[67] In most cases (see, however, 14. 12), he resisted the temptation to depart from the scheme when events proved recalcitrant to it, even though he was well aware that he would be criticized for failing to provide a continuous account of sieges and other occurrences that disrupted his chronological limits (38. 5. 1–3). Finally, Ephorus's arrangement also had its effect on the Latins, who allowed themselves a certain flexibility in order to satisfy the desire for topical unity.

On balance, Ephorus's arrangement, though it lent itself to chronological imprecision, produced an entirely sensible approach to universal history, and it continues in use to this day (cf. the *Cambridge Ancient History*). It allowed for the insertion of extensive "digressions," such as on historical geography or the colonization movement. It was a framework enabling the historian to bring cultural history and ethnography within his purview as well as the political and military chain of events that were his primary business. Above all, topical arrangement permitted Ephorus to organize intelligibly a sequential narrative consisting of lengthy historical segments that were at once independent and synchronous.

It is significant that most of the writers who attempted universal history after Ephorus also practiced rhetoric or philosophy. The pos-

---

[67] The practice was not altogether satisfactory to history, since the Olympic year began in late July and thus bisected the campaign season. Polybius, in fact, normally reckoned a year from the beginning of the campaign season (i.e., spring, not the preceding late summer). See Walbank, *Commentary*, vol. 1, pp. 35f.

sibilities offered by this vast stage to writers of either camp are easily imagined. By the first century B.C., perhaps because the conclusive political developments of the era invited such an approach, universal history was attempted by the rhetorician Timagenes of Alexandria (*FGrHist* 88) and by Pompeius Trogus, who uncharacteristically wrote in Latin. Diodorus Siculus composed his *Universal Library*, much of which is intact, at the same time. Another contemporary, the Peripatetic Nicolaus of Damascus (*FGrHist* 90), court philosopher of Herod the Great (T 12, F 35) and the biographer of Augustus as well, wrote a universal history filling 143 books. It is obvious from the fragments (see especially F 135) that Nicolaus viewed the past as a splendid storehouse of material waiting to be shaped by skillful writing and sententious observation.

Of far greater intellectual power were the works of Polybius and Posidonius of Apamea. Their histories were "universal" in extent of space but not of time. For Polybius continued Timaeus's history, just as Posidonius continued Polybius's. The obvious analogy is the "perpetual histories" of the Greeks (the *Hellenika*). Like Ephorus, whom he admired, Polybius united East and West, the Hellenistic monarchies, Greece and Rome, Africa and Spain; he too inserted whole books as digressions or supplements—historiographical polemic and historical geography (12, 34).

Of the Latin writers of the empire, Ammianus in the late fourth century A.D. approaches universal history most closely. It is perhaps not accidental that East and West were at that time caught in a process of separation roughly inverse to the coalescence emphasized by Polybius. All in all, it seems providential that a Latin-writing Greek soldier who lived both at Antioch and Rome wrote the last great history at a time when the Greco-Roman world was nearing its end politically, culturally, and religiously. The history encompasses both cultures, all portions of the Empire, and the notable enemies of Rome—Persians, Huns, and others; and it contains within itself many of the historiographical elements developed in the preceding seven hundred years. It is a mighty work, a mirror of his times, that seems in spirit as well as content to be a leave-taking of the ancient world.

II

Research, Orientation, and Explanation in the Greek and Latin Historians

I.

The fact that the Greek word for "inquiry," "research," "investiga-tion" (*historia*) became the name of a particular class of literature leaves no doubt possible about what was early considered the defin-ing characteristic of the genre. When method designates a class of literary works, it is obvious that the activity described is the sine qua non of the genre, a necessary condition of composition. The method itself was straightforward; it consisted basically of the interrogation of witnesses and other informed parties and of the redaction of the answers into a continuous narrative. Herodotus established the method as a principle of historical writing. Indeed, by describing his work as an "exposition of his research" (1. 1), he was instrumental in welding the association of method and subject. History, in other words, became an act of synthesis and validation quite as much as of presentation (*apodeixis*). It could not be the mere obiter dicta of an individual on historical subjects; the method, the obligatory method, consisted instead of piecing out the record in detail on the basis of a search for information from knowledgeable sources, and the resul-tant work attested the diligence of the seeker.

It is interesting to see how quickly this method took root. Thu-cydides, for instance, presupposed it as self-evident and restricted

himself to a discussion of procedure, informing the reader of the care
he would take in evaluating his sources and of the manner in which
he would reproduce things said and done (1. 22). Later writers continued the practice as a matter of course.

Within one definitional framework, therefore, the collection of
oral report *was* history, and inevitably so. Writers were almost totally
reliant on their own recollections and the memories of their contemporaries and elders. That is why they were for the most part the
historians of their own generations or, failing that, excerptors of
those who were. The lifespan of oral tradition was comparatively
brief (cf. Polybius 4. 2. 3). When Herodotus, for example, sought
out contemporary recollections of still living history, he froze a wan-
ing memory. His successors were left with little but the possibility of
improvements in detail. Much might still be garnered from privi-
leged and special sources of information accessible to the local historians.[1] But after Herodotus had written, the witnesses were no
longer there to be interrogated. It was thus a natural law of *historia*
that the historians of each generation establish the record of their
own time.

The arduous nature of the work deserves emphasis, especially
since it is often taken for granted. Herodotus, of course, exemplifies
the traveller; and though it may be doubted that he undertook his
travels in order to write his history, there is no question that, once
begun, he traveled extensively in order to complete it properly. Thucydides' insistence on accurate observation and cross-questioning is
famous (1. 22 with 5. 26). Polybius (12. 25e) insisted on the historian's obligation to travel in order to make personal observations (cf.
12. 4c), and his comparative denigration of book-research as easy
work and vicarious involvement presupposed the same ideal. His polemic against Timaeus, by our standards an indefatigable and enter-
prising scholar, is revealing. Not only did he deride this "armchair"
historian for priding himself on the pains he took to collect books on
the customs of Ligurians, Celts, and Iberians (12. 28a. 3); he even
sneered (12. 27. 4–6) that Timaeus chose Athens as his place of
residence because it possessed a good library where he could work
effortlessly.

[1] See the excellent remarks by Ed. Schwartz, "Über der Verhältnis der Hellenen
zur Geschichte," in *Gesammelte Schriften* (Berlin, 1938), vol. 1, p. 65.

Polybius, captiously though he expressed himself, fairly represents the great tradition of *historia*. The hallmark of the profession was personal observation (autopsy), inquiry, and travel. Now these conditions excluded all but the members of the highest levels of society. Wealth and social contacts were essential to the craft. The nature of what historians intended to investigate—the policies of the leaders of city-states and monarchies, the causes and conduct of wars, the intentions of diplomacy—required mobility, familiarity with the great, and the prestige necessary to ensure the cooperation of strangers. To all this, Theopompus gave clear expression (as paraphrased by Dionysius in *Ad Pomp.* 6 = *FGrHist* 115 T 20a):

> [Theopompus is to be praised for the care he took] and his willingness to undertake difficulties for the sake of his work. For it is obvious [from his preface] that even if he had not written any of it he had made the greatest possible preparations for the task and had spent the most enormous sum of money in the process of collecting the material. In addition he was an observer (*autoptes*) of many of the events and established connections with many of the men who at that time held the first place in the military, politics and philosophy. This he did for the sake of his history. For unlike some people,[2] he did not rate the writing of history as a secondary part of life but as its most essential part.

It is self-evident from the conditions of their endeavor, laborious or gratifying as they may have seemed, that the Greek historians— Herodotus, Thucydides, Theopompus, Callisthenes, Polybius et al.—were fully occupied by it and, in the main, devoted to it the years of their prime. The third-century historian Agatharchides (*FGrHist* 86 F 3) put it in a nutshell when he stated that the labor involved was more than an old man could meet. Naturally, there were exceptions. Xenophon, for example, wrote in retirement; he penned his *Hellenica* with the same wondrous facility and, alas, superficiality that generally mark the corpus of his writings, proving the dictum of Theopompus *e contrario*. The use of reminiscence and

---

[2] This looks like a reminiscence of Polybius 12. 28. 3–4, quoted in the next note. If so, Romans like A. Postumius Albinus are intended. Cf. P. Pédech's note in the Budé edition.

an almost casual selection of data swell a work that is at best nothing more than an unpretentious journal enlivened by vivid conversations and portraits. Then there was Hieronymus (*FGrHist* 154), who lived long enough to commence a second career after serving Eumenes of Cardia and Antigonus I. Recollection played a substantial part in the elaboration of his history as well. Too many men attempted history through the course of too many generations to allow iron-clad generalizations. Nevertheless, it holds true that as a class the Greek historians devoted their best years to their work, regarding it as their full-time occupation even when, as in Polybius's time, some of the more notorious difficulties had been smoothed (3. 59).

The point deserves emphasis, for it sets the Greek writers in sharp contrast to the Latins. It would appear, in fact, that the priorities of the Greek and Latin historians stood in inverse relation to each other. History was for the Roman politician what politics sometimes had been for the Greek historian. This difference, together with the correlative fact that the Latin wrote narrowly Roman history and not ecumenical history of the Greek type, goes far to explain some of the more notable characteristics of their respective historiography.

The contention made here about the orientation of the Greek historian varies somewhat from the general estimate. In the usual view, the Greek and Latin historians (at least those who are held to matter) are conflated to suit the longstanding cliché that history, being of essence political, was written by "men of affairs," "politicians," or "statesmen," when it was not being degraded by the "rhetoricians."[3] But though the terminology may be loose enough to sat-

---

[3] The idea reaches back to Polybius 12. 28. 2–5: "Now Plato says that it will be well for humanity when either philosophers are kings or kings make philosophy. [3] I would say that history will be well when politically experienced individuals undertake to write history—[4] and this not, as is currently the case, as a secondary activity [*parergos*]. They must believe that this too is one of life's necessary and splendid callings and they must devote themselves to this throughout their lives without distraction. [5] Alternatively, potential writers must consider political experience a necessary adjunct of historiography." In one fashion or another, this attitude permeates modern thinking, especially when ancient writers are in question. Felix Jacoby, for example, is typical in his belief that "*der politische Sinn und die politische Parteinahme*" are the essential components of the historian: "Griechische Geschichtschreibung," *Abhandlungen zur griechischen Geschichtschreibung*, ed. H. Bloch (Leiden, 1956), p. 83; cf. p. 99 for his effusive development of this idea, which is currently undergoing a sort of revival in recent books on the subject of the "rise of historical thought." A more acceptable formulation is given simply by Schwartz, *Gesammelte Schriften*, vol. 1, p. 56.

isfy a modern prejudice, it is too flexible to provide a category of analytic value. Though the Greek historians may have been "men of affairs" who were sometimes involved in public duties, it is a misuse of language to identify them primarily as politicians or statesmen.

It is true that many historians, like men of distinction in other fields (Sophocles and Gorgias are two good examples), involved themselves in the political affairs of their city. Hecataeus (a sort of archetype) added his counsel to the deliberations that preceded the Ionian Revolt of 499 (Hdt. 5. 36, 125), and he was perhaps also active in the general pacification that followed it (Diod. 10. 25. 4). But neither the advice given by Hecataeus nor Herodotus's alleged (but unsupported) activity on Pericles' behalf[4] makes either figure a "statesman" in the required sense. The same applies to Thucydides. His brief service as a general in 424 proves his importance at Athens, but above all his possession of great influence in Thrace at a time when Thrace was in jeopardy. It is a special situation; Thucydides was a one-time general, not a "statesman." In any case, Thucydides commenced his history when the war broke out, years before the beginning and the end of his abortive military command.

A new type of *historia* was indeed called forth by the altered conditions of the late fourth century. In a trend anticipated by Xenophon, participants in Alexander's campaign wrote histories based on their experiences. Similarly, subordinates of the great, such as Hieronymus, wrote in retirement of the deeds of their superiors. In Hellenistic times, therefore, with the development of reminiscence-literature, the door to historiography was pushed ajar to allow the entrance of men, some of them gifted and all experienced, who proceeded to write history by virtue of special knowledge gained through personal participation. But the term "statesman" will not suit even this group of writers.[5] Alternatively, those to whom the term does apply—Demetrius of Phalerum, Aratus of Sicyon (*FGrHist* 228, 231)—wrote apologetics, not history. Or they wrote horography.

The attraction to horography is understandable. Not only was the city-chronicle the natural vehicle of the partisan politician but also,

---

[4] Jacoby, *RE* s.v. "Herodotos," cols. 228f.

[5] "Man of affairs" is a term sufficiently vague to include most of them, and there is no question but that the Alexander-historians represent a new tendency in historiography. This branch does indeed consist of individuals possessing by virtue of their activities specific knowledge not easily accessible to others.

unlike history, this branch of literature did not by its nature require the extensive research that would have separated the writer from his city. No disparagement of the third-century Athenian local historian Philochorus (*FGrHist* 328) is intended when we observe that Polybius's ridicule of Timaeus as the least migratory of historians puts Philochorus in proper perspective. The study of the local history of one's city-state required the resolution of a series of problems as difficult in their way as any confronting the historians. The elaboration of a fine web of detail, much of it conjectural, required patience, imagination, and skill. It did not, however, require *historia* in the measure demanded of the historian.

As a class, therefore, the Greek historians were primarily just that, historians—and not a part of that group of writers, in Greece or in Rome, who exchanged the pen for the sword. Though the choice was not one of utter renunciation and mutual exclusivity, they chose history instead of politics (or had the choice made for them, especially Timaeus and Polybius). On the other hand, Greek politicians with an inchoate interest in historiography ended by writing memoirs or local history if they wrote at all; they did not write histories of the Greek world where the importance of their local concerns would necessarily have been diminished. The historians, too, of course, were patriotic and had their share of anger and enthusiasm. Thucydides' detestation of Cleon is a notorious, but not isolated, instance. Moreover, their interest in Hellenic history must often have been connected with the important position in international affairs held by their cities, so that their histories were not disinterested. The Rhodians Antisthenes and Zeno (*FGrHist* 508, 523), accused of partiality by Polybius (16. 14), were perhaps inspired by such favoritism. It is worth noting, however, that both men were, in fact, "statesmen" (523 T 3) and the authors not of *Hellenika* but of local histories, in which they wrote tendentiously of the exploits of their city. In any case, the relevant observation is that the field of vision of the authors of *Hellenika* was not coterminous with the boundaries of the city-state in which they lived their political lives. The assumption of pan-Hellenic objectivity, so justly admired by Jacoby, differentiates these historians from the politician-turned-writer with whom they have often been identified.

The Roman historians were a breed apart, and this not merely in respect to their (at least) initial dedication to an active political career. A number of other associated differences—the distance of the writer from his subject, the requirements of research, and the writer's purpose—firmly place the Roman historian in a distinct category of his own.

Truly remarkable is the change in focus. Perhaps because we tend to think of "Greece" and "Rome" as comparable and somehow equivalent entities, we are apt to forget that the Romans wrote the history of their city and only incidentally that of the world. Though for form and structure the Romans took the pan-Sicilian histories as their first models,[6] the historical viewpoint, which for the Greeks was "the memorable deeds of men, Greek and barbarian," has narrowed drastically. We can perhaps best estimate the difference by postulating its analogue in Greece. The true parallel to the spate of histories written by the Latins from the time of the Gracchi to that of Augustus would be Athenian histories of the Thirty Tyrants written shortly after their fall. Unmistakable in Rome is the immediacy of subject, the direct and new involvement of a writer with his most pertinent interests (cf. Cicero *De off.* 3. 17, 69). The alteration could not be greater: Greek history was about the whole known world or its substantial portions; Roman history first centered on Roman war and conquest and, in its second efflorescence, on Roman revolution.

That the history was written by active members of the Roman ruling class is a correlative development, for the shift in focus imposed new requirements on the putative historian, just as it rendered others less pressing. It may be doubted whether anyone but an insider can write the history of the internal workings of an oligarchy, and it goes without saying that only an insider could hope to be taken seriously. The different traditions from which the Greek and Roman historians emerged were in this context most significant. The pursuit of *historia* by private individuals, whose special claims to knowledge in their own cities were basically irrelevant to the larger problems of Hellenic history, had been replaced by the superior validity of practical experience in the Roman senate.

The *persona* of the historian had altered. The Greek writer had made a career of the practice of history; his connections with the political world were of value (in literary terms) insofar as they

---

[6] See above, chapter 1.

opened up avenues for *historia*. In the Roman world, the historian was himself the informed source, the statesman-historian, an individual whose claim to write history was based on prestige and knowledge gained through active participation in the political life of the community. The requirement for writing the "deeds of the Roman people" was *auctoritas*, the authority of offices held, of armies commanded. Together with its precondition, practical experience, this replaced *historia*, careful research by way of the interrogation of witnesses, as the imprimatur of the historian. Fabius, Postumius, Cato, Fannius, Asellio, and the others wrote about their city-state as members of the ruling elite; the experience and status attained thereby supplied their warrant for writing history.

The line of development and transition is perspicuous. In Herodotus's time, the work was all and the writer little. Like Herodotus, Thucydides introduced himself to his audience in the preface by simple reference to his native city, without mentioning his patronymic, the all-important designation of social standing, and when he referred to his generalship and banishment of 424 (5. 26. 5) it was solely to inform the reader of the opportunity thus afforded him to collect information from both sides; not even by implication does he suggest that his authority stems from more than his devotion to the task at hand.[7] Theopompus sends the same message, though in a more inflated way. Ephorus, too, paid homage to the principle (*FGrHist* 70 F 110); that he is unknown to us except as the author of his history further illustrates the point. From a later epoch, we have the words of a certain Posidonius (*FGrHist* 169 F 1), otherwise unknown, who sanctioned his history of Perseus of Macedonia simply by stating that he was a contemporary and witness of the deeds.

On the other side of the ledger, balancing *historia*, we note the assertion of political and military experience. This desideratum first appears in Polybius, a writer long resident at Rome. Since he departs from the orthodox Greek view that paid exclusive honor to *historia*, it is reasonable to suspect the influence of Roman ideas and practice. Now Polybius allegedly wanted the historian to become involved in politics and to fight in wars (12. 28. 3–6, 25g. 1–2). Naturally, even allowing for a certain exaltation and overstatement, it cannot be ac-

---

[7]6. 55. 1 suggests something more, and it is notable that the context is Athenian local history. Here (by way of exception) we observe the claim to special knowledge (presumably based on family) that became the norm at Rome.

cidental that the position he espoused not only runs counter to the rather more theoretical inclinations of the Greeks, but exactly suits Pictor, Cincius, and the *clarissimi viri*, "distinguished men," Cato included, familiar to Polybius. In any case, Polybius's criteria are satisfied perfectly by the line of Roman historians that began before him and extended through the empire. The idea, which for obvious reasons was not the kind to be expressed blatantly by writers about themselves,[8] was succinctly, but obliquely, formulated by Tacitus (*Historiae* 1. 1). He characterized the band of writers who followed "those great men of talent," *magna illa ingenia*, of the Roman Republic as people who wrote "in ignorance of public affairs as if these were foreign to them."

Predictably, exceptions arise, most notably Coelius Antipater and Livy, both of them rhetoricians.[9] Each writer in his different way is a testimony to the increasing Hellenization of Roman culture and of the consequent advance of literary precedent. It is noteworthy that Coelius wrote the history of a war (the Second Punic War) long since won: such a work stood in no need of the "dignity and weight of personal reputation" (*auctoritas*) we have been speaking of. Livy, too, was buoyed by the swelling tide of the same cultural trend. Sallust had already spoken of the prestige and utility of history and of the value of its practice as an alternative to political life.[10] In this, the generation of Cicero, the independent value of letters and of the writing of history had acquired the status of a received idea. Hereafter, the non-political writer, the rhetorician, and even the freedman could devote themselves to historiography very much in the egalitarian spirit of the Hellenes. These exceptions, however, serve to high-

---

[8] Lucian discusses it in *How to Write History* 37. The concept was accepted as self-evident by Cato (F 2 Peter). He manages to make it self-explanatory that history is written by great men (while poetry is not; cf. W. Schröder, *M. Porcius Cato: Das Erste Buch der Origines* [Meisenheim am Glan, 1971] at F 2). Similarly Tacitus's reference to his own "public honors," *dignitates*, is more than simple candor; it gracefully establishes his credibility before the world (cf. Polybius 12. 5. 1–3). But we must bear in mind that these writers were of an eminence that presupposed instant recognition; it would have been demeaning to underscore what was tacitly understood.

[9] Coelius was "skilled in the law" and the rhetorical teacher of L. Crassus (Cicero *Brutus* 102); he lived in the mid-second century. For Livy see R. G. Walsh, *Livy: His Historical Aims and Methods* (Cambridge, 1961), pp. 1ff., and R. M. Ogilvie, *A Commentary on Livy I–V* (Oxford, 1965), pp. 1–5.

[10] *Catiline* 3. 2. But Sallust is here still "settling in" to the profession of historian, and he defends his choice as second-best.

light the general rule that in Rome, unlike Hellas, the "narration of deeds" was preeminently a senatorial perquisite.

A third element in Roman historiography significantly altered in comparison with the Greek form was *historia* itself. It is indicative that the concept of research finds no place in the Latin prefaces. Indeed, it must be admitted that history would not have acquired its name from any obvious emphasis placed upon that activity by Latin writers. At the same time, knowledge was much more easily acquired since the days of Theopompus, and fortune placed the Latin writers, as the historians of Rome, at the very center of communications.

The Romans enjoyed an access to information that makes us marvel all the more at the incredible industry of those first Greek writers. Since the Romans were not writing ecumenical history, but treated the affairs of other cities and states only when they became relevant to Rome, foreign affairs could be covered without leaving Rome. Armies and legates would eventually return while a stream of information steadily flowed from dispatches to the senate. Here we see in a comparatively small way how great a difference perspective can make to the labors imposed on the historian. The authors of *Hellenika*, for example, are in principle at least obliged to verify the accounts of both sides of an engagement in which their own compatriots will not always, or often, have been involved. But the Latins did not write the history of various wars between various parties: they required only to know the details of Roman engagements. Though it does not follow that they were uninterested in providing an accurate version of military activities, the logic of their position made it reasonable for them to content themselves with the examination of colleagues entrusted with positions of command.

By the time of the Gracchi, moreover, foreign policy was subordinate to domestic politics, and after this time it became interesting in the degree that it became a pawn in the civil wars. Provinces became worthy of report because of Roman military operations by one faction or another, and even the great war against Mithridates was studied in the light of the contending ambitions of Roman commanders. The new situation enormously simplified the difficulties of research. In this small and tight-knit oligarchical community, information both public and secret was easily obtained. In addition to word of mouth and private communications, senatorial decrees[11]

---

[11] *Senatus consulta* were collected by year at least from 146: Cicero *Ad Att* 13. 33. 3.

were preserved in an archive together with the memoranda (*commentarii*) of public officials. From the first consulship of Julius Caesar (59 B.C.) publication was begun both of the proceedings of the senate and, in the proceedings of the people (*acta populi*), of the most notable public and private business transacted in the city (Suet. *Caesar* 20). The latter were a source of sufficient value to make them required reading for Asconius in providing his commentary on Cicero's speeches (first century A.D.).[12] In imperial times, though Augustus ended the publication of the proceedings of the senate (Suet. *Aug.* 36), minutes were nevertheless kept and a record was preserved of senatorial proceedings and imperial speeches (cf. Suet. *Tib.* 28f.). In addition, apart from numerous memoirs, public speeches sometimes were published (cf. Cicero *Brutus* 94ff.) and the political pamphlet was ubiquitous. Not least helpful was the excellence of the mails, for information could expeditiously be gathered from friends in the provinces. Finally, if antiquarian or ethnographical material was desired, the Latin writer, e.g., Sallust, was spared even the efforts of a Timaeus, for excellent private libraries at Rome provided the collections already made by Greeks or Hellenized barbarians. But there is no need to continue: the balance between research and composition had swung to the benefit of the writer. The change could not have been more clearly indicated than it was, quite unintentionally, by Sallust in *Catiline* 3. 2. Praising history for its difficulty, his reasons were "first, because deeds must be equaled by words; secondly, because most people suppose that your condemnation[s] of faults are malevolent and envious statements." It did not occur to him to add, even in third place, what for the Greeks had occupied the first: the problems of acquiring information.

The benefits of what can only be described as a historiographical revolution came opportunely to Rome, where the tradition had been established (by Cato and, presumably, by his predecessors) of writing history in retirement as the proper adjunct to one's public career. To

---

[12] See H. Peter, *Die geschichtliche Litteratur über die römische Kaiserzeit bis Theodosius I und ihre Quellen* (Leipzig, 1897), vol. 1, p. 115. His entire discussion of the *acta senatus* and the *acta populi*, pp. 205–12, is worth consulting. No implication is intended that the Romans were uniquely fortunate in their possession of documentary material. Greek city-states and the Hellenistic monarchies possessed archives as well; indeed, in all probability the Romans emulated the Greeks when they applied internal principles of organization to their city's records. The difference is that the world's business had become Rome's, so that the documents housed at Rome were of central historical value.

what degree, and in what ways, history was transformed thereafter, especially for the writers of the first century, by its liberation from the exorbitant demands of *historia* is, of course, impossible to say. Greater accessibility of sources hardly implies that the final product will be less perfect or less careful; yet ordinary experience suggests that a new type of writer, with different priorities, entered the lists.[13]

Cornelius Sisenna, if anyone, would seem to be a likely representative of the new school of historians I have postulated. Certainly his predecessors, Fannius (Cos. 122) and Asellio, give every indication of devoted historiography (probably) undertaken in retirement after the conclusion of a busy and respected political life. Their *auctoritas*, in other words, was a precondition of their essay at authorship, just as it had been for Cato. Sisenna, however, did not wait to become a gray eminence; he commenced his *Historiae* (covering the years 91–79) in the eighties during an interlude in his political life, while waiting on events. It is a different kind of psychological moment from that which had earlier been catalytic of historiography in Rome. The inference, moreover, is regrettably confirmed by the tradition of how history became his genre of choice. According to Plutarch (*Lucullus* 1. 7), Sisenna, Hortensius, and Lucullus, "in a jest that turned serious," probably at the turn of the year 89, drew lots to see how each would work up an account of the Social War, in prose or poetry, in Greek or Latin. Now although this jeu d'esprit, presumably authentic,[14] is by no means enough to explain Sisenna's accomplishment of the task, it illuminates contemporary attitudes in general and those of Sisenna and his friends in particular. To put it mildly, this decision was not taken with the gravity and the commitment of a Thucydides or Theopompus, of a Fabius or Asellio. When, furthermore, we combine the anecdote with Cicero's description of Sisenna as a "clever but lazy man" (*Brutus* 64, 228), a characterization of his oratory with implications for his historiography (cf. *De legg.* 1. 2, 7), an impression of the writer forms from which we are entitled to deduce a corresponding alteration in the nature of the challenge history presented.

Cicero, though no historian (an act of omission devoutly deplored

---

[13] See, for example, the authors listed and discussed by Peter, *HRR* 2, pp. XVII–LXXI.

[14] It is accepted by E. Badian, "Where was Sisenna?" *Athenaeum*, n.s., 42 (1964): 429.

by Nepos [F 17 Peter II]), helps us to view the new historiography from within, as it were. His criticisms of earlier and contemporary writers revolve around style and literary character. Historians and annalists are alike condemned for their inability to provide a rich historical texture (*De orat.* 2. 12, 53–54). Cicero's objections gain definition from the faint praise he accords Sisenna, for Sisenna tried to emulate the dazzling historian of Alexander, Clitarchus (*Brut.* 64, 228), and from his still stronger praise of Coelius Antipater (*De legg.* 1. 2, 6, *De orat.* 2. 12, 54), the writer of a derivative and rhetorical monograph.[15] Coelius, interestingly enough, thoroughly deserves the charge so often leveled against other works of similar type: here was a history sacrificing substance to form, history to art, truth to effect. And even the art was rudimentary (F 1 Peter = Cicero, *Orat.* 69. 229).[16]

Cicero's insistence on the formal side of historiography is by itself evidence of no more than the desire to combine substance and form into a pleasing whole. Unfortunately, this aesthetic impulse reinforced the propensity of the Latins of the first century B.C. and thereafter to separate conceptually the "raw material" and the "finished work." Caesar's *Commentaries on the Gallic War* reflect the practice of collecting together the "raw materials" of history, even if he originally intended to depart from custom and publish them in their own right. Cicero's work on his consulship, submitted to the famous historian Posidonius in the hope that he would make a history of it (*Ad Att.* 2. 1), like the materials he would dispense to Lucceius, "his memoranda on every matter" (*Ad fam.* 5. 12. 10), was also conceived as "raw material," however much he may have polished it. Theoretically, of course, there is nothing reprehensible in this; nevertheless, the practice, for so we must view it,[17] implies a

---

[15] The work was patterned on Greek models and may have owed much to Silenus (F 11 Peter). It contained dreams and prodigies (F 11, 34, 39–40), discussions of local history when relevant (e.g., of Capua, F 53–54), probably a description of the Alps (F 13), and even a discussion of the shape of the continents (F 56).

[16] Coelius is estimated more highly by moderns than by the ancients. See. for example, R. Klingner, *Römische Geisteswelt*[5] (Munich, 1965), p. 81, and E. Badian, "The Early Historians," in *The Latin Historians*, ed. T. A. Dorey (London, 1966), p. 17. Cicero's relatively cool assessment (see the passages in *HRR* 1, p. CCXVI) is our best guide. Neither Sisenna nor Sallust looked to Coelius Antipater; like him they looked to (different) Greek models.

[17] See Lucian *How to Write History* 16 and G. Avenarius, *Lukiens Schrift zur Geschichtsschreibung* (Meisenheim am Glan, 1956), pp. 85ff. with Lucian 47f.

dichotomy of form and substance elevating the former. We are reminded of the activities of L. Ateius Praetextatus Philologus, the assistant employed by Sallust and then by Pollio. Pollio said (Suet. *De gramm.* 10) that Ateius was "the greatest help" in Sallust's imitation of archaic language. According to Suetonius, he composed for Sallust's use a "breviary of all things Roman" from which to select what he wished. For Pollio, he composed a treatise on composition.[18] The character of historical writing had clearly changed.

The use of a professionally skilled amanuensis and other such helpers, like the commissioning of a personal breviary, indicates that the historian is beginning to regard himself as the orchestrator of a symphony. He is a great man with stylistic pretensions and, as he believes, with historical insight. In the nineteenth century, he would have written memoirs. Since the avocation was prestigious and not unduly laborious, it could therefore attract the dilettante as well as the serious historian. Pliny the Younger is an example, and his polite demurral to a friend who urged him to write history (an eloquent detail!) illustrates the point (*Ep.* 5. 8). Accepting the premise that a man like himself should indeed write history, Pliny toys with the possibilities:

> [Shall I write of] those remote times which have been treated of already by others? Here, indeed, the materials will be ready to my hands, but the collating of the several historians will be extremely troublesome. Or shall I write of the present times, and those wherein no other author has gone before me? If so, I may probably give offense to many and please but few. [trans. W. Melmoth]

If his silence is our guide, he did not fear or expect "onerous research" from a contemporary theme.

If something extraordinary has gone out of historiography because of this alteration in the concept and the labor of *historia*, nevertheless the results prove at least as interesting. Great historians still emerge, and a higher degree of conscious artistry is infused into the so-called "raw material." For nothing indicates that standards were correspondingly relaxed. Rather, perhaps, they became easier to

---

[18] On the use of assistants and freedmen, see H. Peter, *Wahrheit und Kunst* (Leipzig, 1911), p. 309.

maintain. Asinius Pollio's criticism of Caesar's *Commentaries* is in this respect a salutary reminder of the accuracy expected of all historical authors:

> Asinius Pollio believes that the work is too carelessly and not quite truthfully written. Caesar rashly credited many things that had been done by others and he gave out falsely many things which had been done by himself, whether on purpose or because of a slip of memory. ***Pollio believes that he intended to rewrite and correct them.*** [Suet. *Caesar* 56]

II.

To attempt to characterize Greek historiography, or even its separate varieties, as a whole would be to seek specious uniformity in a medium that more than most takes shape and character from the conditions of its political and cultural environment. By the time of the battle of Actium (31 B.C.), historiography had flourished for more than four hundred years, and another four hundred lay open to it under a progressively monarchical system of government. It was a uniquely long continuum, nevertheless punctuated by great convulsions and dramatic upheavals, and always under the pressure of more subtle, but not less profound, societal changes. The beginning of the epoch was marked by the successful defense of the Greeks against an Asian army of stupendous proportions; then they liberated their people in Ionia and suffered the consequences of a disastrous general war. They allowed the Great King of Persia to arrange their internal affairs; they witnessed the atrophy of the city-state, the rise of federalism, and the development of Hellenistic monarchy. Then they watched the Romans conquer them one by one. Then the Romans witnessed the end of their own liberty and endured the transference of power to men from the once-conquered provinces and finally even the replication of their proud capitol by the shores of the Bosphorus. To be sure, it would be misleading to compare this great epoch, eventful though it was, with an equivalent epoch in modern times. Ancient society underwent no such structural and intellectual transformation as, for example, occurred in the West between A.D. 1100 and the present day. Moreoever, Greek historiographical tradition was continuous and assimilative. Even so, it is beyond doubt that "new wine was poured into old bottles," that radical shifts in approach, method, and style were implemented by scores of writers. Unfortunately, the possibility of studying these trends in all their variety (and, no doubt, illogic) and, above all, in detailed and uninterrupted sequence, is closed to us. The lacunae are simply too extensive.

It is possible, nevertheless, to isolate some of the more salient and enduring characteristics of Greek historiography even as we observe their modification over the course of time. The most important of these are its lack of parochialism and its striving for, and affectation of, neutrality.

The force of Homer's example, here as elsewhere, proved definitive. The tone of the *Iliad* is one of universal sympathy; the tensions are individual: Achilles-Agamemnon, Hector-Achilles; human relations transcended the battlefield: Glaucus-Diomedes, Achilles-Priam. Greek though he is, Homer's sympathies are dictated by the ordinary impulses of human nature and not by ethnic antipathy; he tended to be gentler in his treatment of the doomed (Hector, Andromache, Priam) than of the victors, while his evocation of the cause of the war, Helen, is unsurpassed in its gentle and humane understanding. In general, although Homer described the exploits and griefs of his heroes primarily from the vantage point of the Achaeans in their camp, his depiction of their Trojan opponents is suffused by his perception of their common humanity.

In view of Homer's sway and, especially, the role that the *Iliad* must have played, consciously or unconsciously, in the crystallization of Herodotus's strategies, it is not too much to say that Herodotus assimilated from Homer the fundamental artistic (and historical) rule that the participants on both sides of his great war must be sympathetically portrayed. Individuals were not necessarily good or bad because of the side they represented or because they were Greeks or barbarians. Even in a work intended for the winning side, there was no room for the caricature of an opponent simply because he was an opponent; rational or logical explanations—not the innate evil of one's antagonist—became necessary to account for major confrontations. Political, social, or specifically personal defects (of intrinsic credibility) were required to motivate imperialism and to explain victory and defeat. Hence the articulation of societal judgments: despotism could explain military and moral inferiority, precisely as freedom was the prerequisite for success, at least for the short term. Thus Herodotus characterized the Ionians (of 494) as effeminate in order to explain the collapse of the Ionian Revolt "satisfactorily," and Thucydides used the same motif to explain the ease with which the Ionians fell under the thrall of the Athenians.

The decision (or predisposition) to treat individuals and groups without the intentional distortions that open partisanship would have encouraged was formative of the future. Just as Herodotus made *historia* the prerequisite of any history of the deeds of men, so did his assumption of impartiality and catholicity of viewpoint carry over thereafter to the *persona* of the historian. Thucydides, for example, never tells us his opinion of the merits of his debaters, and puts thoughts into the minds of others when providing a subjective characterization of individuals. Much later, Tacitus testified to the continuity of this tradition when in the *Annales* 1. 4 he presented the case for and against Augustus as if at second hand. Human nature being what it is, these limits were, of course, overstepped. But the ideal was forged and henceforth a categorical distinction prevailed, separating history from the polemics and eulogizing of oratory.

Equally important was Homer's influence in regard to subject. The *klea andron*, "famous deeds of men," arise not in the spheres of ethics and politics but in wars. By making a historical development centering on the Great Persian War his subject, Herodotus provided a definition of theme that again proved lasting. The precedent was critical, as much for what was thereby excluded as for what would be allowed. One could not write about the "deeds" of a city-state; how categorically different from Herodotus's history is Aristotle's *Constitution of the Athenians* is immediately obvious. The constitutional history of Athens or, rather, elements of it, might indeed be relevant to the "deeds of men." The liberation of Athens and Themistocles' naval law are two Herodotean examples (5. 55ff., 7. 144). But its general consideration belongs to political philosophy, not (in the ancient world) to history. A more interesting exclusion, perhaps, is that of civil war. No Greek could have made *this* the subject of history, not only because history transcended the local boundaries of the city-state but because civil discord (*stasis*) resisted inclusion among the "memorable deeds of men." The Homeric-Herodotean tradition had invested history with a sort of poetic nobility, and its impress was never effaced. However debatable the glory of a general war (cf. Hdt. 8. 3. 1), the Greeks knew that civil war was inappropriate to the Muse.

Emphasis on the "famous deeds of men" continued more undiluted than did objectivity. The latter was endangered both by rhetorical practice and by inescapable partisan sympathies. Thucydides managed to maintain a balance; his resolute objectivity is marked, even though he viewed the war from an Athenian perspective. A change is detectable with Callisthenes, both in his rhetorically grandiloquent monograph of the Sacred War of 355–46 (see *FGrHist* 124 F 1) and in his history of Alexander, where Callisthenes deliberately utilized Homeric associations to cast a heroic luster over Alexander and his exploits.[19] The technique bears superficial resemblance to Herodotus's use of Homer, but Homer's influence, though pervasive, is in Herodotus always unspecific; Herodotus did not set up analogues of the Homeric heroes or expect epic associations to be transferred to the characters of his history. Callisthenes wanted Alexander to appear a modern Achilles, and he embroidered his history in such a way as to prompt the reader to observe striking similarities between the epic poem and the history.

That Callisthenes simply acted out of sycophancy is unlikely. On the contrary, he is on record as believing that the historian did not reflect greatness, but was its source. "He did not come to Alexander in order to acquire reputation but in order to make him famous among men" is a statement attributed to him by Arrian (*An.* 4. 12). In a word, elevation of Alexander implied elevation of self; and we may presume that Callisthenes engaged in more or less self-conscious emulation of Homer, the prize being immortality. In these circumstances, it is not surprising that history veered from the course originally set by Herodotus. The procedure that "enriches" a story by interpolating into it well-known literary motifs intended to evoke significant associations signals the arrival of the overtly artful historian—the writer whose art is purposefully obtrusive. We are reading Callisthenes on Alexander, not a history of Alexander as composed by Callisthenes.

The distortive effects of Callisthenes' technique can readily be imagined. When a writer attempts to invest his history with signifi-

---

[19] See L. Pearson, *The Lost Histories of Alexander the Great*, APA Monograph no. 20 (1960), pp. 40ff.

cancies external to it and, in addition, strives for literary brilliance, the magnification of his subject must follow. Wars are greater than ever, battles more fierce, the sacks of cities more violent, command-ers more brave, tragedies deeper. Once popularized (preeminently by Clitarchus, again with Alexander as the subject), this approach to historiography filled a need strong enough in the third century to prompt Duris of Samos to develop an aesthetic specifically applicable to it. Duris demanded that historians excite the reader's emotions by imitating the reality of history's wondrous course.[20] Naturally, this was to unlock the last barriers of the imagination: the historian was hereby encouraged to heighten the effect of spectacular or surprising occurrences.

The striving for literary effect, like the urge to rhetorical display on the part of some others (see, for example, Polybius 12. 26. 9), must, however, be kept in proper perspective. These are the ex-cesses of art, not the emotions. Some writers there were, as in all cultures, who applied techniques of this type to gain reward (see, e.g., *FGrHist* 161–63, 188) or to vent malice (Timaeus, *FGrHist* 566 F 34f.). But we should not be simplistic or unduly cynical, for admiration can be selfless, and often the affiliations between author and subject were in the first instance intellectual and indirect. A large number of Greek historians wrote as they did for reasons appar-ently external to their own immediate circumstances—Sosylus of Lacedaemonia (*FGrHist* 176), the contemporary historian of Hanni-bal; Duris on Agathocles; Phylarchus (*FGrHist* 81) on Agis and Cleomenes. The literary and dramatic possibilities, or the sheer his-torical importance of what was impending, drew these writers as moths to a candle.

As might be expected, the framework within which the Greek historians chose to describe the deeds of men varied in accordance with their more special purposes. The most obvious and important development, as has been stated, was an increasing emphasis on the deeds of leading individuals. Here several tendencies exercised joint influence. Since the fifth century, a social and political transforma-tion of society produced a weakening of the old order of the city-state and the raising up of monarchs, tyrants, and other powerful individuals. Since they now stood at the center of events, it fol-

[20] See chapter 3.

lowed naturally that Hellenic histories came to be organized around their deeds. Some historians, however, chose to write about the deeds of individuals rather more because of a compelling interest in the people themselves than because of their political significance. The careers of famous men often possessed storybook qualities. Agathocles (361–289), Duris's subject, for example, rose from low birth to tyranny and pursued a military career that included the gain and loss of North Africa. We may legitimately distinguish, then, even within the "biographical" context, between writers with a political orientation and those with primarily artistic-personal interests.

Unmistakable is the natural correlation between subject and technique. The possibilities for developing emotional resonance are progressively limited by extension of the field of study. Thucydides was uniquely successful in imparting character and life to such collective entities as cities and armies; to lesser writers or, more fairly, historians living in less favorable times, when the city-state had lost its special character as the personification of its people, comparable tensions could only be induced by emphasizing the fortunes of individuals. When, therefore, a group of writers from Clitarchus to Phylarchus, a group including Hieronymus, organize their history around dynasties or individuals, its interests are rather more than simply historical. In part, it is what in modern times incites biography. To this we must add political interest, fascination with power, the vicarious appreciation of boundless resources, and, without doubt, literary ambition. For if history became high literature because of the dignity of the subject and the intrinsic greatness of even its ordinary themes, having become high literature it naturally attracted the gifted writer who intended to work in prose.

As stated, however, the opportunity to exploit the human emotions stood in inverse proportion to the breadth of the historical canvas and receded with its enlargement. In this context, the work of Agatharchides of Cnidus, of the second century (*FGrHist* 86), Polybius, and Posidonius acquires special interest. For although the sweep of universal history, as Polybius saw (1 *ad init.*), possesses a drama and intellectual excitement unrivalled in their own way, the more human sentiments are less likely to be stirred and the satisfaction of playing upon them is proportionately reduced. It is not, of course, a case of all or nothing. Brilliant portraiture such as Posidonius's picture of the Athenian tyrant Athenaion (87 F 36), admiring human interest such as that displayed by Polybius for the first Africanus (e.g., 10. 2. 1ff., 23. 14), and such vivid description as that provided by Agatharchides in his account of the Red Sea (GGM 1. 111ff.), were all, in fact, found in these writers. But these elements are subordinate to a grander intellectualization of history reversing the priorities of Clitarchus-Duris-Phylarchus. History is practiced more purely for its own sake than for the literary possibilities inherent in the plot.

In contrast with Greek multiplicity and variety, the series of Latin historians commencing in Gracchan times and extending into the empire gives every appearance of a relay race. Rome's first historians, as we have seen, had been Greek-inspired in subject as well as method, for the history of Roman expansion was the history of war. One fundamental difference from the Greek approach even for these first writers, however, as well as for those who followed, was their simultaneous concentration on local politics. To Roman historians, the internal and external business of the city were naturally two sides of the same coin.[21] But an essentially new beginning was nevertheless made by the Gracchan writers: they and their successors display remarkable uniformity in their single-minded attention to the civil discord erupting before their eyes.

The historians naturally separate into two groups, republican and imperial. Each group seems homogeneous—unless it is an illusion fostered by our deep ignorance of most of these writers. With the exception of Livy, not one continuous page of any of the histories of the republican writers is preserved, and even in Livy's case the most important segment for our purposes, his account of the late republic, is lost. As for Sallust, although the fragments of his *Historiae* are relatively numerous, he would possess nothing like his current standing were it not for the survival of his two monographs (the *Catiline* and *The Jugurthine War*). Works of historians of imperial times are also poorly preserved. (Velleius Paterculus, the Emperor Tiberius's encomiast, though of imperial times, is a writer of an altogether different type.) Tacitus is our only guide, and we shall never know exactly how unique or typical he was, to what extent his attitudes are

---

[21] Thus Sallust defines his subject in the preface of the *Historiae* (F 1 M.) as "the affairs of the Roman people, both at war and at home," while long after, when Rome's actual importance was drastically reduced, Ammianus Marcellinus still feels compelled to provide an almost yearly report of the happenings at Rome.

conventional, or whether he is, in fact, the quintessence of what preceded. But even if we allow for oversimplification, it is not too much to conclude that members of each of these groups, in their different ways—the republican writers from Fannius to the transitional figures, Pollio and Cremutius Cordus,[22] and the imperial writers from Aufidius Bassus to Cluvius Rufus, Fabius Rusticus,[23] and Tacitus—all unite as the students and critics of a single historical process. Naturally, they viewed this process from (as it were) opposite directions. The pressing subject of the earlier group of writers was the political and moral disintegration of the Roman city-state. The imperial writers agonized over the deprivation of liberty ending this process and they viewed the actions of the emperor as a consequence, but also as a further cause, of their humiliation. It was a baffled and angry group aware of the undesirability of a return to the anarchy of the late republic and yet theoretically and practically appalled by the nature of the new regime. We observe, therefore, a tradition of historical writing lasting for more than two hundred years, whose uniform theme is treated by individuals involved with, and suffering from, the very conditions they attempt to describe and analyze.

Within the unanimity of concern indicated by the concentration of these writers on the local political scene, some significant differences appear as well. This historiography seems to have commenced with a spirit of desperate optimism, which was subsequently transformed into a grimly diagnostic mood; this in turn gave way to retrospection.[24] Through all this change, however, most of the historians are distinguished by a deliberate avoidance of partisan pleading. The characteristic is not the less admirable because it ultimately derives from Hellenic tradition (first Polybius, then Thucydides, on his rediscovery), for the Roman revolution tested the participants

[22] A. Cremutius Cordus should be counted, with Pollio, an Augustan writer. He may have read his pro-republican history to Augustus (Peter, *Geschichtliche Litteratur*, vol. 1, p. 66 n. 2, vol. 2, pp. 38f., *HRR* 2 CXIV). He wrote on the years of civil war, including Augustus's generation (Seneca *Ad Marc.* 26. 1 with Dio 57. 24). We possess his account of the treatment of Cicero's corpse (F 1 Peter), a highly rhetorical piece of work.

[23] See Peter, *Geschichtliche Litteratur*, vol. 2, pp. 39–42, R. Syme, *Tacitus* (Oxford, 1958), vol. 1, pp. 271ff.

[24] It is significant in this regard that the contemporary history of the elder Seneca (*HRR* 2 F 1, p. 98) began "from the beginning of the Civil Wars" (Peter, vol. 2, CXCIII). Aufidius Bassus began at the same point.

more radically than any Greek was tried when confronting a general Hellenic war.

The first stage appears to have consisted of didactic optimism, and it is represented by Fannius and Asellio, the Gracchan writers. Fortunately, Asellio's concept of historiography is known (F 1–2 Peter). In an echo of Polybius, he asserted that the knowledge of causes will teach the man of politics not only to defend the state, but to avoid actions to its detriment. The statement stood in book 1 of his work, almost certainly in his introduction, and it therefore does not seem imprudent to assume a correlation between his concept of history and his purpose in writing. As an intellectual successor of Polybius, Asellio wished to apply historical explanation to the improvement of the future. Factional strife arising from the Gracchan crisis must be repressed; history containing the knowledge gained from the past and the present is a valid means of attaining that end. The assumption that Fannius took a similar view, though a large one, is supported by a statement occurring in the introduction to his work (F 1 Peter). Fannius made the sententious observation that it is often the case that things that at first sight seem to be good in themselves turn out otherwise. If the statement is programmatic, as its location suggests, it carries a message essentially identical to Asellio's: history, as the study of origins, of causes, teaches what is likely to be dangerous even if it seems good on its initial appearance or (perhaps) is prompted by good intentions. Implicit in both historians, therefore, is the conviction that the city-state is not beyond the reach of good counsel.

The composition by Fannius and Asellio of their histories with the *auctoritas* of statesmen hoping to explain, anticipate, and forestall political disaster necessarily implies that they rose above faction and addressed themselves to the entire body politic. So much can be allowed them on the basis of the little evidence we possess. Thus, although Fannius's loyalties lay with Scipio Aemilianus (F 4, 7 Peter), and he was therefore the opponent of Gracchan extremism, it is vital to observe that he portrayed the military career of Ti. Gracchus sympathetically (F 4). He testified to Tiberius's generous perception of the greatness of Aemilianus and gave him the palm among the youth for discipline and courage, when he and Tiberius were the first to scale a defended wall in Libya. Biographical details are neither neutrally nor innocently provided by the historian; Fannius clearly adopted a conciliatory stance and attempted to present both sides sympathetically. This permits us to appreciate the remarkably strong sign of approval conferred on Fannius by Sallust in the introduction to his *Historiae*. Fannius was praised for "truth." As for Asellio, his adoption of a comparable *persona* follows automatically from his emulation of Polybius. Although his application of Polybius's scientific principles is no guarantee of his objectivity, his adoption of the pose is what chiefly matters to us, for it is incompatible with open partisanship.

Cornelius Sisenna is of interest here chiefly because of his atypical qualities. He is without doubt an exceptional figure in this line of republican writers. In the first place, Sisenna primarily wrote history to praise Sulla, and it does not seem possible that he could also have been driven with even residual objectivity to *explain* a political process. The evidence is quite incontrovertible. Sallust's charge that he wrote "disingenuously" (*BJ* 95. 2) is a harsh judgment by one historian of another; since Sallust could have written nothing more damaging, one would be compelled to assume that the flaw was real, even if the case were unsupported by further indications. In fact, we possess a damaging fragment from Sisenna (F 132) and a very telling remark by Sallust (*Historiae* 1 F. 88 M). Alluding to the follower of Sertorius, T. Didius, Sallust wrote that "he was of great importance in organizing and equipping the soldiery during the Marsian War; many things that had been accomplished because of his leadership at that time received no notice, at first, because of the baseness of the writers and then because of their jealousy." Whoever else may have been in Sallust's mind, Sisenna assuredly was.

We expect adulatory history from annalists, not historians; one of the most admirable qualities of our group is the determination to diagnose without the interjection of narrow partisan interest. It was a prerequisite of their magisterial authority and gave force to their pronouncements as historians. It is, therefore, natural to inquire whether Sisenna may be anomalous in other respects as well, and the answer seems to be that he parted company with them intentionally in aiming to produce a Hellenistic masterpiece, a panegyric history of conventional Greek design. Certainly, his history was redolent of Hellenistic influence; Sisenna even parades Ephorus's (now conventional) stylistic principle that events will be treated topically, not in strict and relative order, "so as not to impede the attention of the readers by tearing apart coherent contexts or jumping back and forth" (F 127 Peter). The principle, which Sallust ignored[25] and Polybius explicitly rejected, implies a concern with the reader and his pleasure that is typical of the "literary" Greek historians. Part of the same pattern is his use of the non-historical excursus (F 5, 123), his recondite, various, and entertaining style (Ovid *Trist.* 2. 44. 3–4) and his pursuit of vivid writing (F 26, 60, 78f., 103, 107).

At this point it is useful to remember that, according to Cicero, Sisenna's historical model was the famous Clitarchus, renowned for his encomiastic and brilliant portrait of Alexander the Great. "In history [Sisenna] strains for childish effects with the result that he appears to have read no one but Clitarchus and no other Greek besides. Clitarchus, however, he seems at least to wish to imitate. Even if he were to do so successfully, he would nevertheless fall considerably short of excellence" (*De legg.* 1. 2, 7).

The evidence, therefore, uniformly suggests that Sisenna's history was a work of literary art, a *Kunstwerk*, as well as a history of the Social War. Normally, the possession of such literary goals would deserve no special comment beyond the observation that Sisenna was, in fact, in the forefront of the Hellenization of historiography desiderated by Cicero.[26] In the line, however, of Fannius-Sallust, it makes Sisenna an exception. Naturally, the work must have had merit even so; it was ample and presumably well informed. That Sallust began where Sisenna left off (assuming the conjunction was intentional) indicates the acceptability of his history as part of the continuous record begun by the Gracchan writers. But nothing suggests it was a great work, and it was soon unread.

Sallust takes up the thread spun by Fannius and Asellio. As his criticism of Sisenna and his praise of Fannius underscore, Sallust, perhaps with the ostentation rendered obligatory by the behavior of his predecessor, adopted the persona of an objective observer of the partisan spectacle. Unlike Fannius and Asellio, however, who also

---

[25] Although Sallust did not blindly follow the annalistic pattern, his treatment of the Sertorian War is in direct opposition to Sisenna's advocacy of the topical arrangement of such campaigns.

[26] The most likely interpretation of Varro's choice of Sisenna for the *logistoricus* entitled "Sisenna; or, On History" is that Sisenna was made the spokesman for what looked to be the "new historiography."

strove to be above "party," but who simultaneously tried to teach and to repair by their histories the damage that was daily increasing, Sallust at most taught implicitly—if it were teaching to inveigh against the moral corruption he considered the root cause of Rome's plight. His real purpose, however, was to provide a vivid and indelible picture of the symptoms and the progress of the civil wars.[27]

Sallust's conception of his duty as a historian argues a view of historical utility one step removed from Polybius's and one step closer to that of Thucydides.[28] Thucydides described what to Roman eyes looked like a "civil war of Greece," and he attempted to diagnose its causes and development without evident utilitarian purpose, rather like a fascinated doctor who describes the ravages of an interesting and fatal disease. Now, in Rome, matters had grown too serious, too irreparable, to permit history to be written by an optimistic didact or partisan writer, whose respective nostrums—political education or the triumph of faction—were patently delusive. Sallust thus adopted the persona of Thucydides and emulated his style and objectivity. Of this no better example can be found than those concluding speeches of Caesar and Cato in Sallust's *Catiline*. Eduard Schwartz was as certain that Caesar was praised to the disadvantage of Cato as other scholars have been convinced of the opposite.[29] So also is Cicero judged to have been maligned, ignored, or treated fairly in the same work. Surely such disparate appraisals suggest that we are injecting our own impressions into a designedly neutral text. Sallust concealed his predilections; for the sake of historical truth, he repressed his loyalties and took (or tried to take) an objective view of the entire situation, which was one of competing virtues and corollary vices.[30] The real and notorious historical deficiencies of the *Catiline*

[27] So also K. Latte, *Sallust* (Leipzig, 1935), p. 56. According to V. Paladini, *Sallustio* (Milan, 1948), p. 195, Sallust undertook to restore virtue to the Romans. Sallust's "truest self" has by turns been found in a partisan "impressionistic painter" (Mommsen), tragic historian (Schwartz), philosopher (Schur) and *éminence grise* (Büchner). See C. Becker's bibliographical discussion: "Sallust," in *Aufstieg und Niedergang der römischen Welt*, ed. H. Temporini (Berlin, 1973), vol. 1. 3, pp. 720–31. Sallust proves elusive because we demand more from him than he provides; see the sound and conservative estimate given by R. Syme, *Sallust* (Oxford, 1964), pp. 271–73.

[28] See chapter 3.

[29] Schwartz, "Die Berichte über die Catilinarische Verschwörung," *Hermes* 32 (1897): 571ff. See Syme, *Sallust*, p. 115, and Becker, *Aufstieg*, vol. 1. 3, pp. 731–42.

[30] If Sallust recognized the necessity of impartiality when describing individuals and events, he also believed that it was necessary and proper to measure them off against an ideal standard centered in moral virtue. *Optimates* and *populares* (the "oligarchi-

and the *Jugurthine War* aside, both works strive for impartiality. But they are not didactic works in either Cato's or Asellio's sense. The works document "new and unwonted precedents" so that the reader will possess a clear picture (if not analytical understanding) of two epochal moments of Rome's dissolution. That the *Historiae* were written in the same spirit need not be doubted, though it cannot be proved. The best indication of Sallust's position in regard to his subject is the admiration he earned from Tacitus, whose emulation would otherwise be inexplicable.

The didacticism of Fannius and Asellio, like the analytical approach of Sallust, correlates with the stages of crisis enveloping them. Similarly, the decision by Livy to write a history of Rome "from the foundation of the city" can reasonably be explained by the circumstance that the republic, as traditionally conceived, had come to an end for better or for worse. Disorienting though the realization must have been,[31] the conception was for the first time grasped of the beginning and end of a definite and tremendous epoch—the entire prior life-span of Rome. Livy was inspired to deliver the eulogy, or, rather, to study the rise in the light of the decline (for each illustrated the other) and, especially, to trace the apparently inevitable process of degeneration, commencing before 146 but accelerating after 133, that was ending the era (*Praef.* 9, 11–12).

Much of this is implicit in the preface to Livy's work. "It will nevertheless be pleasant for me . . . [in spite of the immensity of the task and the rivalry of others] to be mindful of the memory of the

---

cal" and "popular" factions) were studied in the context of their declining ability to place motherland above self (see D. C. Earl, *The Political Thought of Sallust* [Cambridge, 1961], p. 116); every individual was assessed in terms of moral character, for the indissoluble connection of virtue and good government had been axiomatic to every thinker since Plato. For the Romans perhaps no passage is more instructive than Cicero *De re publ.* 5. 1, 1 Ziegler, which should be consulted.

[31] The Romans, of course, operated under the assumption of continuity, i.e., an open-ended, linear (though not progressive) view of history. Now "What will be the result if the core of belief in a linear scheme breaks down . . . ? When this happens, the shock to historical consciousness resembles a geological cataclysm: both leave a palpable void in their respective spheres, mental and physical. Because time *is* history for a linear model, the realization of the model's central goal [or the realization that the line has been ruptured] will 'stop' history, temporarily divorcing it from the sense of time passing. The sensitive observer of such a cataclysm, possessed of an idea of history, will be vulnerable to a profound feeling of discontinuity and disjuncture, a loss of historical bearings." This perceptive observation by G. M. Wilson, "Time and History in Japan," *AHR* 85 (1980): 557, is directly relevant to Livy's realization that the unthinkable had occurred and time, literally, was out of joint.

deeds of the chief people on earth" (*Praef.* 3) implies that the last of the good old days is quite gone. That he mentions the more than seven hundred years of history he will be writing of (4) can be regarded as a rhetorical heightening of the magnitude of his labor. But it can also be understood as an indirect allusion to the longevity of the old Rome that is coming to an end, "falling by its own weight," *magnitudine labor[ans] sua.* For the history of his day is one in which "the strength of a long-since superior people devours itself" (4). It is a "display of ills" that his "generation has witnessed for many years" (5), but which should not embitter his account of the beginnings of Roman history, though the ills must be dealt with in their proper turn (12).

Whether or not Livy was an "Augustan," as he has often been called, is unimportant here, for few would urge that the appellation be understood in any strict sense.[32] Certainly Livy maintained his literary independence. Augustus called him a Pompeian (Tacitus *Annales* 4. 34), and the point of this allusion should not be blunted, especially when he is further described (in the same passage) as "distinguished in the very first rank for his eloquence and his probity." Livy's reputation in imperial times is strictly incompatible with pro-Augustan leanings, for if there was any group inclined to be merciless in its condemnation of any deficiency in properly republican attitudes, it was the historical writers of the early empire.

It is hard to doubt that Livy has often been prejudged because of his rhetorical background. Yet his republican orientation is something that may have required considerably more independence and strength of mind from a rhetorician than it did from a politician (for example, Pollio) whose connections and prestige ensured his safety, however ostentatiously (*FGrHist* 88 T 3) he vaunted his indepen-

---

[32] It is, however, mere *petitio principii* to date his preface as late as possible in order to bring Livy and Augustus into some kind of spiritual conjunction. See J. Bayet, *Tite-Live* (Paris, 1971), vol. 1, pp. xvii–xix for the assumption of an initial publication of books 1–5 between 31–29 B.C. with a "corrected" edition between 27–25 B.C.) (1. 19. 3 with 4. 20. 7, 1. 10. 6–7). R. M. Ogilvie, *A Commentary on Livy* (Oxford, 1965), pp. 2, 564, wants a later date (27–25 B.C. for the completion; nothing undertaken before 29), making Livy share "the mood of optimism that is evident in Virgil's *Georgics*. The arts of peace could flourish once again" (p. 2). Livy's evocation of Sallust in *Praef.* 9–11 carries a different message; and though T. Janson, *Latin Prose Prefaces* (Stockholm, 1964), p. 70, thinks the preface more "up-beat" than "down," the ambiguity thus attested is the best indication of its nature, precisely because it runs counter to ordinary expectations.

dence. Livy's treatment of the "spoils of honor," *spolia opima*, won by Cossus (4. 20) is a case in point. Confronted with an assertion by Augustus that ran counter to his own information, and this on a matter of immediate political importance to Augustus (because of the force of historical precedent), Livy registered Augustus's observation *but did not change his own story* and by implication let it stand. In any event, two threads of the many that run through Livy's work are important to us in this context. The first is his continuous development of the theme of civil turmoil at Rome, the second the onset of "avarice, extravagance and lust" (*Praef.* 12). In both cases, he followed his predecessors, and, especially in his account of the Struggle of the Orders, he retrojected his own conceptions as well as those of his sources. But the pursuit of these themes, of the historical process of decline, unites him with the great republican writers.[33]

Of Pollio, who is unfortunately known to us only through a meagre scattering of random fragments, it is impossible to say whether he is the last of the republican writers or the first of the new age; in truth, he seems to be neither. Something hangs on the determination: we should like to know the purposes of his work and the spirit in which it was written. Fortunately, the chronological limits he chose supply a valuable clue. The fact that Pollio commenced his history in 60 B.C. (Sallust broke off at 67) combines with his decision to end with Caesar's death (or Philippi) to suggest that he wrote a monograph rather than a continuative history picking up on the work of his predecessors. His choice of 60 B.C. as the starting point is only suitable as the prelude to the great final act of the Civil Wars. For a history of Roman *stasis*, however, the date was unsatisfactory. By presenting Caesar as an established politician and by dismissing (except, undoubtedly, in mere summary form) the critical period 67–61, the causative framework was arbitrarily cut. It is, therefore, difficult to believe that Pollio intended to provide a history of the type offered by Fannius and Sallust, devoted to the study of the unresolved and exacerbating crisis. Here comparison with Sallust proves instructive. Sallust, too, wrote after Caesar's death; yet he went back in time as far as the death of Sulla in order to chart the course

[33] See T. J. Luce, *Livy: The Composition of his History* (Princeton, N.J., 1977), pp. 276ff. Many moderns endeavor to attribute a protreptic, or hortatory, aim to Livy quite unsubstantiated by the history itself; it is based, if on anything, on the occurrence of perfunctory rhetorical commonplaces (*topoi*) as in e.g., *Praef.* 10.

of revolution. That he was guided by the substance of the story rather than by an inherently desirable pattern of events cannot be doubted: Sallust yielded to the requirements of *perpetuae historiae*, the provision of a continuous sequence by historians writing in a chain of succession. Pollio, on the other hand, selected a period of dramatic unity. If the implications are valid, we lost in his history a dramatic and artistic work more similar in compositional technique to Sisenna's than to Sallust's. More important, it would have been a work embodying a certain artistic distance, retrospective in tone, and written rather more with the desire to record brilliantly than to explain. In this sense, it foreshadowed imperial historiography.

The historians of the empire, viz., the senatorial writers, are represented for us by Tacitus. They are the direct continuators of the republican series, except that it fell to their lot only to record the untoward consequences of a fait accompli. If Tacitus is a reliable guide, they wrote in the bitter diagnostic style affected by Sallust, maintaining at least the forms of objectivity.[34] As Sallust had described *stasis* at Rome, so Tacitus attempted to provide a sharply etched picture of Rome under the emperors. The species is the same, though it is naturally and automatically modified to reflect altered conditions. But it is senatorial history, focused on the source of power and its abuses at Rome.

III.

Greek historical writing begins with a grand question and continues with the elucidation of a myriad subordinate ones. Herodotus wrote to preserve the memory of great deeds of Greek and barbarian "and especially to tell the cause, why they fought each other." His arrangement of historical material was dictated, therefore, by a preconceived inquiry into causes, and the history itself is a nest of questions and answers framed in the form of explanatory digressions. A paradigm is supplied in the introduction to the *Iliad*:

> Sing, goddess, the anger of Peleus' son Achilleus
> and its devastation, which put pains thousandfold upon the
>   Achaians,

[34] Tacitus, who truly wrote without hope of favor or revenge for past mistreatment, would have seen no inconsistency with these forms in despising the principate and depicting it as despicable. The tradition went back to Thucydides and his account of Cleon.

hurled in their multitudes to the house of Hades strong souls
of heroes, but gave their bodies to be the delicate feasting
of dogs, of all birds, and the will of Zeus was accomplished
since that time when first there stood in division of conflict
Atreus' son the lord of men and brilliant Achilleus.
What god was it then set them together in bitter collision?
Zeus' son and Leto's, Apollo, who in anger at the king drove
the foul pestilence along the host, and the people perished,
since Atreus' son had dishonored Chryses, priest of Apollo,
when he came beside the fast ships of the Achaians to ransom
back his daughter. . . . [trans. R. Lattimore]

As we see, Homer, after stating his theme, Achilles' anger, asks in
the eighth verse the name of the god responsible for the quarrel.
Having named Apollo, he states the cause that indirectly precipitated the violent debate between Agamemnon and Achilles: Apollo
visited the Achaeans with a plague because he had been angered by
them. Now Homer explains the reason for Apollo's anger by presenting a scene (a flashback) eventuating in the humiliation of
Chryses, his priest. The method of question and answer, involving
anterior explanations, is identical with that of Herodotus (just as
the motive causes of events are closely similar). The difference lies
in Herodotus's transformation of the direct rhetorical question into
declaratory statements of intent.[35] That the method, though stylized, approximates the normal manner of unaffected narration is
readily apparent.

Herodotus was not, of course, a poet, and since he was also firmly
fixed in the fifth century, he dispensed with the routine interference
of the Olympian gods in human affairs, normally explaining events
in terms of the usual, predictable human reactions. On the other
hand, he is unique among Greek historians in also accepting the historical importance of the supernatural. It is not here a question of
his belief in the true prophecy by Apollo as interpreted by his priests
at Delphi (1. 13. 2 with 91); the conviction that there existed a sympathy between the gods and the world of men rendering possible the
divine origin of oracles, dreams, and prodigies lingered throughout
antiquity. Nor was he so credulous as to believe in the Homeric pan-

---

[35] E.g., 1. 95. 1: "The course of my history now compels me to inquire who this
Cyrus was by whom the Lydian empire was destroyed, and by what means the Persians
had become the lords of Asia."

theon. The gods (excepting oracular Apollo) have lost their personal identity, and when they are named individually (e.g., 7. 129. 4), it is metonymy. What renders Herodotus unique and, indeed, Homer-like, is that he assigned actual paramountcy in human affairs to "fate" or "divine power." [36]

Herodotus presupposed a moral universe in which fate or the divine power was intelligent and operative. Insolence was punished and the human condition (as the episode of Polycrates' ring so well shows) was confined within its proper limits; the gods permitted beatitude to none. Herodotus seems to have believed that the divine intelligence considered it as much a part of its function to deny perfect happiness to mortals as it was to punish wrongdoing. Now although this world-view was devoid of originality (cf. Aeschylus Choeph. 1065ff.), the manner in which Herodotus harnessed it to historiography was bold and impressive. As we read Herodotus, the conviction grows within us of history unfolding at the silent direction of invisible powers who will interpose themselves on the rare occasion when their will is likely to be thwarted. In most cases, to be sure, the causes of actions were straightforward on the purely human plane; by and large Herodotus was able to construct a history that was fully intelligible without reference to divine agency (though its operation was implicit). Thus, for Herodotus, the sequence of historical deeds pivoted on the act of injustice. Now since he was the historian of war, and unprovoked aggression was of all injustice the most blatant, the causes of war must (ordinarily) be either revenge or immoral ambition. The revenging parties, when successful, acquired prosperity—and insolence. Thus was precipitated an endless chain of retributive actions and reactions, which, though "fated to be," were caused by human agency.

But of most interest to us is Herodotus's "higher" vision, or rather his fierce determination to persuade the reader that history conforms to a divine plan that, like the will of Zeus, must be fulfilled. That is why he produced a recalcitrant Xerxes and the wisdom of Artabanus

[36] It would be ingenuity misspent to seek for real distinctions within the broad range of his terminology. He assigns control alternatively to "the divine" (to theion), "the gods" (theoi), "divine power" (daimon), "fate" (moira), "destiny" (moros), "the fated" ([moira] pepromene), and "divine fortune" (theia tyche). H. Strasburger, Die Wesensbestimmung der Geschichte durch die antike Geschichtsschreibung (Wiesbaden, 1966), p. 70, observes that Herodotus was the first and the last representative of "theological" historiography.

in unsuccessful opposition to an invincible divine power at the most critically important moment of the entire *Histories*—when the question of whether or not to invade Greece required decision. The passage (7. 8–18) may be paraphrased briefly. First comes a meeting of the royal council, with Xerxes and Mardonius specifying reasons for attacking Greece. All of them were good reasons and in another context might have carried the day. Artabanus counters with arguments of moderation that Herodotus's whole history had prepared the reader to accept as undeniably correct. Here another surprise: contrary to expectations raised by the now familiar Herodotean pattern, *Xerxes is actually persuaded* by Artabanus. This intrusion of the unexpected—a wise course consistent with the principles of divine order has been willingly adopted—motivates the entrance of divinity in the form of a dream. Twice the dream comes to Xerxes, and on the second occasion he is threatened with speedy destruction unless he commits himself to march and sail on Greece. Artabanus would have Xerxes ignore the vision: dreams (he says) are not really divine messengers, but scattered recollections of the day's concerns. But at Xerxes' insistence Artabanus dons the royal garments and sleeps in the royal bed, and is himself visited by the apparition. It promises *his* destruction because he "tried to prevent what is fated to happen." Artabanus naturally withdraws his opposition since "this impulse has clearly come from god."

Herodotus has in this episode purposefully overstepped his usual limits by allowing a divinely sent dream to *change Xerxes' mind*, to his incalculable woe. It should be stressed, perhaps, that the final misinterpretation of the dream (according to which the Persians will triumph) is entirely secondary to its unremitting insistence, accompanied by threats of destruction, that the invasion must take place. In this great and pivotal passage, Herodotus insists that, no matter how convincing the arguments may be for or against a decisive action (cf. 1. 34ff.), it will take place because it is fated to be.

Thucydides no more recognized Fate than Chance[37] as a force in

---

[37] In contemporary oratory, Chance, or *Tyche*, could serve as a specious explanation of success, failure, misfortune, and the unanticipated (cf. Antiphon 1. 2, Lysias 13. 63, Demosth. 18. 194). These rhetorical uses of the concept (applied in speeches twenty times) are manifest in Thucydides; *in propria persona*, the word signifies luck to him (4. 55. 3, 5. 75. 3), an occurrence independent of one's own enterprise (7. 33. 6), paradox (4. 12. 3, 14. 3), coincidence (5. 37. 3), and the operation of natural phenomena (3. 49. 4, 4. 3. 1).

human events. In explaining the causes of his war, fear, honor, and self-interest become the motive forces behind the deeds of men.[38] But it is easier to speak in general of such elements of human nature than it is to decide when they are specifically to be applied. And here Thucydides faced a much more complex problem than did Herodotus, whose historical perspective was clarified by the passage of time and the simplifying tendency of oral tradition. Thucydides wrote contemporary history as it unfolded: he needed to explain the causes of his war by analyzing a multitude of circumstances and by assessing the numerous public and individual allegations made on both sides. Ignoring the easy and superficial view that Pericles or the Corcyraean alliance or Potidaea or the Megarian decrees caused the war, he developed a view of causation distinguishing between what we may term "direct" and "real" causes:

> To the question why they broke the treaty, I answer by placing first an account of their grounds of complaint (*aitiai*) and points of difference (*diaphoroi*), that no one may ever have to ask the immediate [or direct] cause which plunged the Hellenes into a war of such magnitude. The real cause (*prophasis*) I consider to be the one which was formally most kept out of sight. The growth of the power of Athens, and the alarm which this inspired in Lacedaemon, made war inevitable. [1. 23. 5–6, trans. R. Crawley]

Although the meaning Thucydides intended to convey with these terms has been much debated,[39] some holding that *aitiai* and *diaphorai* mean "immediate," "proximate," or "direct" causes, while others understand them as "pretexts," it is sufficient to observe here that "fear," since it is a psychological state, requires some specific excitation if it is to result in a declaration of war. If we recognize this, we must recognize also that a so-called "pretext" is, in fact, a "direct cause" when it functions as the rationale of such a declaration. It seems clear, therefore, that Thucydides attempted to explain the outbreak of the war on two levels—in terms of the immediate

---

[38] 1. 75. 3, in the speech of the Athenians at Sparta. Parts of the doctrine, with its ramifications, are nakedly expressed in the Melian Dialogue, 5. 87–111.

[39] See A. W. Gomme, *HCT* I, pp. 153ff., K. von Fritz, *Die griechische Geschichtsschreibung* (Berlin, 1967), vol. 1, pp. 623ff., and G. E. M. de Ste. Croix, *The Origins of the Peloponnesian War* (London, 1972), pp. 51ff. A truer translation of the last sentence quoted may be found in R. Sealey, *CP* 70 (1975), 92.

political circumstances and by way of a long-developing psychology that invested those circumstances with deadly significance.

After Thucydides the terminology and method of inquiry were firmly in place; how wars began, how alignments were made and unmade, were the primary questions investigated by the historian. For these a variety of explanations, often mutually supporting, could be pressed into service. One only was excepted, the supernatural, for belief in divinity had become irrelevant to historical explanation. As the author of *Airs Waters Places* affirmed of certain Scythians,

> The natives believe that this disease is sent by God, and they reverence and worship its victims, in fear of being stricken by it themselves. I too am quite ready to admit that these phenomena are caused by God, but I take the same view about all phenomena and hold that no single phenomenon is more or less divine in origin than any other. All are uniform and all may be divine, but each phenomenon obeys a law, and natural law knows no exceptions.[40]

Nor were matters altered if one regarded *Tyche*, or Chance, as a potent force in the world,[41] for *Tyche* was by definition incalculable. As "the friend of variety" and "the enemy of stability" (Cicero *ND* 2. 43) its works could be pointed out only after the event. Similarly, though for an altogether different reason, Stoic fate, guided by *Pronoia*, or Forethought, was beyond the comprehension of the historian and had to be accepted in retrospect. To ascribe a historical movement to *Pronoia* was not the same as to attribute human agency to its controlling force. The difference is plain in Polybius's preface where, although something very like Stoic *Pronoia* (providential *Tyche*, or purposeful Chance)[42] is invoked in a general estimate of Rome's remarkable rise, no special appeal whatever is made to active intervention in human affairs. The absence of the concept, in other words, would leave Polybius's account totally unaffected. It is the same with the Latin writers. Livy could believe that Rome was fated to be built and to rule the world. But this conception of *Pronoia* did

---

[40]Quoted from Arnold Toynbee, "History," in *Legacy of Greece*, ed. R. W. Livingstone (Oxford, 1921), pp. 306f.

[41]For thorough discussion with abundant citation of texts see G. Herzog-Hauser, *RE* s.v. "Tyche," cols. 1650ff. See also below chapter 3.

[42]See F. W. Walbank, *A Historical Commentary on Polybius* (Oxford, 1957), vol. 1, pp. 21ff., P. Pédech, *La méthode historique de Polybe* (Paris, 1964), pp. 332ff.

not require that the historian shape events in order to bring them into corresponsion with his notion of the mandates of heaven; he simply inferred the will of heaven from the shape events took on earth.

Of the numerous types of explanation open to the Greeks, fifth-century environmental theory is one of the most interesting. This theory held that a correlation obtained between climate, diet, and moral attributes. That the concept shaped Herodotus's thinking appears from the closing chapter to his history. The recognition that an interconnection existed between climate and abundance and that luxurious living renders men effeminate led naturally to the view that "hard countries breed hard men" thereby possessed of the will to resist subjugation. This view, which seemed so eminently sensible, quickly became truistic (see [Xen.] 2. 7) and functioned axiomatically in Greek historiography. As to the attribution of specific causes, much naturally depended on the insight of the writer, who might choose to emphasize ancestral enmities and friendships, the psychology of a city, ideals, retribution, faction, greed, lust.

An interesting trend gradually becomes apparent in the work of Xenophon, Ephorus, Theopompus, and Callisthenes, where the explanation of political events is sought in the personality of leading individuals. As Dionysius of Halicarnassus noted, "Theopompus not only observes and narrates that which is evident to most people with reference to each specific action, but he analyzes the concealed causes of deeds, the motives of those responsible for them, the emotions in their hearts, something most people do not easily comprehend, and he reveals all the mysteries of alleged virtue and unsuspected vice" (FGrHist 115 T 20 [7]). This "secret history"—Geheimgeschichte, as it has been called—is only partly the result of Theopompus's cynicism. It is a method of explanation perfectly suited to the historical study of monarchs, whether Philip II, Philip V, or, indeed, Tiberius Caesar. It was next to useless to attempt political explanations of the actions of Philip and his son: any such attempt could be undercut and be regarded as a screen hiding the workings of personal ambition, animosity, or sheer viciousness. In fact, the decline of political democracy—or rather, the rise of Hellenistic monarchy—necessarily centered explanation in the individual. Theopompus's psychological approach was perhaps extreme and subjective, but in a more acceptable form it was adopted by the later writers, Polybius included (e.g.,

5. 108. 5), who were equally obliged to explain the actions of monarchs and their attendants. Only in democracies and in leagues could the standard "political" explanations be invoked, as we see from Polybius's accounts of the deliberations of the Achaean League. Even so, whatever the focus, whether political or personal, the foreign policy of monarchs, city-states, and leagues continued to be the standard subject of historical explanation.

Concern with causes of an altogether different type was introduced into historical analysis by Polybius. For in addition to charting the course of Roman hegemony, a process that required the kind of explanations we have been considering, Polybius provided a second order of explanation for Roman success—her superior government. To explain the nature of this superiority, he had resort to political theory and the notion of the "mixed constitution."[43] Thus Polybius superimposed one explanatory system upon another by introducing political philosophy into history (6. 5. 1–2). Rome acquired hegemony by way of the usual collisions, attended by uniform success; but Rome's career was (really) successful because of the peculiar nature of her constitution. These are separate levels of explanation: the opponents of Rome were defeated by superior armies, not by the constitution, yet the Roman constitution became the anterior cause of their superiority.

The difference between Polybius's approach and the conventional mode may be seen by comparing it with Xenophon's analysis of the power of Jason of Pherae in Hellenica 6. 1. 4ff. Jason's superiority is shown to consist in his control of Thessalian cities, possession of excellent mercenaries, and extraordinary bravery. Power was thus explained primarily in terms of commensurable units—resources, fleets, trained soldiers. Naturally, the connection between the form of government and the quality of the citizenry was not unknown before Polybius. Herodotus recognized the relation of Spartan bravery to the Eunomia, as Sparta's "well-ordered" government was called.[44] Thucydides invested oligarchy and democracy with what he considered apposite qualities (though it would perhaps be truer to state that he characterized oligarchy and democracy in accordance with

---

[43] See F. W. Walbank, *Polybius* (Berkeley and Los Angeles, 1972), pp. 130ff.

[44] 1. 65, with which Thuc. 1. 18 and 84. 4 may be compared. So also the Athenians, when "liberated" from their tyranny, became militarily successful (Hdt. 5. 66. 1ff,), thus taking a stride forward analogous with the Spartans'.

his perception of the "nature" of Spartans and Athenians). But Polybius went a step beyond this by arguing that the Roman constitution was the primary explanation of Rome's conquest of the rest of
the world. An inversion of explanatory priorities has taken place. A
contributory element (e.g., Athenian resiliency in Thucydides) has
become primary; elements heretofore primary (men, material, sea
power, and so on) are explained in terms of an allegedly higher
principle.

A theory dedicated to explaining a successful enterprise is ipso
facto impossible to shake, and Polybius's simplistic analysis of the
"mixed constitution" would have been no exception. However,
Polybius lived to see the signs of the dissolution of the Roman government. The events of 146 B.C., when Carthage and Corinth were
needlessly destroyed, and of 133, when the tribunate of Ti. Gracchus
threatened the peace of the city and the loyalty of the allies, unequivocally showed that a sickness had set in. The question thus
raised—what had happened to the *Roman people?*—would dominate
the historiography of the Roman Republic. In other words, an inversion of explanatory priorities heralded by Polybius became standard:
it was not Roman superiority that required explanation; it was the
breakdown of Roman government. The Roman historians from Fannius to Livy would naturally continue to explain the usual historical
developments in the usual way, in the pragmatic mode established
by Herodotus, Thucydides, and Polybius. But these elementary sequences now had to be adjusted to an entirely new context. The
chief question in the minds of the Latins was one with which Greek
historiography had never attempted to deal (except incidentally and
superficially),[45] for the decline of a city-state or kingdom was sufficiently accounted for in the context of ecumenical history by its defeat in war.

Polybius had, in fact, shown the way by remarking the ultimate
instability of even the "mixed constitution." Deterioration of the
government, as he supposed, must result from an impairment of natural balances and from the rise of demagogy, itself a consequence of

---

[45] Theopompus, Duris, and others stressed the cultural differences dividing one antagonist from another (the hardy Macedonians, the luxurious Demetrius of Phalerum)
and the very substantial ethnographical research of writers from Ephorus to Timaeus
emphasized such variations. But they had no reason to make the devolution of a city-
state, monarchy, or nation (*ethnos*) their central subject.

the deterioration of the moral character of the people. That Rome's strength lay in the character of its people was also the traditional Roman view, and it had been enunciated most forcefully by Cato. And, by a coincidence more apparent than real, the finest thinkers of the age were reaching similar conclusions. The geographer, philosopher, and historian Agatharchides of Cnidus (*FGrHist* 86), who was a contemporary of Polybius's, studied the *mores* and social problems of his historical subjects, observing especially closely the marks of luxury and excess displayed by nations and single individuals (*FGrHist* 86 F 2–3, 7, 11–12). His work (entitled *Asia and Europe*) renewed the old Ionian methods and interests, whereby the entire environment of a man or a people was studied systematically with especial reference to character and customs. There emerged a concept of ethnic identity (cf. Polybius 4. 20f.) fully developed by Posidonius (see, e.g., *FGrHist* 87 F 105), the most authoritative philosopher and historian of the first century B.C. and a thinker unquestionably influenced by Agatharchides.[46] Now Posidonius seems to have correlated Roman successes with Roman fidelity to ethnic tradition, simplicity of life, and adroit but limited borrowings of foreign ways (i.e., weapons but not debilitating foods). Thus he underscored the plainness of Roman living habits and the concomitant lack of ceremony. Scipio Africanus, he noted, had gone off to organize the kingdoms of Asia attended by only five servants. The contrast with Rome of the first century could not have been greater.

The relevance of this kind of analysis to the preoccupations of the Romans of the generation of Polybius and thereafter is apparent, and its continuous application to Rome from Polybius to the authors of the first century is equally plain. Polybius had made prosperity (*eudaimonia*) the engine of the degeneration of a government that was not subverted from without:

> For when a regime wards off great dangers **and thereafter attains superiority and unshakable power**, it is clear that, once *eudaimonia* has firmly been established, **people live lives of greater luxury** and the men vie for office and for other perquisites more ardently than they should. [6] When this situation intensifies, **political ambition** and fear of losing face, to-

[46] See H. Strasburger, "Poseidonios on Problems of the Roman Empire," *JRS* 55 (1965): 48f.

gether with **pretentiousness and luxurious living**, prompt a change for the worse. [7] The *demos* will receive the credit for the change when it comes to believe that it is being injured by the over-reaching ambition of some and it is rendered foolish by others who flatter it to gain office. [8] At that point the *demos* becomes savage and, considering all measures with passion, is no longer willing to listen to its leaders or even to be their equals, but wishes to have the entire preeminence. [6. 57. 5–8]

The explanation of Roman decline presented by Polybius,[47] whether entirely his own or also inspired by Roman thought, was seized upon by the Latins of the first century, although they differed in their emphasis on one or another component of the theory. In this sense, one may loosely distinguish between two "schools" of thought. One group, represented for us by Sallust, sought the explanation of political *stasis* from 133 in the Roman success achieved by the destruction of Carthage in 146. "Fear of the enemy [*metus hostilis*] had kept the Romans prudent and moral" (*BJ* 41. 3); a flood of evil qualities corrupted the people and their leaders once that menace was removed. The same writer, in the *Historiae* (1. F 11 M.), alleged that "discord, avarice, political bribery and the other ills that tend to arise when things go well were greatly increased after the destruction of Carthage." In the same fragment, he was careful to add that political discord and economic injustice had also prevailed during the early republic, until ended by the fear arising from the Second Punic War, a view of earlier times supported, if not derived, from the abundant (though hollow) testimony of the annalists. The same theory appears in Diodorus Siculus (34–35. 33. 3–6), who attributes its formulation to Scipio Nasica Corculum, the opponent of Cato in the debates over Carthage and the unsuccessful advocate for its preservation. (Naturally, Polybius knew the speech.) The theory belongs to Posidonius as well; to what extent the ideas of both Corculum and Posidonius have been amalgamated by Diodorus cannot even be guessed, but no reason suggests that Corculum was

[47] That Polybius wrote these words, and interpolated them into book 6, after the events of 146–33 is a distinct possibility (one might even say "likelihood") although Walbank, *Polybius*, p. 134, remains of the opinion that nothing "requires the hypothesis of a date later than around 150 B.C. for its composition." Everything turns on whether or not Polybius's experience of events before 150 could have led him to commit himself to the idea of a popular revolution *in Rome*.

made the mouthpiece of a speech invented at a later time.[48] "Fear of the enemy" had evidently early become regarded in the conventional wisdom as an instrument of domestic peace.

The other "school" of thought is best represented by Livy. It held that Rome's disequilibrium resulted primarily from erosion of moral character. Foreign conquest had introduced luxury to Rome, notably in 187, with predictable results. But the concept of "fear of the enemy" played its part in this scheme too (just as *luxuria* operated in the other), as is clear from the following epitome of Dio Cassius (from 21):[49]

> Scipio Nasica still advised sparing the Carthaginians. And thereupon the senate became involved in a great dispute and contention, until someone declared that for the Romans' own sake, if for no other reason, it must be considered necessary to spare them. With this nation for antagonists they would be sure to practice valour instead of turning aside to pleasures and luxury; whereas if those who were able to compel them to practice warlike pursuits should be removed from the scene, they might deteriorate from want of practice, through a lack of worthy competitors. [Zonaras 9. 30, trans E. Cary]

Fear of the enemy, therefore, would preserve the people from decadence and ensure domestic peace and harmony. As Livy himself stated,

> This enemy [the Ligurians, with whom the Romans were waging war in 187] seemed as if born to the role of preserving Roman military discipline in the periods intervening between the great wars. Nor was any other province a better whetstone for military virtue. For Asia with its pleasant cities and abundance of good things on land and sea and the effeminacy of the enemy and its royal wealth made the armies richer, not braver. [39. 1. 2–4]

It would appear, therefore, that by the first century a single complex of ideas suitable to diverse emphasis by different parties had de-

---

[48] See chapter 4.

[49] Dio seems to have known his Livy; see F. Millar, *A Study of Cassius Dio* (Oxford, 1964), p. 34; W. Soltau, *Livius' Geschichtswerk* (Leipzig, 1897), pp. 190–92, minimized the dependancy of Dio on Livy.

veloped. Sallust's ultimate cause was the removal of Roman apprehension, Livy's the deterioration of national character through luxury. But the precondition of each theory was the primary cause of the other. In this connection, it is noteworthy that Sallust rounded an epoch with the war against Perseus (171–68),[50] even though he also insisted that concord and relatively sound *mores* continued at Rome until 146 (*Historiae* 1. F 8 with 11 M.): fear kept degeneration in check and *mores* sound in spite of the introduction of luxury into Rome after Perseus's fall. Livy's comments on the results of the Roman defeat of Perseus and Antiochus (39. 6. 7–9) perfectly explain Sallust's theory of competing influences:

> The origin of foreign luxury was its transportation into the city by the army of Asia. These were the first men to carry to Rome couches with bronze feet, expensive carpets, curtains and other textiles, and also pedestal tables and marble-topped sideboards, items which at that time were considered magnificent pieces of furniture. At that time females who played the lute and sambuca and various other convivial delights were added to the banquets. The dining itself began to be prepared for with greater care and expense. At that time a cook, a possession of the lowest value to the ancients both in monetary terms and in function, became expensive and his ministry began to be reckoned as an art. These things, **scarcely noted at the time, were the seeds of future luxury.**[51]

It will be noticed that not even Livy suggested that the infusion of foreign wealth destroyed Roman *mores* in 167.

Whatever the exact relationship of Polybius, Posidonius, the annalists, Sallust, and Livy, the nature of their problem is clear: Roman historiography was concerned with explanation that in intractability and in type was utterly different from that attempted by the Greeks. A shift was made from the study of "pragmatic causes" to the cultural-philosophical question of Rome's decline.[52] Unfortu-

---

[50] F. Klingner's adjustment of Bertold Maurenbrecher's fragments of *Historiae* 1 in *Studien zur griechischen und römischen Literatur* (Zurich, 1964), pp. 577ff. is skillful but uncertain; it would be circular to use the fragments (as rearranged) to equip Sallust with a simplified "theory of historical development."

[51] Cf. Dio Cassius 19. 64.

[52] Thus Hippolyte Taine, in his sparkling *Essai sur Tite-Live* (1856; reprint ed., Paris, 1923), pp. 132f., put the cart before the horse in charging that Livy was a moral-

nately, questions of this type do not admit of "pragmatic explanations." An inversion of priorities therefore came about, so that "higher causes" superseded in interest the strict investigation of the historical record. We observe the change in Sallust's *Catiline* and *Jugurthine War*, where no attempt is made to analyze the political and social causes of faction; instead we are presented with its symptoms. Livy, too, is lazy and indifferent about details. It has, for example, been pointed out that Livy modeled his narrative in such a way as to avoid problematic chronological attribution; evasion was preferable to investigation and resolution.[53] He cannot be exculpated from the blame attaching to such practices on the ground that chronology was a "foreign science." The truth is that Livy simply was not interested; the actual record of events was of less importance to him than the trend they foreshadowed. And this was a result of the inversion of causal priorities.

The imperial writers, who no longer concern themselves with the causes of the Civil Wars and took the decline for granted (Lucan *Phars.* 1. 158ff.), recall the Greek writers of the line descending from Theopompus. What Dionysius wrote of Theopompus applies to Tacitus, who sought to read the motives of the (in this respect) unfortunate men who were placed in the position of being the natural adversaries of the senatorial aristocracy. The focus in the *Annals* on successive emperors permits the scrutiny of these men precisely as the critic studies actors on the stage, noting and interpreting their gestures with an abnormal sensitivity.[54] *Geheimgeschichte* was renewed in an atmosphere of distrust and uncertainty. After 27 B.C., writes Dio Cassius,

---

ist because rhetoric is above all things moralistic. His approach was mandated by what he perceived to be the fundamental nature of the problem.

[53] H. Tränkle, *Livius und Polybios* (Basel, 1977), pp. 48f., Bayet, *Tite-Live*, p. xxiv n. 5.

[54] Tacitus's depiction of the emperors, especially of Tiberius, is of course famous for its simmering malevolence. But we must keep in mind that his main problem was to interpret character. Operating on the assumption that individuals do not change, but reveal their true selves when circumstances liberate them from constraint (the clear message of *Annales* 6. 51. 6), Tiberius (it followed) must at first hypocritically have repressed and concealed his flaws, screening them with conduct that retrospect proved ambiguous and deceptive. Tacitus sought to correlate the exterior and interior self, which in fact converged by stages, attaining identity only at the last, when all checks to Tiberius had fallen away—Augustus, Germanicus and Drusus, Livia, Sejanus. "Finally he rushed into wickedness and disgrace, after the removal of the need to feel shame and fear, when he simply acted according to his own nature" (6. 51. 6).

most business began to be conducted secretly and was kept hidden purposefully. If something were in fact published, it was distrusted because it could not be tested. The suspicion was general that all speech and action was accommodated to the wishes of the rulers and their colleagues. [4] Thus many things that did not happen received wide circulation, much that very definitely occurred was unknown, and virtually everything was reported differently from the way it happened. [53. 19. 3–4]

III

The Theoretical Foundations of Greco-Roman Historiography and their Application

History's Definition

Startling though it may seem, the concept of history in the *objective* sense, that is, as the aggregate of past events—was unknown to antiquity. It is a major difference from modern historical thought; the reason behind it, together with its ramifications, goes far to explain what seem to us to be the serious conceptual limitations of ancient historiography taken as a whole. In a vague way, unquestionably, people must have thought of just such an aggregate of events when they spoke of "the past," and they must dimly have contemplated a similar totality when referring abstractly to "the future." But this is not the same as a concept of history identifying the two; it is only we who make the association. It is essential to recognize that, to the Greeks and Romans, "history" was not an aspect of time; "the past" and history were no more intrinsically related than were "the present" and history. The relation was identical for both: "history" was written both of the present and of the past. Now without the idea of "objective history," "subjective history," an idea we take for granted, is impossible to conceive of. To be sure, history may be encomiastic or vituperative or biased in some other way (cf. Polybius 16. 14. 6–10, 1. 14), but these are mere deficiencies in the character of the historian, not limitations imposed by his finite capacity. To believe (as we do) that historiography is a partial and imperfect selection of data out of a veritable universe of occurrences, it is necessary first to postulate the existence of "objective history" and to compare this vast ocean with the few buckets of water we draw from it. This concept having been formulated, it becomes desirable and pressing to refine historical technique and to expand the range of material brought to bear on individual subjects in order to achieve a closer and closer approximation to the "whole truth." Alternatively, in the absence of such a concept, such a technique will no more develop than will the idea of seeking after "the whole truth."

The explanation for this conceptual divergency lies in the fact that the definition of history has expanded cumulatively through time in the West. From our perspective, the Greco-Roman definition *is* rudimentary. "History" is an abstract word to moderns (except when applied to a particular work); to ancients, the notion was concrete even before the word *historia* came to designate it. When we write history, we conceive of our work as a partial and incomplete selection from a theoretical totality of past events, developments, occurrences, and so on. By definition, written history can never attain the "whole truth" after which it searches. But the ancients did not begin or end by considering history as a sum total. History was for them a specific and sharply delineated slice of the present or the past. The definition they started with was that of Herodotus, who defined his subject as the memorable deeds of men, and this definition, with some expansions relating to the treatment of notable individuals, remained standard thereafter.

History, therefore, was *res gestae*, accomplishments, of a particular kind. Herodotus did not intend to write a history of all that he knew about the epoch he described or even (we may suppose) about the critical events at the center of his account. He wrote about what was (or should be) "well known," "splendid," "worthy of relation." His purpose was to inquire into the precise circumstances of well-known deeds. This definition excludes the possibility of omission (a modern dread arising from our concept of "objective history") or, more realistically, it confines that possibility within narrow limits.[1] This particularity of approach proved decisive. Although a "history

---

[1] Variation, in other words, is merely a matter of degree. Thus Polybius notes that "the Romans will read his work because it contains the most famous and the greatest number of their deeds" (31. 22. 8); cf. 16. 14. 7.

of the past" implies the existence of the total aggregate of human experiences, "the history of famous deeds" does not. History is not "whatever happened" but the famous achievements of men with respect to a specific subject, originally military activity.

Aristotle's views, which some have interpreted to indicate a different, more catholic, view of history, in fact prove corroborative of the position outlined here. In a difficult passage in the *Poetics* (1459A), he gave a definition of history in the form of advice to the epic poet. The subject of an epic poem, he wrote, should be dramatic and deal with

> a single action that is whole and complete and has beginning, middle, and end, so that like a single complete organism it may produce the pleasure proper to it. It is also clear [from the preceding] that the structure should not resemble [that of] histories[2] in which of necessity an explanation [*delosis*] is rendered not of a single transaction but [A] of a single period of time, i.e., all the things that happened in it to an individual or to more than one individual.[3] Each of these events is related to the others accidentally [= by no necessary tie]. For [B] in the same way that the sea battle at Salamis and the battle with the Carthaginians in Sicily took place in the same time and in no way led to the same result, so too [A] in a strict sequence of time it sometimes happens that different events follow each other from which no single result is produced.

It is important to be clear about what Aristotle does *not* assert here about history. We must not incorporate his commonsense simile (B), one developed to explain something he perceived to be intrinsic to history, into his definition of history itself. In addition to Aristotle's unproblematic description of the way histories were written (A), he supplies an analogy (B) to elucidate his sophisticated observation about the intrinsically random relationship of events in series. He is clarifying his objection to the adoption by a poet of the principles of historical composition. The poet ought not to write

[2] So with R. Kassel in the Oxford Classical Text (1965), as originally emended by Dacier (1692) and confirmed by the manuscript ER[1]. See A. Gudeman, *Aristoteles Poetik* (Berlin, 1934), ad loc. For arguments in support of the traditional reading, see R. Weil, *Aristote et l'histoire* (Paris, 1960), pp. 163–73.

[3] The phraseology makes it certain that Aristotle contemplates (written) history centering on a small minority of leading individuals.

about the achievements of an individual (Heracles, Theseus) or about any subject defined temporally (the war against Troy). The events of which the sequence consists, Aristotle observes, stand in no essential relationship to one another, and so the resultant plot will be less compelling and less satisfying. In order to illustrate the point, Aristotle selects an example not from "history"—for it is the fallacy of the historical plot, *with its specious unity*, that he wishes to expose—but from its analogue, the "real world." Just as the two battles mentioned were irrelevant to each other, though they occurred on the same planet at the same time, so in history (A) events follow one another that are organically unrelated even though they occur in the same sequence.[4]

Aristotle does not, therefore, imply that "history" is the record of all events anywhere; he states that a chronological progression must perforce include events of disparate origins unified by the larger subject (Theseus's adventures, the war between the Peloponnesians and the Athenians) and not by their intimate mutual relation. Hence his characterization of history in 1451B 5–7 (where the same line of thought is pursued) as less philosophical than poetry. When Aristotle asserted that the poet must provide "a sequence of events that is possible in the sense of being credible or inevitable,"[5] he presumed that there was nothing inherently and necessarily *credible* or *inevitable* in any historical sequence. To Aristotle, historical sequences may, perhaps, always be *explicable*, and, as his use of the comparative suggests in the famous phrase "poetry is more philosophical than history," events in sequence may on occasion even be credible or inevitable.[6] But it is not the nature of history to collect events with a

[4] That is to say, just as the battles occurring everywhere in Hellas are (obviously) unrelated to one another since they form part of unconnected wars, so are the battles connected by time within a unified history, *qua* battles, essentially unrelated, mere episodes (like the labors of Heracles). The point, if recognized, would have obviated some implausible discussions. Thus G. Avenarius, *Lukians Schrift zur Geschichtsschreibung* (Meisenheim am Glan, 1956), p. 112, regards (B) as part of Aristotle's definition of history—so that Aristotle is allegedly warning the poet against the possibility of composing a drama consisting of a sequence of unrelated matters. M. Mazza, *Storia e ideologia in Tito Livio* (Catania, n.d.), p. 43 n. 14, seems to hold the same view, though he expresses it differently; he asserts that Aristotle is defining the difference between unity of time (= history) and of action (= drama).

[5] This is the translation of L. Cooper, *Aristotle on the Art of Poetry*[2] (Ithaca, N.Y., 1947).

[6] Much of the discussion centering on this phrase and its implications (see F. W. Walbank, "History and Tragedy," *Historia* 9 [1960]: 216ff.) is complicated by such ques-

view to these qualities, any more than it is a property of life (in contrast with art) to produce them for the historian. The historian reproduces particulars because they are memorable, not because they are credible; the poet selects from particulars and forms them into a credible sequence.

We must bear in mind, therefore, that Aristotle does not advert to a sequence of events all of which are credible individually (this is "history") but to a *sequence* that is credible because it consists of organically related events, one growing naturally from the next. The historian, on the other hand, must weld a chain of categorically different links—land battles, sea battles, helot revolts, internal revolutions, plagues, disputes among allies, etc. These particulars are collected in accordance with a principle that is indifferent to their genesis and concerned only with their effects, in a word, indifferent to their mutual interdependence and propriety to art. Thus, Aristotle says,

> No art [science: *techne*] has the particular in view, medicine, for instance [considers not] what is good for Socrates or Callias, but what is good for this or that class of persons (for this is a matter that comes within the province of an art, whereas the particular is infinite and cannot be the subject of a true science); similarly, therefore, Rhetoric will not consider what seems probable in each individual case, for instance to Socrates or Hippias, but that which seems probable to this or that class of persons. It is the same with Dialectic, which does not draw conclusions from any random premises—for even madmen have some fancies. [*Rhetoric* 1356B, trans. J. H. Freese]

The relevance to history and tragedy could not be greater. Tragedy, too, must select events with a view to their general credibility, and it would be a mad poet who would seek a plot from history because of its random credibilities. If suitable material can be found in history, it is accidental to the nature of the craft.

To return to *Poetics* 1459A and Aristotle's definition of history, it remains to consider what exactly he understood by "all the things that happened in a single period of time to an individual or to more

---

tions as whether history is "really" philosophical. In fact, when we philosophize from history, it is on the basis of a highly selective procedure (not unlike that which Aristotle recommends to the poet).

than one individual." Did he mean "everything" or "everything important"?

Aristotle's words, taken alone, are susceptible to either interpretation and rather favor the idea of complete inclusivity. The context makes it apparent, however, that Aristotle limited himself to "everything memorable." In the first place, he is describing real histories or plots of comparable type, and these made no attempt at inclusivity. Secondly, the poet would not stand in any need of Aristotle's advice if "history" were everything that happened. No poet would be in the slightest danger even of contemplating the possibilities of such a choice; in fact, the danger exists because poets, like historians, write about everything that is memorable, not everything that happens. The danger faced by the poet is his inclination to integrate into one plot a series of actions that are important in themselves but intrinsically unrelated. That is the objection to history. Single transactions possess cumulative weight, not organic connection. What Alcibiades did or suffered, what Hellas did or suffered, are in the nature of discrete actions, logically associated only from the viewpoint of the actor. Just as there is no intrinsic connection between the labors of Theseus, so the events in history are only unified in respect to the subject, like multifarious flowers in a meadow all picked by the same hand. Thucydides' plague, for instance, or Phormion's battle at Naupactus or the Athenian capture of Pylos are events of this kind exactly, intrinsically separate episodes. But as to the nature of the events themselves, it is clear that they are to Aristotle of one and the same kind: the memorable and important, exactly as Herodotus had defined the subject.

It has already been observed that Herodotus shaped history in conformity with the themes of the epic, which sang the *klea andron*, the famous deeds of men. "This is the exhibition of the research of Herodotus of Halicarnassus, so that human events may not become faded through time, and so that great and amazing deeds,[7] some of them achieved by the Hellenes, others by the barbarians, may not lose their fame, and, especially [to set down] the reason why they fought against each other" (1 *ad init.*). By limiting the discussion (in principle) to the "great and amazing deeds" accomplished in war or otherwise, Herodotus perhaps united epic theme with Ionian

---

[7]Jacoby, *RE* s.v. "Herodotus," col. 334, took "deeds" (*erga*) to mean monumental constructions as well as deeds. Though the usage is attested, it is inappropriate here. Physical monuments will not lose their fame through time.

method. The importance of the events described must transcend normality and, in fact, be worthy of "inquiry." Hence the methodologically important statement that

> Harpagus subjugated the territories of lower Asia while Cyrus himself subjugated its upper portions, conquering every nation and passing none of them by. Now we shall ignore the greater part of them; but those that gave him the greatest trouble and are most worthy of relation shall I make remembrance of. [1. 177]

The definition of history remained constant thereafter, although its limits were widened as time passed and new concepts of the "historically important" replaced the old, especially among the Latins. But the selective principle endured; even the voluble Dionysius of Halicarnassus stated (*AR* 2. 30. 1) that he would relate those deeds of Romulus in war and in the city "which can be reckoned worthy of historical interest," and even at the very close of classical antiquity Ammianus abode by the same rule (e.g., 17. 7. 1, 11. 5).

Herodotus's definition of history's proper subject was accepted by Thucydides and, if anything, concentrated still further. For Thucydides confined himself to "the things that were done" in the war, and by this he meant (some of) the speeches that were delivered and the military engagements that ensued (1. 22. 1–2). It is significant (and lamentable) that this definition precluded his discussion of such mundane matters as domestic politics. To the modern historian, the state of mind in the city and the opinions of various segments of the population are pieces of information sorely missed; Thucydides, however, was singly concerned with the resultant "memorable" acts (cf. 3. 90. 1 with 7. 30. 3).

How narrow a slice of the present or of the past constituted history for the writers of Thucydides' generation and the next is well indicated by a complaint from Xenophon (*Hellenica* 5. 1. 4). "Now I well know," he wrote, "that this matter pertains to no expenditure [*dapanema*] or danger [*kindynon*] or contrivance [*mechanema*] that is worthy of relation [*axiologon*]. But, by Zeus, I think it worthwhile for a man to understand what it was that Teleutias did to dispose his men toward him in this way." We may infer from Xenophon's words the formation of a clear-cut and commonly accepted theoretic or definitional framework. The proper subject of history had become a settled thing, limited to the notable activities of men at war and, by extension, between wars. Hence the enumeration by Isocrates (*Antidosis* 45) of the four main kinds of prose writing, as follows: "For some men have spent their lives investigating the families of the heroes, others have made the poets their study, others have wished to collect together [*synagagein*] the deeds accomplished in war," while still others write dialogues. This restrictive convention, as Xenophon shows by his resentment of it, defined "deeds" (*praxeis*) invidiously and, as it were, externally, to comprise the actual operations of war. Xenophon reveals the tension developing between a burgeoning desire to study the notable characteristics of individuals and the "law" of history affirming the priority of events and deeds.

This definition, confining though it was, did not subsequently alter. Aristotle, as we have seen, presupposed it in the *Poetics* and underscored it in *Rhetoric* 1. 1360A.35 where he defined history as "the investigations [*historiai*] of those who write about *the* deeds."[8] Polybius, moreover, reaffirms the principle in words that echo Xenophon's complaint that history is supposed to limit itself to expenditures, danger, and contrivances—the formulation must have become standard. Thus he explains his omission of Egyptian affairs in the appropriate part of his history on the ground that Ptolemy had relapsed into a dissolute life and achieved nothing of moment: "This man, except for the cruelty and license of his court, performed neither a land battle nor a sea battle nor the siege of a city nor any other thing worthy of remembrance" (14. 12).[9] Thereafter the meaning of the word remained basically the same. In spite of the inevitable and numerous infractions, history continued to be an account of the important deeds of men, principally in warfare. As a poet of the time of Domitian, Statius, wrote, history was

> armed conflicts
> And the distinguished deeds of men and fields pouring over
>   with blood
>
> [*Silvae* 1. 2. 96f.]

---

[8] Elsewhere (*Poetics* 1451B, 1459A) he refers to "history" as a self-explanatory concept. His inconsistent usage suggests that the general meaning of *historia* narrowed to embrace history in our sense in Aristotle's time. The word could of course still be used in the original sense, context making clear the intended meaning. See, e.g., Geminus in Polybius 36. 1. 8.

[9] Cf. 39. 12. 1–4. The same categories of history appear in Plutarch *Alex.* 1.

Objectivity

As we turn our attention from the ancient concept of history's province to some of the more important principles and theoretical developments shaping its form and content, we are struck immediately by the numerous and sometimes conflicting demands imposed on the historian. Unlike writers in other literary genres, in which the play of the imagination enjoys free scope and the objective connection with the world of reality is attenuated, the historian was obliged to approximate reality while at the same time presenting a cogent, ordered, self-explanatory account. This practitioner of *mimesis* was, in short, torn by these competing requirements, which he took as necessary and desirable in themselves, but which came into collision in fact if not in theory. He must tell the truth, and do it brilliantly and meaningfully. He must capture the reader by his art, instruct, edify, and eternalize virtue and infamy—especially infamy. At his most ambitious, the historian was an artist seeking by means of his art, but in fidelity to the truth, to be the teacher or the conscience of his people, or both. Conversely, he sought to capture the vividity and drama of the world he described for the delight and fascination of his readers. Clearly the historian was in the awkward position of serving two masters, what we call art and science.

Of the various principles laid down by the ancients, none is more fundamental than the honest and impartial presentation of the facts, and it is entirely consistent with their clarity of vision and intellectual emancipation that the Greeks gave it to the world. The principle was a natural, indeed, reflexive inheritance from the ethnographic-scientific Ionian school: *historia*, unless accurate, is a contradiction in terms.[10] The line of succession from Hecataeus to Herodotus is here direct and unproblematic, while Thucydides probably deserves the credit for solidifying precedent into a rule by his unmistakable demonstration of intellectual honesty and severe impartiality. Thus a veracious report of what men actually had said evolved into a veracious narrative of what actually had happened, based on the collation and sifting of the reports of informants. The historian who determines the truth from his sources has evolved

[10] It is immaterial, of course, whether or not the story is a fiction; what matters is its authenticity as a story.

from the writer whose purpose it is to collect and repeat with accuracy the "stories" or "accounts" of others.

Since the historian must now weigh his sources and exercise his independent criticism, he has become far more than "the reporter of tradition," and it is perhaps remarkable, therefore, that neither Herodotus nor Thucydides found it necessary to assert his intellectual independence and freedom from bias. The point was hardly academic: Herodotus perforce disposed of the reputations of the jealous and contentious city-states taking part in the Persian War at a time when recent enmity, the outbreak of the Peloponnesian War, had sharpened the significance of his characterization of them. Thucydides, moreover, was a citizen of one of the leading cities contending in the war, and was thus directly concerned with its issue. Yet both could rely upon at least conditional acceptance of their work as an objective contribution, and for this their simple statements of intention in the introductions to their work was apparently enough. It was sufficient for Thucydides blandly to observe that the reports reaching him were sometimes tainted by favoritism, and that it was difficult for him to ascertain their truth (1. 22. 3). In any case, their fulfillment of the tacit requirement made honesty and objectivity a rule of the genre for subsequent writers.

The cardinal importance of the contract between author and reader should not be underestimated. A theoretical norm based on incontrovertible propriety cannot easily be outraged. It established a field or parameters beyond which the historian was unlikely to stray, even when he departed from strict observance of the rule; departure from the norm was, therefore, always qualified when not prevented. Just as Xenophon had to keep his admiration of Agesilaus within reasonable bounds in the *Hellenica* (though not, of course, in the *Agesilaus*), and Phylarchus and Polybius had to frame their case for Cleomenes and Aratus within the conventional restrictions history imposed, so the Romans—in the equivalent sphere of their history, Roman politics—refrained from the exploitation of history to serve narrow political ends. *If*, for example (as I do not believe), Cato dished up what he regarded as self-serving propaganda when he inserted speeches of his own into the *Origines*,[11] later writers did not

[11] So E. Badian, "The Early Historians," in *The Latin Historians*, ed. T. A. Dorey (London, 1966), p. 9. A. E. Astin, *Cato the Censor* (Oxford, 1978), p. 234, is cautious.

follow his example so far as can be known; they seem to have repressed, instead, their factional interests for the sake of a formally
objective account consistent with the "dignity" and "authority" of
history.[12] Sallust articulated the concept when he praised Fannius for
truth (*Hist.* 1. 4 M.), castigated Sisenna for sycophancy (*BJ* 95. 2),
and said of himself (*Hist.* F 6 M), "nor has my political enmity in
the civil strife moved me from the truth." Now although it is reasonable to doubt that Asellio, Sallust, Livy, Pollio, Tacitus, Ammianus,
and others succeeded in transcending their enmities and loyalties,
no evidence whatever suggests that they or their fellows intended to
write propaganda; on the contrary, we have every reason to believe
that the dictates of convention and the assumption of the *persona* of
the historian made the contemporary writers strive to be the impartial analysts of their recent past. On the other hand—and the fact is
correlative—since *ex parte* "history" was as irrepressible as it was improper to the spirit of the genre, a special place for it was made in
the autobiography and the memoir.[13]

The belief has been expressed by some, however, that partiality
was actually and explicitly condoned, at least in the monograph.[14]
Apart from the indisputable observation that monography often
centers on individuals, while the selection of such a subject often
implies the adoption of a position pro or contra, the basis of this
assumption is a somewhat mystifying interpretation of Cicero's letter
to Lucceius (*Ad fam.* 5. 12), a justly famous little essay on history.
However, the letter presents not a theoretical justification for panegyric historiography but a forceful plea for such a work as a favor to
Cicero. In essence, the letter exposes to our view in candid language
the surreptitious pulling and tugging to which historians were apt to
be subjected. With a candor amiably neutralizing the impropriety of
his request, Cicero avows that he "burns with a tremendous desire"
to see "his name rendered illustrious and famous" in a work by Lucceius (1); he asks Lucceius to "embellish my deeds **more emphatically than perhaps you feel that they deserve**, and that in this work
you neglect the laws of history . . . and dispense something more

---

[12] See above chapter 2.
[13] See chapter 5. This was the proper vehicle for self-glorification and *ex parte* writing, and it is a grave misestimation of the importance of genre to confound memoirs
with history, whatever the stylistic excellence of the former.
[14] See, especially, R. Reitzenstein, *Hellenistische Wundererzählungen*[2] (Stuttgart,
1963), p. 89.

for the sake of my love than the truth concedes" (3). Now Cicero clearly has not asserted that the laws of the monograph abet distortion or magnification; on the contrary, he would like the laws of history bent in a monograph about himself. Indeed, the main reason for his solicitation of a monograph is impatience; otherwise he would have waited for his place in a conventional history. But Lucceius is still finishing up that part of his history concerned with the Marsic War (91–83) (2) and Cicero wishes to be immortalized while still alive. We can be certain, therefore, that the same request (with suitably altered arguments) would have been made of Lucceius if his regular history had reached the appropriate point in time. To be sure, as Cicero makes plain in the letter, he is aware that the monographic form will best fulfill his hopes. But this lies in the nature of a monograph; it is not the consequence of a special theory about them. Cicero must needs be center-stage in a monograph about the year 63 (unless Sallust were its author—his *Catiline* places Cicero in the wings).

Although Cicero's letter fails to suggest the elaboration of a theory calculated to extenuate favoritism, it reveals the importunities to which historians were exposed. Unless enemies were to be made on principle, tact was necessary, especially in Rome. For the men who made history and who wrote it belonged to the same comparatively small circle of the social elite; the former regarded it as their due to be treated with circumspection if not laudatorily and there were always some, like Cicero, who expected something more.[15] Something of the atmosphere, though in a later time, can be sensed from a letter of Pliny's (9. 19); more compelling testimony, perhaps, can be extracted from the words of Ammianus Marcellinus: "Now [after the death of Jovian, A.D. 364] that the order of events has been related to the limits of my own special recollection with very considerable diligence, it would be expedient to decline the description of matters of comparative common knowledge if the dangers frequently attaching to the truth are to be avoided" (26. 1. 1).

Yet it seems evident that monographs of contemporary subjects, quite apart from the influence of friendships and the dangers of enmity, tended by their very nature to be panegyric or defamatory. When someone like Arrian, remote from his subject and merely

[15] For an interesting example of the same principle in reverse see Cicero *De republ.* 1. 1.

bathed in sentimental nostalgia, can be prompted to write his history of Alexander in the persuasion that "no other man performed so many or such monumental deeds, whether in number or magnitude, among Greeks or barbarians alike" (1. 12. 4), it is apparent that the spell of a living and dynamic individual could easily melt impartiality away.

Treatment of important individuals calibrates more or less precisely with the political atmosphere and with the presence or absence of political freedom and professional independence. Of the so-called encomiastic historians, there is a dividing line between pre-imperial and imperial writers, though the traditions of the republic managed to live on until at least the time of Tacitus. However, the decline that was already in progress, and of which Velleius Paterculus had already been a sign, touched its nadir with the crowd of sycophants of the second century A.D. (*FGrHist* 203–10) excoriated by Lucian in *How to Write History* (7, 13ff.). History became the province of opportunists. A contemporary letter of the emperor Lucius Verus (161–69) to the rhetor M. Cornelius Fronto, gives the picture.[16] Verus informs Fronto that he will be supplied with military reports, letters clarifying Verus's intentions, illustrations, commentaries written by himself and his field generals, his bulletins to the senate, addresses to the army, and colloquies with the barbarians. In return, Fronto will write a history in Latin to throw Verus's accomplishments into high relief—"in order to make clear how much I have accomplished"—by emphasizing the low state of affairs preceding his intervention in the East. He closes with a veiled threat: "my deeds will appear as great as your wish to portray them as such."

The historian has degenerated into a professional rhetorician, whose chief purpose is to compile skillfully, to mould disparate material, all of it flattering, into a unitary historical narrative displaying the refinements of art (cf. Herodian 1. 1) and devoted to the glorification of the emperor. The data furnished by Verus for the commissioned history (which never saw the light) was of its nature inimical to sober historiography; the emperor, his staff, and his generals, even his artists, will contribute a suitably glowing and self-serving version of events, to which Fronto will add his own adornments, superimposing Verus's figure over that of Alexander. The old correlation be-

---

[16] P. 134 Nab; see Peter, *Die geschichtliche Litteratur über die römische Kaiserzeit bis Theodosius I und ihre Quellen* (Leipzig, 1897), vol. 1, pp. 378ff.

tween political freedom, intellectual honesty, and historical objectivity could not be plainer than by this example e contrario.

The relation of emperor and courtier was special to the times, and implied an abrupt derogation from the dignity earlier claimed by the historian. Although there always were writers eager for fame and wealth (cf. Polyb. 16. 14. 3) on the literary fringes of power, the prestige of history long enabled its practitioners to assert their intellectual independence from the heroes of their histories. Callisthenes, the Hannibalic historians, Polybius in his monograph on the Numantine War, and Posidonius (who wrote on Pompey) all attempted to keep their obligations in balance, though we would deceive ourselves if we denied that these writers prepared the evil of sycophancy by aggrandizing their central characters. The commitment implied by Callisthenes when he followed Alexander in the hope of an Asian conquest, like that of Polybius when he recorded the destruction of Numantia, was confining, even if entered into voluntarily. The admiration felt by Chaereas and Sosylus for Hannibal, though not strictly incompatible with an objective historical account, rendered it practically impossible.[17] But the evil was recognized as such (cf. Dionys. Ad. Pomp. 5. 2), and we may believe that its worst manifestations were carefully avoided. Renunciation of impartiality entailed the invalidation of one's work and the impairment of one's fame.[18]

On balance, therefore, tendentiousness, though an omnipresent danger, probably threatened the integrity of historiography no more than in present times. The intellectual tradition had evolved a code defining and emphasizing its impropriety, obvious partisanship was repugnant to the persona of the historian, and the evil was too transparently obvious to escape detection. Until imperial times, with predictable exceptions, propaganda was reserved for the open letter, the memoir, autobiography, and the pamphlet.

History's purpose

If the Latin writers and the Greeks before them were largely able to protect themselves from so vulgar and transparent a threat to their

---

[17] How fine was the line dividing history from panegyric is, incidentally, shown by Cicero in De legg. 1. 3, 8, where Atticus is made to say of Cicero that if he chooses to write contemporary history "he will render Pompey's renown illustrious."

[18] Ammianus's words (relative to Julian) well illustrate the point: "Now whatever I

integrity as self-interest and sycophancy, their defences were permeable to more insidious influences capable of producing distortion. Fortunately or unfortunately, history was harnessed early on to "higher purposes," was made to subserve ethics and patriotism, and simultaneously was conceived of as an instrument of "pleasure." Although none of this is theoretically incompatible with a strictly veracious account, the reader will readily perceive that the potential for distortion, even unintentional distortion, was great.

In this connection, the first of the historians, Herodotus and Thucydides, perhaps because they were the first, occupy an anomalous position when viewed within the larger context of Greco-Roman historiography. Although Herodotus (1 *ad init.*) considered it self-evident that important deeds should be preserved in memory,[19] he was moved neither by utilitarian nor by "scientific purpose," as has sometimes been alleged.[20] On the contrary, he expounded a philosophy of history, or, rather, he wrote a history incorporating that philosophy for the edification of his readers. But Herodotus not only believed and tried to show that (within the larger design woven by fate) good fortune was unstable and intrinsically corrupting, whether for individuals or for city-states and kingdoms. It seems clear that he also invested past actions with present relevance by making the Persian Wars foreshadow and illuminate the conditions in Greece in his own time, when the Peloponnesian War had broken out. It is a question how far this technique can be reconciled with the elementary rules of "objective" historical composition, for if Herodotus was guided in his selection of fact by contemporary considerations, it unfortunately follows that (through him) we have been viewing the Persian Wars through a distorted lens.

Thucydides, on the other hand, probably in reaction to Herodotus, pursued an indubitably "scientific" purpose. No other historian of antiquity treasured *akribeia*, strict accuracy, so much as he, and he is unique in estimating factual detail as important for its own sake.

---

shall tell (and no wordy deceit adorns my tale, but untrammelled faithfulness to fact, based upon clear proofs, composes it) will almost belong to the domain of the panegyric" [trans. J. C. Rolfe]. For signs of evenhandedness, see 22. 3. 7, 4. 1, 7. 3, 10. 3.

[19] In this connection 7. 224. 1 is a passage of exceptional interest. Herodotus states that he learned (though he does not publish) the names of all three hundred Spartiates who fell at Thermopylae "because they had become worthy men."

[20] A. W. Gomme, *The Greek Attitude to Poetry and History* (Berkeley and Los Angeles, 1954), p. 78.

As to the value of his history, Thucydides claimed for it no more and no less than the knowledge gained of the great war that was his subject, denoting his work, however, as "useful" (*ophelima*, 1. 22. 4)—a word not used by Herodotus.

What Thucydides understood by "useful" has been disputed, some holding that he provided lessons for the statesman, others that he offered knowledge that was not directly utilitarian.[21] The first of these opinions seems to be nothing more than a nineteenth-century prejudice. History and the historian were elevated by making the latter a clear-eyed statesman descanting upon matters of high import for other members of the same select order.[22] The concept of political utility has simply been interpolated into Thucydides' account without assistance from the author. Although, for example, it has been stated that the speeches at Sparta or in the Mytilenian Debate serve as *exempla*, examples of situations and policies to be avoided or pursued, it is a contradiction in terms to speak of *exempla* written by an author who concealed their alleged point and who constructed his intellectual commentary on events in the form of antithetical presentations of equivalent intellectual power. The way a didactic historian explicates his material is clear from Polybius (e.g., 3. 7. 4–7); a wide gulf separates the method of the two writers. The kind of utility Thucydides intended his history to provide is defined in 1. 22. 4; it will permit the reader "to contemplate the clear actuality" of the Peloponnesian War: and, by extension, comparable cataclysms of the future. The purpose is knowledge, not the manipulation of events by way of an education in probability. *That* purpose was rhetorical (cf. Andocides *On the Peace* 2), not historical, as Thucydides understood the term.

A Socratic writer was the first to introduce the moral lesson into history. In *Hellenica* 5. 1. 4, Xenophon asserts that it is of more value to show how Teleutias treated his men than it is to set down what conventionally is defined as "worthy of relation." In 5. 3. 7 an "example" or "lesson" occurs:

[21] The older view (see, for example, Felix Jacoby, "Griechische Geschichtschreibung," in *Abhandlungen zur griechischen Geschichtschreibung*, ed. H. Bloch [Leiden, 1956], p. 88) that Thucydides intended to convey information of political utility has been recently advocated by H. Erbse, "Die politische Lehre des Thukydides," *Gymnasium* 76 (1969): 393–416, in opposition to H.-P. Stahl, *Thukydides*, Zetemata, no. 40 (1966), pp. 14ff.

[22] See chapter 2.

From experiences of this type I assert that men learn above all that it is not right to punish even slaves in anger. For it is frequently the case that masters have suffered more harm when they have been angry than they have meted out. But as to one's opponents, it is a complete error to engage them in anger and not with judgment. For anger is regardless of consequences, while judgment is as much concerned to suffer no harm as to injure the enemy.

It may be noted that Thucydides was himself fond of inserting general maxims into his speeches. They function, however, as logical premises to actions either advocated or opposed by the speaker, not as conclusions extracted by the author from what has been described. The difference is symptomatic.

By the end of the fourth century, history became openly judgmental. The historian asserted his obligation (as he viewed it) to confer praise and blame in his own voice upon individual deeds, the entire life of a man, and the policies of a city-state. The idea was no more intrinsic to history proper than to other types of historical writing (ethnography, horography) and, as is well known, it was resisted even in something so rich in opportunities as Suetonian biography. Herodotus and Thucydides had on occasion pointed the record in what they considered to be the proper direction and had "guided" the reader to the appropriate judgment; when feasible, they also attributed their opinions to collectives like the "public mind."[23] This restraint proved, however, too austere to satisfy the newly developed interests and enthusiasms of the next generation. The Socratic movement reflected and intensified a new and predominating interest in ethical questions, while corresponding exaltation of the individual naturally turned the spotlight from city-states to persons. Meanwhile, the historical writer by now had inherited some of the prestige of his subject and the reflected genius of his predecessors: he had earned the right (as he supposed) to speak with authority *in propria persona*. A new relationship between the historian and his work

[23] See I. Bruns, *Das literarische Porträt der Griechen* (Berlin, 1896), pp. 71ff. (Herodotus), pp. 3ff. (Thucydides). Herodotus occasionally broke this inchoate convention, most notably when he praised the Athenians in 7. 139. Thucydides drew perilously near to an expression of personal opinion in 2. 65, and a moralistic attack against Alcibiades lurks in 5. 43. 2.

thus evolved: he not only can write history but will lecture the reader by providing his assessment of the historical data.

Late in the *Hellenica*, Xenophon increasingly asserted his personal opinions: specific praise can be found in 6. 2. 32, 39 and 7. 5. 8. Philistus of Syracuse (*FGrHist* 556), an early fourth-century historian, provided bulletins of "praise and blame" (T 16a). These additions to the narrative are all the more notable because Philistus was otherwise notoriously an imitator of Thucydides (T 16a–b). To be sure, Dionysius of Halicarnassus minimized the extent to which Philistus allocated praise and blame. This, however, was colored by a perspective involving comparison with subsequent writers; from ours, it is significant that he provided these bulletins at all.

The practice, in any case, became a recognized theoretical adjunct of history when it was adopted by Ephorus.[24] Polybius, who admired greatly his so-called "critical appraisals" (*hoi epemetrountes logoi* [12. 28. 10]),[25] describes them as *intrinsic* to history (8. 10. 7), de rigueur in historical works (1. 14. 5, 7. 7. 7, 16. 28. 5). Cicero therefore reflects an orthodox view when, in his letter to Lucceius (*Ad fam.* 5. 12. 4), he enlarges on the historical possibilities of a monograph on himself, "when you condemn what you will consider reprehensible and approve what pleases you with all due elaboration of your reasons."

The technique has rhetorical origins, and can be viewed in part as a carry-over from epideictic or demonstrative oratory (such as that practiced by Gorgias and Isocrates), for the specific object of this kind of speech was to praise or blame (Arist. *Rhet.* 1358B, Quintil. 3. 7. 1). But other influences can also be detected, most especially the eulogy, which perhaps explains why Polybius preferred to embody the "critical appraisal" or evaluation of someone's mental and moral attributes (*proaireseis*)[26] in an obituary notice, i.e., at that point in the narrative when the death of a notable personage was

[24] See P. Scheller, *De hellenistica historiae conscribendae arte* (Leipzig, 1911), pp. 48ff., G. Avenarius, *Lukians Schrift zur Geschichtsschreibung* (Diss., Meisenheim am Glan, 1956), pp. 161ff.

[25] The term signifies a supplementary discourse, an addition to the objective relation of fact. Its function is to pass in review the actions and policies of individuals and larger groups. The allocation of praise and blame need not, of course, be restricted to moralistic judgements; see, for example, Polyb. 32. 21. Polybius generally used it for "pragmatic" appraisals; see 15. 34 and P. Pédech, *La méthode historique de Polybe* (Paris, 1964), pp. 408–10.

[26] See Polyb. 2. 61. 6 and Diod. 15. 88. 1 (from Ephorus).

related. Indeed, Seneca the Elder (*Suas.* 6. 23) regarded the "critical appraisal" and the eulogy (*laudatio*) as the same thing. Whatever the antecedents of the "appraisal," however, it is important to bear in mind that Polybius's praise of Ephorus's application of this device (12. 28. 10) implies, in the absence of counter-indications, that Ephorus behaved much more responsibly when assigning credit or blame than modern writers presume. The standard view, in fact, is that Ephorus did not confine himself to "critical appraisals" as a sort of running commentary on events, but actually went so far as to select and shape his material in order to incite the reader to virtue. On this view, history became a moralistic schoolroom, providing lessons of praiseworthy and culpable conduct for the instruction of the reader.[27] In short, Ephorus is credited with the notorious dictum of [Dionysius] 11. 2 that "history is philosophy by paradigm."

The charge is a serious one, for it presupposes the fourth-century convergence of history and rhetorical theory ("teaching by example") and therefore postulates an evolution of Greek historiography that, if it is correct, presumes the early debasement of the genre. Now it must be clearly understood that what is imputed to Ephorus transcends the mere use by him of didactic judgments in "critical appraisals." He has been accused of the intentional and methodical introduction into historiography of specimens of behavior in order to work some salutary effect upon the reader. Apparently, the alleged association with Isocrates has been enough to convince the moderns of Ephorus's guilt,[28] while the prevalence of this didactic practice in the first century becomes confirmatory evidence. Someone injected the method into the historiographical mainstream and, if so, who but Ephorus? As we shall see, however, a radically different development seems indicated. In fact, the idea of introducing "lessons" for their own sake into Greek historiography seems to have proceeded not from abstract moral considerations but instead from the urge to make history an instrument of political utility. Once the principle of the lesson was admitted into Greek history by that route, it followed inevitably that *exempla* of moral philosophy gained entrance as well.

Paul Scheller[29] noticed the rather puzzling fact that Ephorus's al-

---

[27] See Scheller, *De hellenistica arte*, pp. 77f.

[28] The ancients *assumed* (as the lack of hard biographical data shows) a connection between Ephorus and Isocrates on the basis of style. Moderns have carried the identification one step further, as if oratory and history (therefore) became identical genres.

[29] Scheller, *De hellenistica arte*, pp. 77f.

leged paradigmatical view of history does not present itself until the first century, when (after Asellio) it was "revived" by Sallust, Livy, Diodorus, and Dionysius. Scheller, however, let his observation drop. Since it was taken as certain that Ephorus had introduced this approach, accidents of preservation no doubt explained the three-century hiatus. But the certainty primarily arose from guilt by association; Ephorus was, after all, a student of Isocrates, and Isocrates clearly believed that one of the functions of the rhetorician was to set forth paradigms or models to incite people to virtue (9. 76f., 1. 51, 5. 113). As he wrote to the son of Hipponicus,

> I have exhibited a sample of the nature of Hipponicus; you must relate your life to his as if it were a paradigm, regarding his character as your law, and becoming the imitator and emulator of your father's virtue. For it would be shameful for painters to represent figures of beauty and for children not to imitate the noblest of their race. [1. 11]

Nevertheless, a link was necessary to connect Ephorus with Isocrates for the conception and use of the paradigm *in history*, and it seemed to be found in *FGrHist* 70 F 42. The passage requires close attention, for I think it will become clear that the desire to produce a parallel with Isocrates may have substantially enhanced our readiness to accept one. The fragment derives from Strabo (7. 3. 9), who quotes Ephorus as follows:

> He says that the mode of life of the Sauromatians is different from the rest of the Scythians. He says that these latter are un-civilized [cannibalistic] but the others refrain from the meat of all creatures. "Now the other writers," he says, "speak about the bloody cruelty [of the Scythians]. They know that fearful and amazing things have startling impact." But [Ephorus] says that it is necessary both to report the opposite and to give examples [of these opposites]. Thus [Ephorus] will himself write about the Scythians who possess the justest customs. For some of the nomadic Scythians are nourished [not on human food but] on the milk of horses and are distinguished above all men in justice. The poets mention them: Homer . . . Hesiod . . . Choerilus. . . .

The usual rendering of the sentence I have translated[30] as "to re-

---

[30] *Dein de tànantia kai legein kai paradeigmata poieisthai.*

port the opposite and to give examples" is "to say the opposite and to provide a paradigm or model [of what is good instead of bad]." In this view, Ephorus asserted the duty of the historian to provide examples of good conduct with all of the historical irresponsibility we associate with Isocrates. But is it not apparent that the context cannot sustain this interpretation?

In the first place, Strabo's summary makes it evident that Ephorus has provided no paradigm. He has rather listed the traditional authorities (starting from Homer) who testify to the righteousness of one group of Scythians—he has given examples, in other words, of the opposite way of life in proof of his assertion that the Scythians were good as well as bad. Secondly, even Jacoby admitted (in his commentary to the fragment, *FGrHist* 2C, p. 51) that "the idealization [allegedly intended by Ephorus and on which the entire interpretation is based] was not carried out; Ephorus rather establishes the existence of *anomoiotes* [the dissimilarity of sub-groups], because he united all the peoples of the north, the Homeric Abioi and Galactophagoi as well as the Androphagoi and Hippomolgoi of the *Wunderepos* . . . and the real Scyths of the north of the Pontus into one great Scythian people of the north." Ephorus, in other words, did not do what he is alleged to have intended to do; he dealt with what he regarded as the entire Scythian nation, paying due regard to the salient characteristics of individual tribes and providing testimony for his assertions. If there is a correlation between purpose and procedure (and here we must infer the former from the latter), it follows that his intention was not to provide a "paradigm" of good but instead to correct a serious distortion in the ethnographical tradition. The predilection of others to tell shocking stories for the sake of sensationalism required a corrective for the sake of a balanced presentation.

It should have been noticed, perhaps, that the specific meaning of "paradigm," as the term was used in a moralistic-historical context, is quite inapplicable to such things as the customs of barbarous or pacific Scythians. Ephorus could hardly advocate that the Greeks take some Scythians or an individual such as the Scythian wonder-worker and servant of Apollo, Abaris, for their model. Whether, on the other hand, Abaris or other Scyths, individually or collectively, were used by Ephorus as exponents of ideas critical of Greek customs is another question; one need not deny that Ephorus may have utilized this topic for moralistic purposes of his own. But that is not what is ordinarily inferred from F 42. In sum, the fragment indicates that Ephorus wished to rectify an imbalance in ethnographical tradition and for this reason was compelled "to speak the opposite," with examples, of what other writers had already said about this people.

Thus the positive evidence suggesting that Ephorus possessed a view of history reducing it essentially to a repository of *exempla* falls away. But the evidence of "probability," the taint of his association with Isocrates, remains, and this it would be virtually impossible to dismiss (in spite of the absence of any sign of the recurrence of his system until the first century) were it not for the happy circumstance that Polybius assigned to *himself* the responsibility for the introduction of this historical approach. His purpose was political utility.

As is well known, Polybius added to the moral element already resident in history an emphatic insistence on that element's political usefulness.[31] He stressed history's utility for men of affairs (1. 35. 9) and dwelt on the benefits accruing from a true perception of events —"how, for what reason and from what source each event takes its beginning" (3. 7. 6). Indeed, Polybius went so far as to claim that a true reading of history would permit predictions of the future (12. 25b, 30. 6. 4). One principal passage on the value of history reads as follows:

> Some injudicious readers of these matters [concerning the origin of the Second Punic War] will perhaps say that we have been unnecessarily exhaustive. [2] As for me, I would say that if someone supposed himself to be all-sufficing in every situation, in that case knowledge of past events is a good thing but not, perhaps, necessary. [3] But since no one can dare to say this in regard to his affairs private or public, inasmuch as he is merely a human being, because no thinking person can ever reasonably secure his hope of the future even if he enjoys success at the present moment, [4] I affirm that knowledge of past events is not only a good thing but, because of this, all the more necessary. [5] For how can one find support and allies when he or his

---

[31] Whatever the precise definition of "pragmatic history" (9. 1. 4, 1. 6; see Pédech, *La méthode*, pp. 21–32), we can infer the force of the word "pragmatic" from Polybius's insistence that his work was useful because it described how "things were done" in the world of politics and war; note especially the implications of 12. 27a. It is pragmatic because a causative history of contemporary politics presents the politician with a guide for future action.

fatherland is injured? Or how can he impel associates to join his endeavors if he wishes to acquire more territory and begin hostilities? [6] How will he justly motivate them to support his political aims and to preserve his form of government when he is satisfied with the present dispensation, if he knows nothing of the past actions of each [potential ally]? [7] For men always manage to accommodate themselves to present circumstances and to play a part; all speak and act such things as to make it hard to perceive their actual disposition and to darken the truth in many things. [8] Past actions, however, are tested by the results and truly reveal the mental attitudes and sentiments of each; they show who it is that owes us gratitude, requital of good, assistance and, similarly, those who owe the converse. [9] From this it is often possible to identify for a variety of purposes the one who will pity us, join in our anger, assist in our vengeance. [10] All of this provides the greatest assistance to human existence both publicly and privately. [11] That is why neither the writers nor the readers of history should consider the recital of the facts themselves as much as the circumstances preceding, accompanying and following the deeds. [12] For if one subtracts from history the why, the how, the purpose for which a deed was done, and also whether the end was predictable, what is left is a prize composition [*agonisma*] but not a lesson, [13] and though it give momentary pleasure, it provides no utility at all for the future. [3. 31]

If, as this passage shows, Polybius treasured the study of history as a sound inferential basis for present and future political activity, it would be an error to suppose that rationalistic bias made him blind to its *hortatory* value. Indeed, like his follower Asellio, he fully respected the importance of this moral component of political utility. In fact, what has been generally assumed of Ephorus applies to him: Polybius is the first Greek historian known to have indicated the desirability of including exemplary actions in history specifically to serve as models of behavior. (Let it be emphasized that we are speaking not of the presence of *exempla* in history but of the doctrine that such *exempla* belong in history in order to subserve an edifying purpose.) One could, of course, try to "explain" Polybius by Ephorus F 42, just as Ephorus is "explained" by Isocrates. But this Byzantine procedure is categorically invalidated by Polybius 10. 21. 2–4:

Since that point in our history has been reached where the deeds of Philopoemen begin, we think it is fitting, just as we have tried to display the training and character of the other memorable [*axiologoi*] men, to do the same with him. [3] For it is a peculiar thing that although historians describe with precision the foundations of cities—when, how and by whom they were established, and also their political arrangement and condition—they are silent about the training and goals of political leaders, though this is a far more useful thing. [4] For to the extent that one is able to **emulate and copy noble men** [32] rather than inanimate constructions is it probable that discussion devoted to them will bear comparable benefit.

It is an important declaration. Polybius's categorical exclusion of prior Greek historians certainly excludes the assumption that he has been influenced by Ephorus. Alternately, the transmission of a concept from Isocrates to Polybius without the mediation of Ephorus would be a major miracle in the history of the dissemination of ideas. Though Isocrates and Polybius are united by a similar paradigmatic approach, a fundamental difference separates them. Isocrates wished to teach moral virtue; Polybius wanted to inculcate patriotism and teach the craft of statesmanship by example. Polybius's historiographical innovation does not flow from Isocratean springs.

Polybius's inspiration must be sought in Rome. In fact, his adoption of an approach to history hitherto absent in Greek historiography but already present in the work of Fabius Pictor can only be explained by the influence of Roman culture. Polybius, we must remember, for more than fifteen years of his intellectual prime was a resident of the city, and it is hardly to be supposed that the experience left him unchanged. Now the Romans fully recognized, indeed, instinctively felt, the interconnection of present and past; not only the deeds but especially the lives of exemplary men, connected by blood as well as by citizenship, continued immanent through constant recollection. Each generation subsumed the experiences of the preceding ones and was taught to emulate the best of them. Something of the intensity of the feeling can be read in the gravestones of the Scipiones (see, especially, Dessau No. 6). The attitude was en-

---

[32] Keeping the original reading, which Schweighäuser emended to "men who were alive."

forced and exemplified by the funeral customs so shrewdly analyzed by Polybius in 6. 54. 1–3:

> The orator, when he completes his laudation of the individual, begins with the other members of the family [whose images are present], commencing with the most ancient, and he describes the successes and deeds of each. [2] This usage constantly keeps fresh the fame of the virtue of these great men; the glory of those who have accomplished some splendid thing is rendered immortal and the repute of the benefactors of the fatherland becomes well known to the many and is bequeathed to their descendants. [3] Most important, *the young are incited to undergo any difficulty for the republic in order to acquire the glory that accompanies those men who become great.*

Consistently with his aim of political utility, Polybius has therefore introduced the equivalent of a protreptic, or hortatory, laudation into Greek historiography (see, e.g., 10. 2–5). The fact that in 31. 30 he described his excursus on the second Scipio as "useful for the young," the same reason given in 6. 54. 3 for public funerals, shows the intimate connection in his mind between the two. As we might expect, however, Polybius accepts the utility of Roman conventions from a certain intellectual distance. Subsequent emphasis of the same theme by Roman writers throbs with passion. Nothing in Greek historical literature, for example, is comparable with Sallust *Jugurtha* 4. 5:

> For I have often heard that Q. Maximus, P. Scipio and, beyond this, other distinguished men of our city used to say that when they looked upon the waxen masks [*imagines*] of their ancestors, their minds were powerfully incited to virtue. Certainly it is not the wax or its outlines that possesses so much power; that flame leaps up in the hearts of eminent men because of the memory of their ancestors' deeds, and it does not diminish until their own virtue has rivalled the fame and glory of these men.[33]

Here we must bear in mind that although Roman historiography adopted Greek forms and terminology, the manners and careers (*mores vitaeque*) of the ancestors possessed a concrete historical rele-

---

[33] Cf. Tacitus *Agricola* 46.

vance to the Roman present far transcending the more intellectual approach of the Greeks. The ethical interest in character exhibited by the Hellenes or the political utility discerned in it by Polybius pale in comparison. In any case, an important conclusion follows: the Greco-Romans of the first century, chiefly prompted by the Roman habit of thinking in terms of models, though also aided to it by Polybius, extended the definition of history by adding the life and character of famous men to speeches and deeds as the proper subject of history.

That we are witness to a redefinition of history and not merely a material expansion of the range of information history would willingly accommodate follows from the new phraseology of several first-century writers, whose unanimity would otherwise be perplexing in the extreme. Indeed, as the following quotations will show, we can actually observe the suture connecting the old definition with the new. Dionysius of Halicarnassus, perhaps not surprisingly, presents this new view with a note of apology:

> I am absolutely convinced that it is appropriate for writers of history not only to narrate the warlike deeds of distinguished commanders and whatever beneficial and salutary political measures they may have contrived for their cities **but also to exhibit their lives**, if they were moderate, self-controlled and **kept to the customs of their homeland**. [AR 5. 48. 1]

(Note how the third characteristic listed suggests the Roman provenance of the entire topic.) Remarkably similar is Cicero:

> [History requires] that all the causes be explained, whether they arise from accident, wisdom, or rashness. History requires of the participants themselves not only an account of their deeds **but also** of the life and character of each man who excels in fame and name. [De orat. 2.15, 63][34]

It would be as rash as it is unnecessary to deny the influence of the rhetorical schools in making this expanded definition of history acceptable. As the preface of Diodorus Siculus attests , history had indeed become philosophy by example.[35] One must concede the oper-

---

[34] The entire passage is quoted on pp. 138f.

[35] This, the major preface, unlike some others, where the substance is inimical to

ation of mutually enforcing theoretical principles combining with still other influences to bring about intellectual change. The important point is that in history the lives of individuals had finally attained a status coordinate with that of their deeds, apparently primarily as a result of the conflation of Roman priorities with Greek theory. The theoretical scaffold was now in place for the imperial writers, the concept of history having been brought into conformity with its practice.

One negative result of placing a value on history for the examples it provided of men's virtue and vice, strength and weakness, was a disinclination to engage in the kind of revisionist research that might have resulted in a closer approach to the historical truth. One might write history better than one's predecessors, perhaps, as Q. Cicero supposed of his brother (*De legg.* 1. 3, 8) and as Livy actually demonstrated; but new "hard" data were irrelevant to the task of tendentiously presenting traditional knowledge in order to allow history, "life's teacher" (*magistra vitae*), to give her own message. The task of history, as we may see, for example, from the first-century writer Pompeius Trogus, was to present historical pictures of the rewards of moderation (Justin 4. 2. 4–5, 13. 6. 19), military discipline (12. 4. 10), the consequences of laziness (6. 9. 2), the advent of retribution (16. 2. 5), and the expiation of evil (1. 9. 2).[36] From this perspective, clear analysis and painstaking investigation became superfluous, even complicating. Sharper characterization with a deft literary touch was more useful.

In the service of this end, authors like Trogus (and Livy) devoted themselves not to the accumulation of new facts but to the elaboration of stereotypes agreeable to the prejudices and expectations of

---

some of Diodorus's own concepts (and to concepts contained in still other of the prefaces and is reasonably attributable to his sources), should be conceded to Diodorus himself, as A. D. Nock, "Poseidonius," *JRS* 49 (1959): 5, observed. It is worth adding that the assumption that the proemia are not his own because of their allegedly richer diction and stylistic differentiation (M. Kunz, *Zur Beurteilung der Prooemien in Diodors historischer Bibliothek* [Diss., Zurich, 1935], p. 67) has been invalidated by the study of J. Palm, *Über Sprache und Stil des Diodoros von Sizilien* (Lund, 1955), who concludes, pp. 194ff., that *stylistically* Diodorus gave the material "a new modern dress." Naturally, this leaves unaffected the conclusion that Diodorus reproduces the theoretical arguments of some of his major sources.

[36] See E. Schneider, *De Pompei Trogi Historiarum Philippicarum considio et arte* (Diss., Weidae Thuringerum, 1913), pp. 9ff.

reader and writer alike. They write, therefore, from a slightly different point of view than did Rome's earlier and decidedly hortatory
writers, for example, Cato and Asellio, who had created [37] or emphasized *exempla* (e.g., Cato's Q. Caedicius, F 83 Peter) with a view to
their immediately beneficial effect upon Roman citizens. A definite
line separates the invention of characteristics in order to provide an
exemplum (as Cato and Piso had done) from the shaping of *exempla*
in order to perfect their nature; Livy, Nicolaus of Damascus, and
Pompeius Trogus are writers of the second category.

For although we are apt to make Livy responsible for the didactic
purpose of his *exempla*, we must bear in mind that his gallery of heroes was long in place when Livy undertook his work. Figures like
Mucius Scaevola and the two Decii had acquired their clear-cut
identity and paradigmatic quality well before Cicero (*Pro Sestio* 21,
48). Yet we somehow regard Livy as a creator of significancies, when
in reality his objective was to do with *exempla* what he did with (for
example) Quadrigarius's description of the single combat of Corvi-
nus (compare F 12 Peter with Livy 7. 25. 13, 26)—develop the latent potentialities of the material. In view of the intellectual milieu,
and the total public recognition of these stock figures of Roman antiquity, it is reasonable to deduce that art and patriotism, not the
desire to teach moral virtue to his contemporaries, primarily motivated his treatment of the standard *exempla*. Certainly, to infer from
the presence of *exempla*—of museum-pieces—in Livy that he wrote
Roman history in order to improve the morals of the Roman people
is to confuse his conception of history and of "those great men of
yore" with his purpose in writing. He wished to make his readers
comprehend how great Rome had been; there is no apparent basis
for the belief that he also wished to use his picture of Rome in order
to make his contemporaries great.

Thereafter, in imperial times, the connection of examples and didacticism (in the ordinary sense) was severed completely—though
Tacitus payed lip-service to the concept (*Annales* 3. 65). [38] Perhaps it
would be truer to say that Tacitus held up the entire epoch as *the*
example of tyrannous and base government, consigning the emperors to hell in the conviction that history was the proper place for

[37] I do not suggest that they did so dishonestly; *that* procedure was left to the annalists. For one example, see the treatment of Romulus by Piso Frugi in F 8 Peter.
[38] He expresses a more conventional view in *Agricola* 1. 1.

eternal praise and retributive justice (*ibid.*), and that the task of the historian was to be judge and jury. It is a fascinating concept (anticipated by Theopompus), presupposing the possession of a long and continuous historical tradition taken as the analogy for the writer's own expectations of future generations. That the shouldering of such an obligation was inherently prejudicial to the balanced presentation of character needs no argument. If the purpose of history is punitive, the writer will not seek to modify his verdict by the consideration of extenuating circumstances. On the contrary, the "true evil" of a miscreant like Nero must be exposed to view by banishing deceitful appearances. Dwelling on counter-indications would obscure and conceal a villain's merited place in the annals of history. As the poet Claudian wrote in 398 A.D.:

> The annals speak of the wrongs committed by the men of old and the stains will remain always. Who will not for eternity condemn the monstrous actions of the House of Caesar, the dreadful murders of Nero, the disgusting cliffs of Capri inhabited by a filthy old man? [8. 311–315]

On the other hand, such a concept of historiography, though it might invest the writer with dignity (for example, Livy), power (Sallust), or both (Tacitus), could equally well become a mask for sensationalism, already *en vogue* in the early empire, and capitalized on subsequently by the biographical writers of the *Historia Augusta*. The Byzantine historian, Procopius of Caesarea, epitomized this trend in his *Anecdota*, the "Secret History" of Theodora and Justinian (mid-sixth century A.D.), and his formal justification of the work deserves quotation:

> These considerations moved me to write the history of these deeds. It will be clear to future tyrants that it is not improbable that retribution for their evil deeds will overtake them, just as it befell the subjects of my work. Secondly, their deeds and their character will forever be written up, and from this circumstance they will perhaps be slow to live improperly. For who of future generations would have known about the unrestrained life of Semiramis or of the madness of Sardanapalus and Nero if their remembrances had not been left by the writers of that time? But especially have I written this for those who will suffer similar injustices, if so it be, at the hands of tyrants. This narrative will

be very profitable for them. It is the habit of people who are unfortunate to console themselves by the knowledge that dreadful things have not befallen them alone. [1. 7–9]

How little these guiding principles correspond to the substance and emphases of the *Anecdota* is known to every reader of the work. It remains valuable as a comprehensive statement of what in Procopius's time was the conventional purpose of history.

Pleasure

That "pleasure" was inherent in the nature of history was an accepted idea. Nevertheless, the nature of history's "proper" pleasure and the consequent impropriety of alternative kinds were matters of conviction and principle that sparked discussion, controversy, and contemptuous dismissal. On the most elementary level, the pursuit of overtly pleasurable material for its own sake might well sully the truth of history and damage the reputation of the historian. Thus, although Thucydides was willing to impute "higher" pleasures to history, he scornfully rejected all pleasure attaching to the recital of the fabulous,[39] associated by him with the deliberate distortion of the truth or, at the least, with the easy credulity that will allow the publication of "tall stories." Much later, Tacitus took the same view, considering it "remote from the gravity of [his] work . . . to collect fabulous reports and to delight the minds of [his] readers with fictions" (*Hist.* 2. 50).

It would not seem improper, therefore, to distinguish a "Herodotean" and a "Thucydidean" tradition in accordance with which historical writers through the ages parted company on the issue of the gravity of history and the tolerable limits of pleasure it might afford. Some distinctions, however, are in order. The first generations of historians in Greece are not to be compared with those contemporaries of Tacitus whom he accuses of deliberate frivolity. There is a

[39]Gomme, *Greek Attitude to Poetry and History*, p. 117, believed that *to mythodes* ("the fabulous") refers to Herodotus's stories about Candaules and Gyges, the birth of Cyrus, and so on. The meaning of the term should rather be extracted from Thucydides' preceding sentence (which insists on the pains he took to sift his information) and therefore suggests "storytelling" only in the restricted sense of "exaggerative hearsay." The best commentary on the word is Arist. *Meteor.* 1. 13, quoted by Richard Jebb at verse 1248 of *Oedipus at Colonus.* Thucydides is objecting to what we might call embellishments.

world of difference and four hundred years between a Theopompus[40] and a Mucianus.[41] We must bear in mind that the inclusion of marvels "worthy of relation" uncovered by *historia* had formed an integral part of historiography since its inception, and that it was regarded as proper to the genre to retail fabulous reports and fictions if they were the authentic expression of learned informants (*logioi andres*). Probably not until the third century, when Alexandrian literary interest in strange and mythical stories induced a more artful and self-conscious approach to historical writing (cf. Phylarchus), were "fabulous reports" and "fictions" exploited specifically to evoke pleasure.

Between the austere practitioners of the craft, to whom something light was vulgar and indecorous, and those others who sought to tantalize the reader by an array of novel stories,[42] there was a middle ground held by writers who believed that the reader required *some* relief and pleasure from the arduous study of serious material, rather as Varro justified his use of humor in the learned Menippean satires: "I sprinkled them with some gaiety mixed with a large amount of abstruse philosophy and dialectical argument. To make the less learned understand these things the more easily, they were invited to read because of the pleasure provided" (Cicero *Acad*. 1. 2, 8). As is well known, Lucretius (1. 935ff.) offers a comparable justification for the poetic flights interspersing his exposition of Epicurus's philosophy.

On a level removed, and always theoretically legitimate, was the intellectual pleasure arising from the rehearsal of great deeds—that fundamental pleasure consisting in the acquisition of significant

[40] One may safely assume, for example, that Theopompus was not primarily concerned to purvey pleasure (though he was certainly aware of its provision) when he gave his account of magic-workers (*FGrHist* 115 F 67 b), recorded the striking tenets of Zoroaster and the magi, included their raising of the dead, discussed the miracles at Sardis in 546 B.C. (F 66), and discoursed on Epimenides of Crete (67–69). From a later vantage point, however, when the *logoi* of the historian were attached to him directly (see Cicero *De offic*. 3. 39 for the application of this procedure to Plato), these authors were accused of "lies" and "misrepresentations."

[41] For the work of this extraordinary man, who helped Vespasian to the throne, see *HRR*, vol. 2, pp. 101–7. His taste for marvels is indicated by F 1, 8, 10–11, 12 (a Greek-writing elephant), 13–14, 16 (a fish story), 28. Other writers with a similar bent were Tanusius Geminus (Peter, vol. 2, p. 49, F 1) and Suetonius Paulinus (Peter, vol. 2, p. 101).

[42] See the implied criticism of the Elder Pliny (*NH*, *Praef*. 12) and Lucian (*How to Write History* 9–13).

knowledge—and the pleasure of learning the explanations behind great events. Both ideas seem to have been implicitly endorsed by Thucydides, and that they persisted we may best observe from Polybius's preface.[43] His repeated reference to the readers of his work as "men who take pleasure in the acquisition of knowledge" (*philomathountes*)[44] underscores this fundamental pleasure. Among the Romans, a third type developed with Cato (F 1 Peter)—the pleasure of reviewing the record of one's past. This self-indulgent and patriotic approach to history naturally altered with the change in Rome's fortunes, and Livy, though he echoed the sentiment (*Praef.* 3), gave it deeper meaning: "While I hearken back to those ancient times, I avert my gaze from the observation of present evils, free from all cares which can trouble me even if they cannot turn my mind from the truth" (*Praef.* 5). Later writers accepted this principle (Tacitus *Hist.* 2. 50, *Annales* 4. 33) but inverted it by presenting a lamentable story evoking not pleasure but indignation and pain. Cato's principle thus paradoxically lived on through dark times.

The pleasure of knowledge is, of course, not unique to history, and one can indulge in patriotic sentiment by reading historical epics and plays as well as epideictic orations; the delight in the fabulous, too, can be satisfied by the novel or romance. The question therefore arose, as we might expect from a people who analytically explored the unique character and genius of the genres of their creation, "What was the pleasure peculiar to History?" Though details are scant and conjecture must be pressed, it is clear that the debate had already been opened by the fourth century B.C. Unfortunately, its reconstruction is a little like arranging the pieces of a partially damaged puzzle, for Lucian (second century A.D.), in *How to Write History* (8–13), provides the first extant synthesis of some of the material. Plato had discussed the nature of pleasure itself on the most fundamental level (*Rep.* 583A–85A, *Phileb.* 31E–42C). He issued the opinion (*Phileb.* 20B) that every pleasure except philosophy was

---

[43] See, especially, 1. 1. 6, 4. 11. Cf. Cicero *De republ.* 1. 13 and *De fin.* 4. 5, 12; 7, 18.

[44] See 1. 13. 9, 69. 5, 7. 7. 8 and 9. 2. 5 (at 1. 13. 9 Walbank translates the term as "students of history"). In 9. 1. 5 Polybius wrote that "my work will not bring pleasure [will not be psychagogic] *to the greater number* of [possible] readers" because of its strictly political subject. Cf. 15. 36. 3 and 31. 30. 1. The *philomathountes* obtain the intellectual pleasure of learning something useful, while the other type, the "curious reader," loves anything that is superficially interesting. See 7. 7. 8 and 15. 36. 3.

a bewitchment (*goeteia*). It can be taken as certain that under the circumstances some higher justification of the pleasures of competing genres was sought by their exponents. In a superficial and general way, Isocrates (*Antidosis* 47) had already asserted that men not only take as much delight in listening to epideictic oratory as they do in hearing poetry but they also hope for instruction from it. At this point, it was natural for Ephorus, the historian, to advance the claims of history in this competition of genres. In his great introduction,[45] he made a comparison of poetry, oratory, and history, and in view of the now standardized terms of the debate, it must have turned on "pleasure," at least in part. Since he objected to poetry (*FGrHist* 70 F 8) because it "was introduced among men as a deception and bewitchment [*goeteia*]," and argued the superiority of history over demonstrative or epideictic rhetoric (Polybius 12. 28. 8, 11), he must have stressed its superior validity and the authenticity of the pleasure it afforded. Ephorus's comparison of the genres became famous, for such is the implication of its mention by Polybius in 4. 20. 5 and of the polemic directed against it by Timaeus (Polybius 12. 28). That we do not possess Ephorus's words on the subject is singularly unfortunate.

The differentiation of the pleasure evoked by epideictic oratory, poetry, and history, and the intrinsic propriety of such distinctions, was presupposed by Aristotle in *Poetics* 1453B. In this famous passage, he asserted, speaking of the tragic emotions, that the tragedian "must not seek every pleasure from a tragedy but [only] the pleasure that is proper to it." This proper pleasure, he continues, is one derived from pity and fear arising from the imitation (*mimesis*) of pitiful and fearful things. Unfortunately, history receives only enough attention in this work to imply that its pleasure (if it has one) must differ from that of epic poetry and the drama. But in view of the different natures of these genres, as Aristotle understood them, that conclusion is self-evident. A discipline devoted to the exposition of what Alcibiades did or had done to him is not intrinsically concerned with the excitation of fear and pity.

[45] The idea (expressed by Jacoby in his commentary) that Ephorus, in his great introduction, compared history and music (*FGrHist* 70 F8) and yet avoided the obvious and obligatory contrast with history's categorical competitor, epideictic oratory (F 111), is impossible to accept in the absence of counter-indications. There is no reason for Jacoby to place F111 in *another* preface.

In a very interesting, but unfortunately enigmatic, development Duris of Samos (ca. 340–260 B.C.) took quite a different view, helped to it, however, by Aristotle's own poetic theory. According to Duris (*FGrHist* 76 F 1), Ephorus and Theopompus wrote perfunctorily and without verisimilitude.[46] But the reason he gave for their "falling short of reality" is that their works were devoid of *mimesis* and pleasure. That Duris developed a theory of imitation or representation in history with reference to the specific pleasure that was proper to historical description is a necessary inference from his words, abbreviated though they are by Photius, the source of the fragment. It is also evident that the theory relates to the categories of representation and pleasure that Aristotle applied to tragedy and epic in the *Poetics*. For we observe the application of one and the same aesthetic equation: just as (for Aristotle) the *pleasure* of tragedy is produced through the *imitation* of fear and pity, the emotions peculiar to tragedy (1452B), so the *pleasure* of history is produced through the *imitation* of the emotions raised by history.[47] Duris has applied an Aristotelian concept, whatever his specification of the "historical emotions" and his identification of the proper pleasure of history. The importance of this step should not be underrated: a new theory of historiography has made its appearance. It was, moreover, quite revolutionary, for of the two kinds of literary theory honored in ancient times, rhetorical and poetic, Duris was the first historian to urge the substitution in history of the latter for the didacticism of the former: the "pleasure" of history becomes an end in itself.

When we attempt greater precision, matters become more difficult. No definitions attaching to Duris's name are known to us, and we can only speculate about the emotions he sought to portray, or to

---

[46] So I understand *ton genomenon pleiston apeleiphthesan*. It is a difficult phrase, not helped by comparison with Diod. 20. 43. 7. In addition to Jacoby, see Scheller, *De hellenistica arte*, p. 69, Avenarius, *Lukians Schrift*, p. 134. The all-important second sentence is as follows: *oute gar mimeseos metelabon oudemias oute hedones en toi phrasai, autou de tou graphein monon epemelethesan.*

[47] Eduard Schwartz, *RE* s.v. "Duris," col. 1855, understood this "pleasure" as one induced by language. Scheller, *De hellenistica arte*, pp. 68f.; Jacoby at *FGrHist* 70 F 1; F. Wehrli, "Die Geschichtsschreibung im Lichte der antiken Theorie," in *Eumusia: Festgabe für Ernst Howald* (Erlenbach, 1947), p. 63; and Avenarius, *Lukians Schrift*, p. 134, take the phrase basically as I do: pleasure induced from the imitation, i.e., realistic description, of the objective actions and subjective reactions of the historical characters. I would add, however, as will appear below, that the vivid portrayal of these actions and reactions are pleasurable not only for their own sake but because they fill the mind of the reader with amazement.

imitate realistically, in order to bring the pleasure of history to the reader. Though it seems obvious that the lighter emotions can be dismissed from consideration, the idea that Duris may have claimed for history the very fear and pity isolated by Aristotle has gained adherents, in spite of its obvious and dismaying implications. One may certainly doubt that Duris would have been prompted to father a theory involving so limited an emotional range—we are speaking, after all, of the genre of history, not simply of the epos, which even so was wider far, in its range, than was tragedy—were it not for the fact that a writer subsequent to Duris, and quite possibly under his influence, the third-century historian Phylarchus, was accused by Polybius (2. 56. 7–12) of confusing tragedy with history in his desire to raise the emotions of fear and pity. Polybius accuses Phylarchus of the "desire to incite pity in the readers and to make them respond emotionally to what he has written"; he speaks of Phylarchus's "introduction of scenes of woe" (7); "he does this throughout his history, constantly attempting to set terrible things before the very eyes of the hearer" (8). But, Polybius affirms, the historian must not write like an author of tragedies (10). "The end of tragedy and history is not the same but the opposite. In the former, one must frighten and charm the hearers for the moment by means of persuasive speech. In the latter one must teach and persuade the *philomathountes* forever by means of true deeds and speeches" (11).

Since Phylarchus has been charged with a confusion of the ends of tragedy and history—that is, with implementing a poetic theory of history—and since Duris apparently broke new ground by advocating precisely this, it seems reasonable to associate the two men. We should, at the same time, resist imputing to Duris precisely the technique and aims practiced by Phylarchus. Intellectual affiliation does not imply artistic subservience. It is useful to remember that Thucydides is properly regarded as a successor of the essentially different Herodotus. Similarly, Xenophon followed Thucydides, and Sisenna Clitarchus. That Phylarchus may stand in comparable relationship to Duris is an inadequate basis from which to judge the latter's historiographical theory. It does not seem cogent, therefore, to assume merely from Polybius's polemic, in which we must allow for exaggeration and caricature, that Duris or even Phylarchus simply equated the pleasure of drama with the pleasure of history and generally obliterated the distinctions between them.

Duris assuredly attempted no such identification. He would have made himself ridiculous. There is something artificial and insensitive in the notion that Duris blandly could have equated tragedy and history in this fashion. For the question is not one of the accessory qualities of tragedy and history, but of the pleasure of categorically disparate genres. To equate the intrinsic pleasure of each is not to build on Aristotle, but to pervert him and to make an unholy confusion of all his work on genre. For this reason, if for no other, we must seek some other specific emotion or assume that he regarded the excitation of *all* emotions, whatever the historical narrative might prompt, as desirable. But, in the first place, we must commence by recognizing that Duris, as a proper Peripatetic, would not have started with a shopping list of emotions suitable to be represented in a history. He would have attempted first to isolate the character of history, define its nature, and would then have proceeded to isolate the appropriate emotions in accordance with this identity.

Can we, then, find a pleasure categorically different from tragedy's and arguably consonant with the nature of history itself? Here, though the evidence is slight, I think it probable that Duris fastened specifically on the emotion of "surprise," the inevitable concomitant of the workings of Chance, or *Tyche*, the fundamental principle of Duris's philosophy of history. Such a view, as it happens, also goes far to explain the charge by opponents of this theoretic that it involved a confusion of tragedy and history.

Empedocles (31 B 51 DK) had first imparted philosophical respectability and purpose (as it were) to *Tyche*. The nature of Chance (whose operation Thucydides noted, though it was not integral to his concept of history) was described by Plato in *Laws* 4. 709A as a deluge of random and disturbing occurrences (but cf. *Laws* 10. 904C). The concept gained in popularity and, as we learn from Demetrius of Phalerum, who wrote a treatise on the subject, *Tyche* even attained earthly mastery (though not, of course, over Stoics). Demetrius emphasized the utter instability of good fortune, arguing the case historically, at least in part (F 81 Wehrli = Polyb. 29. 21). Now Duris was the contemporary and fellow Peripatetic of Demetrius. We know, moreover, that he assigned a predominating role to *Tyche*, so that the essence of his history will have consisted in his observation of the vicissitudes it produced. It is possible now to comprehend why Phylarchus and others were likened to "paratragedians" by Polybius. Fear and pity may have been concomitant reasons, but the actual culprit was Chance. Chance worked for these historians as a *dea ex machina*, and the *deus ex machina* had come to epitomize tragic poetry. It was a standard criticism, for example (Plato *Cratylus* 425D, Arist. *Poetics* 15. 1454B.2–6) of *poor* tragic technique to effect a resolution from without by means of the gods. By an easily conceivable extension[48] the abuse of this technique soon became a defining quality of tragic poetry in general. Once the cliché arose that tragic poets were writers who unfolded and resolved their plots by the means of supernatural causes, it is easy to see how the term could have become a useful polemical tool in the hands of a "pragmatic" historian confronting a group of writers using *Tyche*, historical instability, as the ultimate determinant of the actions of men. It is highly relevant that Polybius in the passage partly quoted above observes (13) of Phylarchus that "apart from this, he narrates for us the greatest number of vicissitudes without supplying the cause and manner of the events. Without these it is impossible to feel rational pity or be appropriately angered at any of the events that occur" (cf. 15. 34. 2, 7. 7. 2).

It seems not unreasonable, therefore, to impute this theoretic to Duris, tenuous though the links of argument may be. The vicissitudes of history became a historical cliché, just as "pleasure" became one of the two competing definitions of history's purpose (the other being "knowledge"). Abuse of *peripeteiai* (reversals to elicit pity and fear) was one very emphatic complaint brought by Polybius against Phylarchus. Perhaps most important of all, Duris was convinced of the dominating power of Chance in history. That he would have sought some direct reciprocity between what he considered "the nature of history" and the emotion and pleasure deriving from it seems indisputable. "Surprise," therefore, became his defining criterion, and the pleasure deriving from the reader's constant encounters with the unexpected was the unique "pleasure of history" Duris had in view.

Naturally, insistence on the irrationality of the results of human actions made vivid writing and *mimesis* that much more a requirement of the proper historical style. Surprise betokens strong human emotions, especially pity and fear, for the implication is that individuals and groups so "surprised" are as unprepared for the jolt as is the

---

[48] See Cicero *De natura deorum* 1. 54. 4 (*tragici poetae*) with A. S. Pease's note.

reader. More than this, they are the sports of a goddess to whom justice and injustice are irrelevant; victims must inevitably suffer the more grievously. It is easy to see, therefore, why Polybius attacked Phylarchus as he did, for it is a reasonable inference that Phylarchus sensationalized the theoretic promulgated by Duris. It may be significant that Phylarchus commenced his history where Duris broke off: in Hellas, where a multiplicity of writers flourished, continuing the work of one of them carries an obvious implication. More important is the fact that Phylarchus adopted a style of historiography that correlates with the principles of vivid writing and emotional appeal apparently urged by Duris. More important still is the nature of Polybius's criticism: as stated, it is more than a polemic against one writer's extravagances; it is also an attack on a particular way of writing history (cf. 15. 36).[49] Phylarchus not only writes tragically, but proceeds according to the (misconceived) plan that history should be so written. For Polybius's comparison of history and tragedy in this context (2. 56. 11) would be ludicrous if it were not that Phylarchus's aesthetic, generally recognized as such, was dependent enough on poetic theory to sustain Polybius's charges and give them point. Therefore, unless we are prepared to assume that both Duris and Phylarchus independently developed congruent principles of historiography, the connection of Phylarchus with Duris, and of Duris with "tragic history"—history dominated by sudden reversals, with Chance as the *dea ex machina*—is firm.

We should very much like to know how far Duris went in asserting the mimetic power of the historian and how he viewed the relationship of history to poetry. Here Plutarch may be of help. For, in the first place, it is just possible to infer that Duris argued his case with reference to Thucydides: the otherwise unknown Marcellinus, in the *Vita Thucydidis* 41, indignantly rejects the opinion of "some" who maintain that Thucydides' history belongs to poetry and not to rhetoric. Though the claim is absurd on its face (such a classification would have been impossible at any time),[50] its basis may reasonably

[49] The passages critical of tragic history are collected by F. W. Walbank, *A Historical Commentary on Polybius* (Oxford, 1957), vol. 1, p. 259.

[50] The application of poetic literary theory is another matter. Thus Quintilian 10. 1. 31 (cf. Agathias 2. 135D): "History is very like to poetry [*proxima poetis*] and, in a certain sense, a poem in prose." Quintilian perhaps has in mind the increased use of the *ekphrasis*, or "description," by contemporaries in both genres. It is interesting that, in spite of this approximation, Quintilian mildly repudiated Lucan's poetic

lie in analysis of Thucydides' mimetic skills precisely along the lines adopted by Duris. Now Plutarch (*De gloria Atheniensium* 347A) discusses this question, and the nature of his discussion strongly suggests that he may bridge Duris and Marcellinus for us. Here Plutarch defined as the *most successful historian* that writer who "paints" with "emotion and dramatic characters," "making the hearer a spectator (and) **eagerly desiring to infuse the dizzying and upsetting emotions of the actual participants into the reader.**" On this basis, Plutarch chose Thucydides as "the most successful historian," instancing his descriptions of Demosthenes and Brasidas at Pylos and the battle in Syracuse harbor.

It should not be necessary to insist that the central point for Plutarch is the vivid and dramatic treatment of sudden reversals, dizzying sequences, the unexpected. Though pity and fear may indeed be raised by the spectacle of the battle in Syracuse harbor, these emotions are secondary to the primary note struck by Thucydides: reversal of roles with paradoxical results. It cannot be accidental that the two instances mentioned by Plutarch were stressed by Thucydides for their violence to predictable expectations. Thucydides emphasizes this turn of events in the affair at Pylos (where the Athenian presence was itself a fortuitous development) not only in the speech he attributes to Demosthenes (4. 10) but in concluding remarks that Duris could only have applauded:

> [After the initial attempt by Brasidas and the Spartans to force a landing was prevented,] chance [*tyche*] had so turned that the Athenians were repelling the Lacedaemonians from the land, and Lacedaemonian land at that, while the Lacedaemonians were disembarking from ships and onto their own land, which was hostile to them, against Athenians. For at that time it was the prevalent opinion that [the Spartans] were landsmen and foot soldiers par excellence, while the others were a sea people and far outdistanced [all others] in the use of their fleet. [4. 12. 3]

On the battle in Syracuse harbor, there is no need to comment here; all who know the passage well remember the emotion of suspense and sense of paradox conveyed by Thucydides.

(10. 1. 90). In any case, the categories remained differentiated; see Cicero *De legg.* 1. 1, 4, Quint. 2. 4. 2, Pliny 9. 33, Ausonius 26.

Since Thucydides has been appraised favorably in terms suitable to the (conjectured) aesthetic of Duris, there is reason to think that Duris claimed Thucydides for a precursor and model. Such an assumption would explain the surprising confinement of Duris's criticism to the techniques of his immediate predecessors, the "rhetorical historians," Ephorus and Theopompus. He did not, in other words, criticize all of his predecessors (as an innovator might well do) for a deficiency of pleasure and *mimesis*, and it is credible that he contrasted them unfavorably with the great Athenian and perhaps with some others (Ctesias is a possibility; see Demetrius *On Style* 215).

From Duris himself we learn little more. The fragments (*FGrHist* 76) reveal a florid style. One passage (F 24) moves with commendable rapidity and there is a notable avoidance of participial constructions, Duris here preferring the rapid fire of a series of finite verbs. His narrative, as we may infer from Diodorus 20,[51] was rich in dramatic emphasis. So his description of Agathocles' departure from Syracuse (20. 7. 4), a splendid scene reminiscent of Thucydides, his close interest in the emotional state of people (20. 9–10, 61. 5), his description of lamenting women (15. 4) and, above all, constant observation of the vicissitudes of fortune (13. 4, 33. 2–3, 34. 7, 51. 4).

In Hellenistic times, the literary-historical vocabulary appears to have been substantially enriched by poetic terminology,[52] and it is reasonable to seek the explanation in the popularity of Duris's theories among the critics. A special insistence on visual effects—that history should place a scene before your very eyes—is unmistakable. Thus Duris attempted to add the pleasure of poetry to history's own. The emotions were to be excited, especially pity and fear, by the use of vivid writing pointed toward the description of surprising turns and calamitous events.

We need not wonder at Duris's aesthetic revolution: it is the nature of trends for them to be supplanted, and smooth Isocratean diction had begun to pall. Nevertheless, a lively discussion has raged

[51] That Duris was the primary source (with additions from Timaeus) is a safe assumption, and it is not invalidated by the possibility that Diodorus's procedure was more complicated when his material was more diffuse, e.g., in book 1; see A. Burton, *Diodorus Siculus Book I: A Commentary* (Leiden, 1972). A safe guide to his normal procedure is the Alexander-history of 17 and his use of Ephorus in 11ff. In general, see the relevant fragments of Ephorus with Jacoby's commentary.

[52] See Avenarius, *Lukians Schrift*, pp. 130ff.

about the origin, extent, and even existence of the movement since the publication by Ed. Schwartz of his brilliant *aperçu* identifying "tragic history" in *Fünf Vorträge* (1896) and subsequent works.[53] Much of it has proved repetitive or sterile. Of those who accept the idea of a new historiography, some are chiefly moved to insist that not Duris but Theophrastus or Praxiphanes was its true author. The distinct predisposition to deny the ostensible formulator of a theory credit for its adumbration is observable. It is hard to shake the suspicion that Duris has been bypassed as the theory's prime mover in order to provide it with more authoritative credentials. But Theophrastus has only his connection with Aristotle to recommend him in this respect; he evinces no theoretical interest in historiography. The other candidate, Praxiphanes, in his dialogue *On History* (Marc. *Vita Thuc.* 29 = Wehrli F 18), ought never to have been brought forward. It is alleged that this associate of Theophrastus's and Duris's wrote a dialogue personifying Thucydides as the spokesman of the potentialities of history in argument with representatives of poetry. However, although the hypothesis requires that the Thucydides in question be the famous historian, he is in fact somebody else with the same name. The reader must understand that Praxiphanes' work is mentioned by Marcellinus in the course of his identification of other figures named Thucydides (homonyms); indeed, the collection and identification of homonyms was a common ancient practice. Having finished with the first three bearers of the name, Marcellinus moves to the next:

> The fourth Thucydides **other than the historian was a poet**, of the deme Acherdous, whom Androtion mentions in his *Local History of Athens* [FGrHist 324 F 57], saying that he is the son of Ariston. *He* was a contemporary, as Praxiphanes says in his *On History*, of Plato the comic poet, Agathon the tragic poet, Niceratus the epic poet, Choerilus and Melanippides [the epic

---

[53] A bibliographical discussion is provided by K. von Fritz, "Die Bedeutung des Aristoteles," in *Entretiens Hardt, no. 4, Histoire et historiens* (1956), pp. 106–14. See also F. W. Walbank, "Tragic History: A Reconsideration," *BICS* 2 (1955): 4–14, and "History and Tragedy," *Historia* 9 (1960): 216–34. The premise of authors on either side is that "fear and pity" were the emotions primarily contemplated by Duris. My own refinement may perhaps somewhat strengthen the case for the enunciation of a new historiographical theoretic (since it relieves Duris of the imputation of having acted superficially and mechanically); but the nature of the debate is not thereby fundamentally altered.

and dithyrambic poets]. When Archelaus [of Macedon] was alive [died 399] he enjoyed little fame, as the same Praxiphanes makes plain; later he gained extraordinary repute.

Now Jacoby stated in 1954 (at the fragment of Androtion) that "everything cited from Praxiphanes refers to him (the poet), not, as is generally assumed, to the historian, a sojourn of whom at the Macedonian court is reported neither by Marcellinus nor by anybody else." Only the wish to compose a philosophical-historical fantasia can produce a different interpretation. Praxiphanes may be dismissed from consideration.

Clearly, both Theophrastus and Praxiphanes have been propelled into this context because the search for causes, and for causes of causes, has been pushed to extreme lengths. There is a certain irony in the recruitment of Praxiphanes as the ideological mentor of Duris when Duris, too, was a student of Theophrastus's and, to judge from the extent of his theoretical writings, sufficiently capable to develop his own theoretic, especially for a discipline he decided to make his own. His interests in Homer, tragedy, and painting all combine to make him a plausible originator of the theory expressed and implemented in his work. But to some, apparently, it is better somehow to make Duris the exponent of a corporate philosophy: the Peripatetics have spoken on history. This grandiose notion then acquires grandiose consequences: Duris's theory of stylistic representation and dramatic emphasis (hinging on reversals of expectation, as I would maintain) must be suitably amplified and systematized, and "tragic history" must be ranged against "rhetorical" or "Isocratean history," another will-o'-the-wisp. At this point in the evolution of the controversy, opponents of this inflated view may legitimately point to the lack of evidence of any "school" of "tragic history" written according to rule; Duris's aesthetic, the solid base on which the entire modern reconstruction was erected, is also repudiated.

Taking a different tack, some moderns deny the existence of the theory altogether,[54] pointing out that historians before Duris excited

[54]E.g., F. W. Walbank (see note 53). The desire to keep "theory" in proper perspective (as shown by Kurt Latte in the discussion following von Fritz's paper in *Entretiens Hardt*, no. 4, pp. 129f.) must be warmly supported. The very word will galvanize some scholars. But the pendulum has swung too far, and we begin to deny the existence of theory almost on principle. Here we have a theoretical work (the *Poetics*), an adaptation of its system (Duris), the use of consonant techniques by a writer

the same emotions in tragic descriptions. Even conceding for the sake of argument that the excitation of fear and pity were the primary components of the theory (instead of emphasis on the unpredictability of historical sequences), such practice by earlier writers is surely not an argument against the theory. It need only be credible that neither Ephorus nor Theopompus (and, we should assume, other members of this generation, including Callisthenes) attempted such evocative descriptions. For that, unless there is evidence to the contrary, we must take Duris's word. Needless to state, here we must separate form from substance. For example, Callisthenes' ravens and the prayer at Arbela (*FGrHist* 124 F 14, 36) are not characteristics of "tragic history" (as they have been called) but wonderful details ideally suited to description of the kind. History had by nature always been epic and dramatic by turns, and it is certainly not a consequence of accepting Duris's theory to believe that he was the first historian to be inspired by a sense of theatre. Dramatic influences in earlier historiography are simply irrelevant to Duris's assertion of their theoretical propriety. As we know from Aristotle's *Poetics*, the assertion of an ideal need imply no more than the lack of an intuitive grasp of correct procedure by the practitioners of any art. Indeed, we must bear in mind that although Theopompus and Ephorus "gave neither imitation nor pleasure in their narrative," both of them included events dramatic in the highest degree. The problem was not with what they described but with the means they employed. They "fell short" (*apeleiphthesan*) of the sublimity or pathos inherent in their historical subject, and, above all (as I believe) failed to grasp the staggering incalculability of history's course.

The essence of Duris's theory is captured, I think, by Cicero in his letter to Lucceius, where he calls history a source of pleasure that powerfully affects the mind.

> **For nothing is more suitable to the delight of the reader than changing times and reverses of fortune.** Although mine were not sought for when I experienced them, **they will be pleasant to read.** The recollection in tranquillity of **past suffering has its own pleasure**; for others who have undergone no trouble of

---

(Phylarchus) who is accused of not knowing the difference between tragedy and history, and the adoption of poetical terminology to prose works by literary critics thereafter.

their own *a pleasurable pity arises* when they regard *the mis-fortunes of others*, though these are unaccompanied by their own personal grief. [*Ad fam.* 5. 12. 4]

Historical amplification

That Duris envisaged a technique involving the use of abundant and unverifiable circumstantial detail is a necessary implication of his theory of *mimesis*. He can only have done so, however, because it was long since an established principle that the bare historical facts required both supplementation and deductive interconnection in order to provide a narrative that was at once intellectually and artistically satisfying. From the beginning, with Herodotus and Thucydides, the historian assumed the right to *picture* a scene consistently with the reports of witnesses or common knowledge. In essence, just as the data in his control reflected a sharply reduced image of the reality, with many of its features obliterated, so his account more closely approached the actuality (as pictured) by the refraction of that image and the restoration of the features. If the reality led to the report, it followed that the report led back to reality by inference and empathy. Thus Herodotus pictured the death of Cyrus and the grand debate between Xerxes, Mardonius, and Artabanus; Thucydides similarly collated his evidence for the battle in Syracuse harbor and wrote of it as he visualized its progressive course.[55]

The need for imaginative recreation and inferential elaboration from the facts was the necessary consequence of the demands placed on all subsequent historians by Herodotus when he decided, following Homer, to present events with verisimilitude. Everything from needful circumstantial detail to the virtual reproduction of the thoughts of leading figures was injected into the historical narrative,

---

[55] See Thucydides' comment in 7. 44. 1. In the process, here, of describing the night battle for Epipolae, he observed that the Athenians were thrown into consternation "so that it was not easy to get from one side or the other any detailed account of the affair. By day certainly the combatants have a clearer notion, though even then by no means of all that takes place, no one knowing much of anything that does not go on in his own immediate neighborhood" [trans. R. Crawley]. The description that follows is nevertheless a masterpiece. The very real difficulties in providing a veracious description of any battle, seriously underrated by modern critics, seem fairly indicated by the relative success or failure of Callisthenes (*FGrHist* 124 F 35), who assuredly strove to provide an accurate account of the battle of Issus, of which he was a witness.

often on mere grounds of probability. Thus Aristotle simplified somewhat in *Poetics* 1451B when he distinguished poetry (what might happen) from history (what does happen). The historian often explains how what did happen could have happened. He tries to make a sequence of events "possible in the sense of being believable or inevitable," as Aristotle said of the poet. The demands of art, abhorrence of a spotty and ragged account, and the obviously hypothetical character of what began by being a reconstruction smoothed the integration of fact and inference into a seamless narrative. In this fashion, the requirements of the medium resulted in the fusion of the factual basis of the record with its imaginative reenactment by the writer.

The process here described is irrelevant to the categories of "fact" and "fiction," "truth and falsity," "honesty and dishonesty," so often applied to the discredit of the ancients. Certainly some writers will have been dishonest and others will have written fiction or approached it in their zeal to excite the emotions of their readers and otherwise to pleasure them. Such excess, however, for which there are enough modern parallels, was a gross evasion of the rules of historical responsibility, while the latter were entirely compatible with the process of the imaginative and intuitive reenactment of events.

Since the activity here isolated was inherent to historical composition, it was taken for granted by the Greeks as a natural part of writing. Cicero, however, comes very close to providing a definition of the procedure because of his perception of the absence of this very quality in Latin historical literature. The fundamental discussion is contained in *De legibus* 1. 1–2. Mention of Cicero's historical epic, the *Marius*, prompts the question from Atticus, the historical purist, whether Cicero may not have invented salient details in the epic. There are readers, he notes, who do not know what is true and what false. Cicero replies that a historical poem offers a poet's truth, *not that of a witness*, and Q. Cicero adds that there are different laws for poetry and for history, of which the standards are, respectively, pleasure and truth (1. 1, 5). With this highly important premise set down, there follows a discussion of the limitations of Latin historiography. Though a historical work properly is "more than any other genre rhetoric's very own" (*opus unum hoc oratorium maxime*), Latin historiography is thin (*exile*) and stylistically primitive in comparison with the historical literature of the Greeks. Now the corrective process desiderated by Cicero is indicated by the verb *ornare*,[56] which is why Cicero uses the same word (or rather stem) in *De oratore* 12, 54, where he demands of Latin writers that they become "elaborators" (*exornatores rerum*), not simply "purveyors of the details" (*narratores*). For our purposes, one further and highly relevant use of the same verb by Cicero occurs in the *Brutus* 11, 44. Clitarchus and Stratocles are accused of having invented the dramatic suicide of Themistocles—"for they were able to elaborate this famous death in a rhetorical and tragic manner" (*hanc enim mortem rhetorice et tragice ornare potuerunt*).

One must conclude that the Latin verb means something more than "adorn superficially," "decorate," "embellish." It implies description and amplification, and it extends considerably beyond the mere introduction of political commentary, praise and blame, and other common historical elements. Clitarchus, for example, did not merely brush in strokes but painted a scene, and he not only painted it but invented it. It is vital to note, however, that only the imaginative reenactment is covered by the term *ornare*; the false and contrived nature of the scene is expressed adverbially by *tragice et rhetorice*. *Ornare* in itself is to take a fact and from it to set a scene, developing its latent potentialities. But in a historical work *ornare* subserves the laws of history and is tested by the standard of the truth. Otherwise how could Cicero declare that the law of history was truth and yet condemn the Roman writers for the absence of *ornare*?

Ornare therefore designates a technique that involves much more than stylistic ornamentation, and the implication of the term (in this context) is entirely free from the idea of meretricious adornment. The term comprehends the activity of *mimesis* and, as Cicero well knew, defines a requirement of historiography in which the Greeks far surpassed the Latins. *Ornare* can be applied to true tradition, as the "laws of history" prescribe, or to false tradition in the manner of Clitarchus. Thus, if you develop the inherent possibilities of a true datum, *ornare* is legitimate; if from a fiction (where the psychology may be to delight the reader), the practice is culpable.[57]

---

[56] *De leg.* 1. 2, 5. Your fatherland, says Atticus, deserves to have its history "described with the necessary embellishment and amplification [*ornata*]. For the genre of [proper] history is absent in our literature."

[57] The opinion should never have been imputed to Cicero, on the basis of *Brutus* 11, 42 ("it is granted orators to lie when they relate well-known stories [*in historiis*] so

Naturally, since every writer from Herodotus to Ammianus Marcellinus possessed his own concept of the proper limits to the imaginative restoration of detail and mood, the approach leaves us almost helpless when we attempt to extricate fact from fancy. The ancients, however, would have repudiated any such analytical exercise, for they wrote in the expectation that their histories in fact established the record in a final and conclusive sense.

The Place of Historiographical Theory

Thus far we have attempted to isolate and place in their probable context some of the more important principles and theoretical developments dictating the practice of historiography. Though it may seem surprising to us, especially because of the modern proclivity to works on historiography per se, no evidence suggests that these theoretical developments received systematic treatment in a work written between the fifth century and late Hellenistic times. Since Aristotle had denied that the study of the particular could qualify as a "science" or "art" (*techne*), and the claim that history was a *techne* never was advanced, such a treatise would have lacked a reason for being. Naturally, if someone postulates the existence of a treatise of this type to explain, for example, the theoretical basis of Duris's concept of history, the claim cannot be refuted. Something alleged to have existed for which there is no evidence cannot have its nonexistence demonstrated, even when it is clear that by ancient standards such a work would have been anomalous. On the other hand, in these circumstances the allegation can be dismissed without regret or argument. All the same, it does not seem impossible that something of the kind was attempted at a somewhat later time. If ever there was an epoch ripe for the theoretical speculation postulated for the early third century B.C., it was the first century B.C. This age witnessed the popularity of history, and a sense of its importance, never matched before or since in antiquity; it was a veritable renaissance, reflective and critical as well as creative.

Polybius's thorough discussion of methodology may well have pre-

---

that they can say something clever"), that rhetoricians possessed some kind of license to lie *when they wrote history. In historiis* is equivalent to the Greek rhetorical term *en diegemasin* ("in stories") and simply refers to the historical illustrations supplied by orators in the course of a speech.

pared the way for this movement, and the treatises on history written by Caecilius of Caleacte and (perhaps) Metrododorus of Scepsis
(*FGrHist* 183, 184) may indicate the solidification of principles in a
new synthesis. The study of historiography became intensely practical as well as literary. Latin historians (for example, Sisenna and
Sallust) studied technique from model historians—Philistus, Xenophon, Clitarchus—and subjected the Greek tradition of historiography to review. Probably this explains the rediscovery of Thucydides
in the middle of the first century,[58] and to a generation habituated to
admiration of Polybius, Thucydides' history must have come as a
shock and a revelation. Greater intellectual power and sure methodological grasp combined with spare and muscular prose to produce
a history that was also a work of art.

The intellectual movement indicated by these signs can be perceived in the radical shift in emphasis from the ordinary province of
rhetoric to historical analysis exemplified by Dionysius's study of
Thucydides; and it is an unmistakable sign of the times that Dionysius proceeded to write a history of his own, the *Antiquitates Roma-
nae*. Whether or not he did so in order to advertise himself as a
teacher of rhetoric, as is sometimes assumed, the important observation is that historiography, and one which incorporated a developed
theoretic, was the medium he chose. Above all, there is the seminal
influence of Cicero, in itself an effect and cause of historical interest.
This great literary genius delivered himself of a number of important
theoretical pronouncements and exhibits deep involvement in the
study of Latin historiography. As it happens, some of his remarks,
delivered in the midst of this intensely fruitful period of historical
writing, also locate for us the repository of doctrine.

In *De oratore* Cicero inimitably lists the formal requirements of
history as dictated by current theory:

> **For who is ignorant** that it is the first law of history not to dare
> to say anything false? Not to dare to withhold the truth? To
> avoid while writing the suspicion of currying favor? Of indulg-
> ing animosity? Obviously, *these foundations are known to ev-
> eryone, and also that* its edifice consists of events and speeches.
> The reckoning of events needs temporal order and the descrip-

---

[58] See D. Earl's fascinating discussion, "Prologue-form in Ancient Historiography,"
in *Aufstieg und Niedergang der römischen Welt*, ed. H. Temporini (Berlin, 1972), vol. 1.
2, pp. 854ff.

tion of the sites. Furthermore, since the deliberations, then the deeds and after that the results are awaited, history requires that indication be made of what deliberations are approved by the writer and, as to the actions themselves, that the writer point out not only what was done or said but also the manner in which it was accomplished. When the result is discussed, history requires that all the causes be explained, whether they are accidental or intended. History requires of the participants themselves not only an account of their deeds but also of the life and character of each man who excels in fame and name. [2. 15. 62–63]

How was this "known to everyone" in 55 B.C.? Even assuming that Cicero overstates the diffusion of this knowledge, he nevertheless guarantees that the theory expressed is both accessible and routine. In what kind of work was this material generally available? Cicero tells us a little later on in the same work (64). He points out that the rhetorical manuals and the rhetorical schools provide no precepts for the *implementation* of the very requirements he has admitted to be generally acknowledged. It follows, precisely as Sextus Empiricus later asserted (*Adv. gramm.* 266–68 Mau), that it lay in the province of the rhetoricians to articulate the principles of historical writing and that they had done so in Cicero's time along the lines he sketched—which is why "everybody knew them." It further appears that nothing more ambitious was attempted by them.[59] The result is not entirely negative: we may envisage a process whereby the rhetorical study of the historians from, let us say, the fourth century resulted in the accretion of a set of principles passed on in the schools as a foundation for critical reading and, on occasion, active enterprise. Thus we understand the reason for the close similarity of Cicero's historical *dicta* with the definition of history offered by Dionysius not long afterward:

> I consider that it is not sufficient for the benefit of readers of history to learn [only] of the actual result of the deeds but that everyone also requires a historical account of the causes of what

[59] Though some scholars opine (see Avenarius, *Lukians Schrift*, p. 172) that Cicero's remark does not exclude the existence of substantive treatises on history outside the confines of rhetoric, the evasion is unworthy of the importance of the subject. You do not deplore the absence of material in *x* if it is already present in *y*—unless your concern is not for the material but for the rhetorical handbooks.

occurred, the nature of the deeds, the intention of the actors, divine manifestations, and that they be ignorant of nothing that attends events. I see [also] that the knowledge of these things has a very necessary relation to men in politics, who must be able to apply it as models to the events befalling them. [*AR* 5. 56. 1]

Other aspects of the ruling (syncretistic) historiographical theory are presented to us by Cicero in the letter to Lucceius (*Ad fam.* 5. 12), written in 56 B.C., a year before the *De oratore.* Here he emphasizes (among other things) the importance of variety of episode and the desirability of introducing various acts and many scenes. As we have seen, Richard Reitzenstein recognized that Cicero presupposes a specific theory of historiography, although Reitzenstein limited its scope when he insisted that it applied only to the monograph and not to history in general. Reitzenstein did not observe that the differences separating the monograph from the continuous or annalistic histories (*fortlaufende Geschichte*) are irrelevant to the points contained in Cicero's letter, while these same points (which Reitzenstein used to establish "rules" for the monograph) are common both to the continuous histories and to the monograph. He erred most seriously, however, when he contended that the monograph was believed to be the only suitable form for the *Kunstwerk*, or work of art. Callisthenes, Duris, Phylarchus, and, especially to the point, Sisenna, would not have agreed; the principles of unity and artistic coherence, which of course are especially applicable to the monograph, were also applied to their own creations by writers as diverse as Ephorus and Polybius (1. 4), just as they would be applied in later times by Tacitus and Ammianus.

Cicero argued not that a monograph on his consulship must follow the "rules" of monography (an impertinent request, this, to make of the practiced historian, Lucceius, who presumably knew the rules) but that his consulship was uniquely suitable to historical treatment in a monograph. Cicero is combatting a prejudice long since cogently stated by Polybius:

> Whenever writers take a simple and monographic subject and want to be called historians . . . they must make big things of little, embellish and extend short speeches, turn some marginal actions into major ones, arrange battle-lines and narrate

clashes in which sometimes ten foot soldiers fall. . . . As to sieges and descriptions and the rest, one cannot describe well enough how extensively they elaborate on account of the dearth of material. [29. 12. 2–4]

It is clear, then, that Cicero's purpose was not to set down the rules of the monograph but, quite the contrary, to trumpet its potential. He wanted to prove to Lucceius that his consulship was a brilliant historical subject calculated to satisfy all of Lucceius's desires. The desiderata of every historian, Cicero urged, were present in this single topic.

Cicero's theory, therefore, implies no more than the tailoring of current historiographical theory to the monograph. It was a theory extrapolated from the best and most popular practices of the Greeks and was expounded in the rhetorical schools to all and sundry. Individual historians naturally applied one principle or another as it suited their artistic goals and historical purposes. But as Cicero stated, and Sextus Empiricus categorically affirmed, the theory lay within the province of rhetoric, where classification passed for criticism and historical writing was chiefly interesting because of its extraordinary literary possibilities.

IV

The Speech in Greek and Roman Historiography

It would be almost impossible to overstate the importance of formal speeches in Greco-Roman historiography, for they present us with the reactions, intentions, and expectations of the movers of events and provide a clarification of the issues dividing powers at war or citizens in internal disputes. In a word, they provide history with its innate intellectual dimension. We not only learn what deeds were accomplished, but also acquire a grasp of the complex mental states of leading individuals and their supporters. All of this follows, naturally, *if* the speeches are reliable. Of this there is great doubt; the general inclination today is to dismiss most of the speeches inserted (a tell-tale word!) by the Greco-Roman historians (Polybius and, sometimes, Thucydides excepted) on the ground that they are mere rhetorical constructions, no better or no worse than the intellectual power and aesthetical predilections of the individual writers. The fact that they are not direct quotations, but have the effrontery to masquerade as such, probably has much to do with the formation of this unshakable prejudice, for the practice, to modern eyes, approaches deliberate perjury. Nevertheless it seems to me that a much more positive view is indicated. We must first recognize, however, that the speech was taken seriously by the ancients, at least beginning with Thucydides, who regarded it as a genre with laws and requirements of its own, which authoritatively transcended and disallowed historical irresponsibility. The fact does not seem to have been sufficiently appreciated that the ancients unfailingly endorsed the convention that speeches must be reported accurately. Furthermore, as we shall also see, where the evidence allows us to form a judgment, it is clear that within certain definable limits, they proved faithful to the doctrine.

Theory

THE REPORT OF CONTEMPORARY SPEECHES

Although it was Herodotus who introduced the direct oration into history (Marcellinus *Vita Thuc.* 38), our proper point of departure is the well-considered decision of Thucydides to continue with its use. One should observe that Thucydides takes it as understood that the procedure is appropriate, indeed mandatory, and justifies not the inclusion of the speeches but his method of presenting them (1. 22. 1), actually apologizing for not providing the exact words of the speakers:

> It was difficult for me to remember the exact substance of the speeches I myself heard and for others to remember those they heard elsewhere and told me of. Instead . . . .

Thucydides, in other words, not only accepted the premise that speeches and deeds were the integral elements of "the memorable actions" that comprised history (cf. Plato *Timaeus* 19C) but held, in theory, at least, that verbatim speeches would have been best. The principle that speeches must be presented as a necessary part of the historical narrative proved enduring. Apart from the elusive Cratippus,[1] Pompeius Trogus is the only major writer known to have abjured the direct oration (Justin *Epit.* 38. 3. 11), and Duris himself only wished them shortened (see below, pp. 149ff.).

Thucydides' explanation for his incapacity to present the actual

---

[1] For Cratippus, see Dionys. *De Thuc.* 16 with W. K. Pritchett's commentary, *Dionysius of Halicarnassus: On Thucydides* (Berkeley and Los Angeles, 1975). Cratippus's allegation that Thucydides intended to discontinue the use of the speech has invariably been viewed in isolation from the programmatic statement of 1. 22. Since it is inconceivable that a writer who began with the opinion that speeches were coordinate with deeds as the stuff of history could have come by the end of the war to consider them merely as a literary device, it is best to assume that Cratippus made an improper inference from their absence in book 8. In all probability, Cratippus was a Hellenistic writer justifying his own aversion to the speech at a time when it had become vulnerable to attack. See below, pp. 147ff.

words of the speakers, whether or not it is the sole reason for his adoption of a different procedure, implies a concept of accurate reporting fully consistent with his scrupulous narration of the deeds of the war. Thucydides appraised the speech as an historical event categorically equal to the deed. It is in this context (and not with the tautological assistance of one's impression of the speeches themselves) that one should read the oft-discussed methodological statement of 1. 22. 1:

> I have given the speeches in the manner in which it seemed to me that each of the speakers would best express what needed to be said about the ever-prevailing situation, but I have kept as close as possible to the total opinion expressed by the actual words [*tes xumpases gnomes ton alethos lechthenton*].

Although there is some question about the exact meaning here of the word *gnome*, "opinion" (which I interpret as parallel with 2. 35 and would illustrate by Herodotus's use of the same word in 7. 139), the difficulty with this sentence is not the language, which is clear enough, but the logic. Two competing procedures are presented in the same sentence as if they were compatible—the freedom to make the speakers express what was necessary for the comprehension of events (as Thucydides would retrospectively determine their importance!) and the promise to reproduce the actual opinions of the speaker as closely as possible.

Though it might seem a tempting possibility, the dilemma cannot be evaded by drastically narrowing our interpretation of the word *gnome* so as to exclude from the "opinion" itself all arguments raised by the speaker in support of it. A *gnome* was not, of course, a "yes" or "no" vote, but a considered and reasoned opinion, like Herodotus's in 7. 139 or Nestor's in the *Iliad*. A decision formed a unit indissoluble from its rational basis. Furthermore, Thucydides has deliberately blocked this way out of the impasse by his use of the adjective *xympase*, "all," "the entire" *gnome*, and by his assertion that he will supply "the actual words" [*ton alethos lechthenton*]. Both expressions require his careful selection of material from entire speeches.

It becomes apparent, therefore, that Thucydides was torn between the desire to explain (and foreshadow) significant events, viz., those that will figure in the history, and the obligation to present speeches as *erga*, "deeds." He attempted an uneasy compromise that unfortunately renders impossible the allocation of responsibility for particular arguments in the speeches. For our purposes, however, the frustrating consequences of his procedure are less important than his declaration of intent. The principle was established that speeches were to be recorded accurately, though in the words of the historian, and always with the reservation that the historian could "clarify"— provide arguments expressing what the circumstances required of the speaker when the latter presented his case imperfectly. The existence of this "gray area" is naturally vexatious to us. The reasonable assurance that a given speech is "primarily" Pericles's or Diodotus's is useless when we seek to establish the true author of specific concepts and sometimes breathtaking perceptions. But if we do not possess all that we could wish, it does not follow that what remains is negligible. In theory, at least, Thucydides set down a positive methodological rule: speeches were deeds or actions requiring accurate reproduction in substance, always with the possibility, when necessary, of expansion, truncation, or reduction.

Thucydides' methodological rule proved authoritative. Surprising as it may appear, as we see from *FGrHist* 70 F 9, it was acknowledged even by Ephorus. For by stating that neither the deeds nor the speeches of archaic times were capable of being remembered down to his own time, Ephorus unequivocally registers his intention (now set firm in the historiographical tradition) to report speeches faithfully; indeed, he has entered into a commitment with his readers leading them to expect it: the public proceeded on the expectation that the speeches they would read represented the tenor of what had actually been said.

A refinement of the Thucydidean convention may be traced to Callisthenes (*FGrHist* 124 F 44). This grandnephew of Aristotle's asserted that "anyone attempting to write well must not disregard the speaker. The writer must compose speeches that are appropriate to the speaker as well as to the situation." Some scholars[2] explain this remark with reference to the increased biographical interest associated with the Age of Alexander, fostering the impression that Callisthenes urged an (increased) attention to biographical characterization. However, a consideration of this kind will at most have

---

[2] F. W. Walbank, *Speeches in Greek Historians: The Third J. L. Myres Memorial Lecture* (Oxford, n.d.), p. 5, and P. Pédech, *La méthode historique de Polybe* (Paris, 1964), p. 255 n. 12.

been secondary: Callisthenes is delivering himself of a statement critical of the practice of others; the polemic was directed against writers whose characterizations were *inappropriate*. He was advocating not creative but consequential historiography, possibly influenced (though the assumption is unnecessary) by the new awareness of "typical behavior" as shown, for example, by Aristotle in *NicEth.* 4. 8. 1124B. In all probability, the object of his attack was Thucydides, though perhaps Philistus and Xenophon should be included as well.[3] All wrote speeches "that are written in the same style of language" (Dionys. *De Thuc.* 43).[4] Crucial is the following comment of Dionysius in *De Thuc.* 41, which repeats the charge of Callisthenes almost in his exact words: "It remains to be examined whether he has made the [Melian] Dialogue appropriate to the circumstances and befitting the persons who came together at the conference."

The situation is clear. Callisthenes analyzed Thucydides' statement of method, with which his own remark is closely aligned, and he concluded that Thucydides treated one side of the equation, as it were, unlike the other. Situation and speaker demanded similar treatment; the speaker must not say anything that the circumstances rendered improper or implausible, "not fit to be spoken by either Athenian or any other Greek" (Dionys. *De Thuc.* 40). Conversely, words fit to be spoken could be employed whether they were uttered or not—as long as they did not misrepresent.

Analysis of the theoretical picture becomes more difficult after the generation of Callisthenes. On the one hand, there can be no doubt that the Thucydidean conception of the speech continued as the orthodox view, at least until imperial times. That is clear from Polybius's own assertions (12. 25 a 3) as well as from his condemnation of Timaeus (12. 25 i) as a pariah for having broken the Thucydidean rule—a charge presupposing the rule's general validity and the objective impropriety of Timaeus's conduct. In the first century B.C. in Rome, the view was endorsed by Cicero.[5] On the other hand, solid

---

[3] P. Scheller, *De hellenistica historiae conscribendae arte* (Diss., Leipzig, 1911), p. 52. Jacoby (at the fragment) recognizes the retrospective critical animus of the remark, but rather wildly suggests Isocrates as its target.

[4] The quotation specifically refers only to Thucydides, though it is applicable to the others. See Pritchett, *Dionysius of Halicarnassus*, p. xivf. It is clear that Thucydides' concern with the preservation of the important elements of an orator's speech as part of the historical record overshadowed any incipient desire to present the speaker *in his speech* as an individual in his own right.

[5] In *De oratore* 2. 15, 62 (see above, pp. 138f.), he asserts that the "edifice [of history]

evidence supports the conclusion that a new view of the speech, diminishing its importance and critical of its overuse, came into competition with the orthodox view sometime in the third century B.C., finally to win predominance in imperial times, at least within the main branch of historiography represented by Tacitus and Ammianus.

Since the pedigree of this new theory is both interesting and important and the evidence has been variously interpreted, it will be expedient to consider the matter closely, although it will entail somewhat intricate source-analysis. The theory to which allusion has been made is first enunciated (in our extant sources) by Diodorus Siculus, who wrote in the last half of the first century B.C. The passage, though lengthy, requires quotation in full:

> One might justly censure those who in their histories insert overlong orations or employ frequent speeches; for not only do they **rend asunder the continuity of the narrative** by the ill-timed insertion of speeches, but also they **interrupt the interest of those who are eagerly pressing on** toward a full knowledge of events. [2] Yet surely there is opportunity for those **who wish to display rhetorical prowess** to compose by themselves public discourses and speeches for ambassadors, likewise orations of praise and blame and the like [and thus refrain from introducing them into history]; for by recognizing the classification of literary types and by elaborating each of the two by itself, they might reasonably expect to gain a reputation in both fields of activity. [3] But as it is, some writers **by excessive use of rhetorical passages have made their entire historical work into an appendage of oratory**. Not only does that which is poorly composed give offense, but also that which seems to have hit the mark in other respects yet has gone astray from the themes and occasions that belong to its peculiar type. [4] Therefore, even of those who read such works, some skip over the orations although they appear to be entirely successful, and others, wearied in spirit by the historian's wordiness and lack of taste, abandon the reading entirely; [5] and this attitude is not without reason, for the genre [*genos*] of history **is simple and self-**

consists of events and speeches"—a Thucydidean formulation. A necessary implication of his further observation that the historian must indicate his approval or disapproval of the speeches is that they have been correctly reported.

consistent and as a whole is like a living organism. If it is man-
gled, it is stripped of its living charm; but if it retains its necessary integrity it is duly preserved and, by the unity of the whole
composition, renders the reading pleasurable and clear. [2. 1]
Nevertheless, in disapproving rhetorical speeches, we do not
ban them wholly from historical works; for, since history needs
to be adorned with variety, in certain places it is necessary to
call to our aid even such passages. [20. 1–2. 2, trans. R. M.
Geer, with modifications].

It is apparent at once that the ultimate source of this passage—
Diodorus is not in question, except for 2. 1, which includes elements
of first-century rhetorical theory—was a theorist of more than ordinary perspicuity and intelligence. His objection to rhetorical
speeches avoids obvious superficialities such as fulsome language and
tedious orations, and he is even willing to concede that some orations "appear to be entirely successful." Our theorist argues his case
from the nature of history as he conceived it—an urgent, pressing
flow of events—and from the artistic and historical requirements of
the genre itself. Now although some scholars, following Laqueur,[6]
assume that this theorist was Ephorus, the identification cannot
stand. Quite apart from the fact that by book 20 Diodorus was no
longer following Ephorus, so that the alleged use of one of his prefaces becomes problematical, the implication is intolerable that the
historical principles advocated by Thucydides could be attacked
seventy-five years later by a writer himself presupposing the parity of
speech and deed. But the reasons against the identification are
legion. Ephorus was the dominant figure in the new rhetoric, and
although it is wrong to assume that he was a "little Isocrates," it is
surely absurd to picture him as a remorseless opponent of the introduction into history of time-honored rhetorical techniques. Besides,
it was he who introduced the category of "praise and blame" into
history and he again who summoned forth the admiration of Polybius for *logoi epimetrountes,* "critical appraisals," which inevitably rend
asunder the continuity of the narrative and interrupt the interest of
those eager to press on. And of whom can it be said more truly than
of Ephorus that he wished to display his rhetorical prowess in his-

---

[6]"Ephoros," *Hermes* 46 (1911): 161–206, 321–54. Effective criticisms of Laqueur's
method are provided by Kunz, *Zur Beurteilung der Prooemien in Diodors historischer Bibliothek* (Diss., Zurich, 1935), passim.

tory? Finally, the class of writers Ephorus *ex hypothesi* attacked *did not yet exist*. Philistus (*FGrHist* 556 T 1) is said (by the Suda) to have been the first historian to write "in conformity with the rules of rhetoric"; yet this slightly older contemporary of Ephorus broke off his work in 362. Diodorus's source, clearly, must be criticizing the excesses of a generation previous to his own—men whose works were already before the public and who had carried the rhetorical movement to excess. We cannot postulate so early as the time of Ephorus a class of writers who either inserted lengthy orations or larded their work with a great number of speeches. The genre of history was not transformed into an appendage of oratory until Ephorus had left the scene. Modern writers cannot condemn Ephorus for inspiring "rhetorical history" and also make him the opponent of the excesses to which it *eventually* led.

Since the only arguable point of contact between Diodorus 20. 1 and Ephorus centers on the issue of narrational continuity, it may be inferred with confidence that this apparent affiliation is, in fact, the primary reason for attributing the entire passage of Diodorus to Ephorus. Even here, however, the connection made is gratuitous and even misconceived. Ephorus, we recall,[7] opposed Thucydides' adoption of a strict relative chronology and replaced it with a topical arrangement of events. Is it not plain that Diodorus's complaint about the disruption of a continuous narrative by the introduction of display pieces is irrelevant to topical continuity? The insertion of orations may rend asunder the continuity of the narrative, but they assuredly do not interfere with the continuity of the topic, and if Ephorus (for example) chose to include speeches at various points of his narrative of the prehistory of the Peloponnesian War, he would have preserved topical coherence precisely when he had also brought the momentum of events to a halt. The problem faced by Diodorus's source is, in fact, unlikely to disturb a universal historian; the type of historian most likely to be offended by these abuses is one who conceives of his subject as a thematic unity, precisely as Diodorus's words imply.

The source of Diodorus is not Ephorus but Duris of Samos.[8] Like Ephorus, Duris was in his own way exercised by the problem of nar-

---

[7] See chapter 1.

[8] So also C. Gramann, *Quaestiones Diodoreae* (Diss., Göttingen, 1907) pp. 25f. (inaccessible to me), and Kunz, *Zur Beurteilung*, pp. 91f.

rational flow and continuity; indeed, as we may infer from Diodorus 20. 43. 7, also from Duris,[9] he viewed the matter with an intensity of feeling that suits Diodorus 20. 1 perfectly. Duris, as we know, was also a theorist whose aesthetic would by definition be antagonistic to pieces of rhetoric (*rhetoreia*). The vivid portrayal of events and the excitation of emotions cannot grind to a halt and begin again for the sake of a predictable set of orations that will become mere flotsam in the wake of history's sudden changes. Moreover, we must keep in mind that Duris was not only advocating a new policy but by that same token justifying his repudiation of conventional historiography. The class of writers we seek in vain on the assumption that Ephorus is Diodorus's source is well established by the time of Duris. The group consists of Ephorus (of course), Theopompus, Callisthenes, whose own theory about speeches supplies a pointed contrast, and numerous others whom one could name.

One further consideration deserves mention, for it is relevant to later historiography as well. We have seen the source of Diodorus 20. 1 diminish the importance of the speech in history. Some reflection of the reality as well as of literary abuse may be supposed; indeed, the two go together. By automatic adjustment, political history focuses on those of our institutions that are vigorous and instrumental of policy. If our author considers speeches otiose and disruptive, it seems clear that they have lost a measure of their original importance in the political life of Hellas. This trend, however, was only just commencing in the time of Ephorus; what is presupposed by Diodorus 20. 1 is the entrenchment of Hellenistic monarchy, when public debate either became an empty form or fell into desuetude. The major powers, those attracting the most intense notice, were monarchies; free speech no longer served the critical function it had possessed in Periclean Athens. The reason behind Thucydides' insistence that speeches were an integral part of the actions of the war was no longer valid. Hence the disposition of Duris, the

---

[9] "At this point one might censure the art of history, when he observes that in life many different actions are consummated at the same time, but that it is necessary for those who record them to interrupt the narrative and to parcel out different times to simultaneous events **contrary to nature**, with the result that, although the actual experience of the event contains the truth, yet the written record, deprived of such power, **while presenting copies of the events** [*mimeisthai*], **falls far short of arranging them as they really were**" [trans. R. M. Geer]. The phraseology is strikingly reminiscent of Duris, F 1.

historian of Agathocles, to regard speeches as rhetorical interludes simply "dragged into" the narrative. On the other hand, Polybius, for his part, necessarily took the opposing view: from his perspective, dominated as it was by Roman politics and even the Achaean League, speeches remained the critically important instrument they had once been for Thucydides. Until, at least, the introduction of the Principate, this assessment of the significance of speeches in historiography must for the same reason have remained orthodox for the Romans.

The question we must now face is whether the theoretic propounded by Duris not only debased the speech but also contemplated its free invention. It should be plain, however, that only Duris's identification with "tragic history" could engender any such suspicion. On purely general grounds, and in the absence of contradictory testimony (whatever the actual practice may have been), it is impossible to believe that so flagrant a departure from the historiographical tradition would have been left unnoticed (for example, by Polybius) whether promoted or merely condoned. It would, moreover, have been entirely unnecessary. Thucydides' "escape clause" allowed the writer to couch the material contained in actual speeches in words of his own. It was, therefore, open to any writer to expand or contract actual speeches as he pleased and to formulate the gist according to his pleasure. It is not a corollary of Duris's theory that speeches should be invented but, quite to the contrary, that they should be avoided or left free from rhetorical embellishment. We may, therefore, infer that although the Thucydidean conception of the speech as equal in importance to the deed was undercut by Duris for reasons that were historically justified in the third century and acquired renewed force three centuries later still, when the empire was founded, the more important principle of reporting the main points of what had actually been said remained (theoretically) an unquestioned rule through Hellenistic times at least.

The establishment of the empire brought radical change. Conditions became analogous for the Latins with those impelling Duris to banish the set oration. Unfortunately, though we have some knowledge of the practice of the historians, there is little explicit theory. Quintilian is interested solely in skillful characterization. His recommendation of character-imitation in declamations as being of the greatest utility to future poets and historians (3. 8. 49), like his

praise of Livy,[10] is consistent with the Thucydidean tradition as modified by Callisthenes. Yet it must be admitted that the impression
one gains from Quintilian is that the historian's inventive powers
ought not to be impeded by anything so crass as the words actually
delivered by historical personages. And certainly that was the view
implied by Lucian, a century later, in *How to Write History* 58. To
Lucian, the elaboration of speeches is an adornment of the narrative, an "addition" providing the historian with an opportunity for
rhetorical display.[11] But even here we must not lose sight of the fact
that rhetoricians take the "raw material" of history for granted and
approach their task of instruction from a purely ahistorical vantage
point.

More can be inferred from the historians themselves. Unmistakable is the fact that two styles of historiography developed under the
empire, one of them "rhetorical" (exemplified by Curtius Rufus),
the other averse to speechifying (Tacitus, Ammianus), at least by
contrast. Writers of the first group chose history as the background
for their exploitation of moral-philosophical themes and rhetorical
skill. Curtius is probably representative—an essentially apolitical
writer (as his subject, Alexander, implies) interested in character
and ethics, indifferent to the battles (compare 7. 9 with Arrian 4. 4.
4–9) unless they allowed scope for epic treatment (9. 5), and superficial about causes (4. 2. 1–5). He was a writer whose emphasis on
individual conduct, the pathetic or the poetic, results in the serious
displacement of the strategic or the political (see, e.g., 9. 4) and,
above all, he writes all categories of rhetorical speeches (e.g., 6. 10,
8. 8. 7–8). That some of them contain, even at a far remove, something of what actually was said, or was believed to have been said, is
likely enough. But we would deceive ourselves if we supposed it a
matter of importance to the author. Working from the established
tradition, he was content to embellish whatever lay to hand.

[10] "His speeches are eloquent beyond description; so admirably adapted is all that is
said both to the circumstances and the speaker [*cum rebus, tum personis accomodata
sunt*]" (10. 1. 101, trans. H. E. Butler). No evidence suggests that Quintilian urged a
"poetic" and ahistorical treatment of speeches (or of history), and his famous comparison of history with poetry in 10. 1. 31 hardly contemplates departure from truth.
He has in mind the need to remove "dullness by the use of recondite words and more
adventurous figures of speech" (ibid.). One may compare the similar equation of rhetoric with poetry made by Cicero in *De oratore* 3. 27.
[11] See chapter 5, below.

In contrast with this group of declaimers to whom history was a secondary interest, we may range the "political historians" of the line represented for us by Tacitus. How *he* managed speeches is a question of obvious importance. It is one we are permitted to answer, fortunately, on the strength of *Annales* 15. 63, which marks him as the continuator of the Hellenic tradition. Here he gives his reason for omitting a speech by Seneca: "Since it has been given to the public in his own words I decline to recast it here" (*invertere supersedeo*). Though the exact meaning of *invertere* is unclear for the lack of exact parallels, the context makes plain that it describes a technique combining stylistic freedom with fidelity to substance. If Tacitus believed that the prior publication of Seneca's speech rendered it superfluous for him to produce one of his own, clearly he believed that the actual speech and the rendering he would have provided would each have served in its way to provide the required historical information. Any doubt that this was his conception of his duty should, moreover, be removed by the basic integrity of his reproduction of the emperor Claudius's speech delivered at Lyons in 48 A.D. For we may compare with Tacitus 11. 24 the actual words of Claudius as preserved on the "Lyons Tablet" (*ILS* 212). It will be sufficient, however, to quote here the comments of Furneaux:

> The fact that the order of these sentences does not in any way correspond to that of those in the original speech would show that Tacitus, in that process of adaptation to his narrative which he describes by the word "invertere," considered himself fully at liberty to rearrange as well as to condense, and to give arguments in what seems to him to be their most appropriate form and order.[12]

Perhaps I misread Furneaux when I infer that he would have been the better pleased if Tacitus had considered himself less fully at liberty to make these alterations in the "documentary evidence." If

<hr/>

[12] H. Furneaux, *The Annals of Tacitus*[2] (Oxford, 1907), vol. 2. p. 55 (after the text of book 11). R. Syme, *Tacitus* (Oxford, 1958), vol. 1, p. 337 n. 10 (cf. *Entretiens Hardt*, no. 4, p. 193), considers "all Tacitus" the speech of Cremutius Cordus given by Tacitus in *Annals* 4. 34 since "Cremutius's writings were not the sole, or even the main, charge against him," as the speech in Tacitus suggests. More specific charges undoubtedly were brought (Seneca *Ad Marc.* 22. 4); why deny, however, that Cremutius would have spoken to the main issue? See *Ad Marc.* 1. 3, 4.

not, it is a good example of how our interpretations are prejudiced by our own concepts of "true history." Instead of being complimented for providing a substantially accurate account of the speech (in the Thucydidean manner), Tacitus is chastised for tampering with the evidence.

The fact that most speeches in the *Annales* are brief reveals Tacitus's intentional avoidance of rhetorical declamation and utter dissociation from the type of writer known from Curtius. If we discount his resort to the quotation of group opinion, a traditional exception to the rule, the little evidence we possess indicates that he presented speeches responsibly, refused to invent them, and searched them out when it was possible to do so. It is notable, for example, that he acquired a copy of the unadulterated speech of Otho's that he "inverted" in *Historiae* 1. 90; he even knew that it was the product of a speechwriter. It is evident, therefore, that Tacitus stands in the tradition established by Duris and, like Ammianus thereafter,[13] he may be viewed as the heir of sound Hellenic theory. For the absence of rhetorical overstatement we perceive in the speeches of Ammianus carries the clear message, particularly from so rhetorical a writer, that he wished there to be no mistake about his faithful reproduction of the substance of the speeches.

Practice

THE REPORT OF CONTEMPORARY SPEECHES

As we inquire into the relation of practice to theory, it is essential to keep in mind the fact that the ancients had unanimously adopted the Thucydidean principle of honest reporting of the things that were said as well as the things that were done. (I naturally exclude from consideration the Declaimers of the empire, who fall into a category of their own.) It perhaps need hardly be said that the existence of this principle matters a great deal: as was mentioned earlier in another context, conventions set the parameters of conduct; we are not entitled to proceed on the assumption that the historians considered themselves at liberty to write up speeches out of their own

---

[13] See J. Szidat, *Historischer Kommentar zu Ammianus XX–XXI*, Historia Einzelschrift, no. 14 (Wiesbaden, 1970), p. 167, for a brief (and inconclusive) discussion citing opposing modern views.

heads. That some or many or most actually did so is perhaps hypothetically conceivable. We must recognize, however, that such a procedure would have been contrary to convention and not, as all too many moderns seem to suppose, a convention in its own right.

Unfortunately, the question of procedure is complicated at the outset by the variety of opinion about the historicity of Thucydides' own speeches.[14] Some of the uncertainty is, however, rather more marginal to the present subject than it perhaps appears. For example, we may willingly accept the fact that Thucydides' powerful and rhetorical prose transformed the sentiments actually expressed by his speakers by making them more abstract, incisive, paradoxical, psychologically consistent. So, too, it is probable that he pointed contingencies expressed by the speakers to have them "prefigure" events subsequent to the speeches. Naturally he edited and reorganized to make the speech as pointed and as relevant as it "should" have been ideally. In this respect Thucydides' speeches will forever be ambiguous documents; we are not (for example) able to separate Thucydides from Nicias when we read his speeches in book 6. But is it not evident that our dilemma is the special dilemma of our own traditional scholarship, of a modern literary and historical criticism disoriented by *our* habituation to quotation marks and unsettled by the need to separate the Thucydidean element from the historical "document"? In other words, our problem arises from our insistence on a clear-cut distinction between objective and subjective truth. Thucydides will give us an ideal speech in his own words reflecting the substance of the arguments of the speaker and our distrust so feeds on the potential for distortion that we forget his promise to remain true to the fundamentals of the speech. That this ancient method is deficient may freely be conceded, but unless there is something in the speeches to invalidate the assumption that Thucydides held to his stated intention, we should suppose that he has fulfilled his purpose and that we possess a record of the arguments and debates held during the Peloponnesian War.

If any speech or its equivalent excites suspicion, it is the so-called Melian Dialogue of 5. 86ff. Yet Thucydides' decision to present this

---

[14] See Gomme, *HCT*, vol. 1, pp. 141ff., and von Fritz, *Die Griechische Geschichtsschreibung* (Berlin, 1967), vol. 1, pp. 618ff. A good bibliography has been compiled in *The Speeches in Thucydides*, ed. P. Stadter (Chapel Hill, N.C., 1973), pp. 129ff.

deliberation in this form violates the letter or the spirit of his stated purpose only if no private meeting took place. The meeting (5. 84. 3–5. 86) has, indeed, been doubted, but the reason would appear to be nothing more than suspicion of the dialogue. We must, of course, grant that the meeting took place as Thucydides alleged: much more than a theory about the speeches is at stake; Thucydides can hardly be accused of inventing specific historical data in order to motivate a set of fictitious conversations unless we abandon all attempts at systematic and coherent criticism based on our observation of the work as a whole. If we grant the private meeting, are we then to take umbrage at the "sophistic" terminology of the speakers? That doctrines of might and right were in the air in the last quarter of the fifth century is certain. This was the time of Thrasymachus of Chalcedon, the famous exponent of the doctrine in Plato (*Republic* 1); how infectious these ideas will have been, and how easily assimilable, is surely apparent, not only from their appearance elsewhere in Thucydides' history (e.g., 1. 76. 2) but from Euripides (*Medea* 314f.) and Sophocles (*Electra* 396), where the principle is presented as a commonplace. One does not need the credentials of a sophist to grasp the main ideas or to promulgate them in support of one's position, even if it is difficult to analyze them and pursue the inquiry to logical extremes. A confrontation between rationalistic Athenians and traditionalist Melians can have taken precisely this turn. No reason suggests that the Athenians would have been coy.

It is hard to doubt that an underlying suspicion attaches to the Melian Dialogue (which then colors our attitude to the speeches themselves) because it *is* a dialogue, and dialogues are literary forms, not garden-variety historical events. If Thucydides allowed himself to experiment in this fashion (so the argument would run), clearly he has greatly distanced himself from the material and is attempting something more grandiose than mere historical reporting, analysis, and explanation. Thucydides unquestionably was prone to experiment with different literary modes; the prose he used in his description of the revolution at Corcyra (3. 82f.) testifies unassailably to his belief that the medium by which events were expressed should be attuned to the nature of the event. Straightforward prose was an inadequate vehicle for the intensity of his reaction to civil war. For that reason the dialogue, with its non-prosaic, dramatic, and perhaps philosophical resonances, was an eloquent and appropriate form for Thucydides to adopt. It was even one which his predecessor had already attempted (Herodotus 3. 80ff.). But this is not to suggest that Thucydides was on the watch for an opportunity to insert a dialogue, like some rhetor of imperial times with a list of devices that he must interpolate at the proper time into his work. When, however, a private colloquy occurred between these poetically contrasting groups, the insignificant Melians and the haughty, power-hungry Athenians, the situation was made to order; Thucydides seized upon the confrontation and recreated it as an orthodox dialogue, subsuming the arguments of individual Athenians and Melians and attributing them to the collective entities, undoubtedly improving and refining their arguments. The process is neither intrinsically suspicious nor deleterious of the principle expounded in 1. 22.

It will now be fruitful to consider the evidence from Polybius. This historian generally presumes that a real correspondence existed between orations actually delivered and the versions reported in histories. Thus he does *not* disparage the practices of "most writers" (36. 1. 2) when they present the case (*hoi enontes logoi*) for one side of an issue or another. Since we well know how much importance he attributed to the faithful rendering of a speech (12. 25a. 3–25b), the allusion implies that he found the general procedure acceptable. Polybius's attacks on Phylarchus and Timaeus acquire their proper significance in this context. Whatever the justice of his charges, the criticism of Timaeus (the greater offender of the two) is that his speeches are pure fabrications (12. 25a. 4): Timaeus has neither reproduced "what was actually spoken [by Hermocrates at Gela in 424] nor the truth of what actually was said." How did Polybius know? Evidently, Timaeus departed from the approved version of Hermocrates' speech, whether given by Thucydides, Antiochus, Philistus, or all three. This passage guarantees that the tradition of faithful reporting (in whatever rhetorical dress) was taken seriously by the historians, and this naturally required that the historians reported them faithfully. The worst that follows from Polybius's criticism of Timaeus is that he ignored the ruling convention.

The method followed by Polybius in the first two books of his history offers further reason to affirm that the historians reported speeches with due regard for the points actually made. Here (e.g., 2. 22. 4–5) Polybius paraphrased speeches that must have been direct orations in the works of Fabius Pictor and Philinus of Acragas, who wrote from the Carthaginian point of view. It is not possible to believe that Polybius summarized as *erga*, actual events, what he supposed were flights of the imagination; Polybius judged that the relation of these speeches to the actual words was close enough to require a summary. We perceive, therefore, the operation of a principle understood by the historians to the effect that arguments of substance in speeches were preserved in the historical text. It follows that the historians practiced what they preached.

For the Latins, the necessary starting point is Tacitus, for we have already observed his inheritance of the tradition of Duris. If so, it becomes mandatory to infer that his predecessors followed the same rule or (to put things in their proper order), rather, that Tacitus applied the standard practice of his predecessors. For the alternative runs counter to reason and likelihood. Did Tacitus after the time of Quintilian, an age in which standards were debased, *tacitly* break with his (irresponsible) Latin models in order to resume a higher ideal of historical writing not practiced since the Hellenistic Age? The idea refutes itself. Tacitus was in the line of Sallust and his method will not arguably have been superior to that of his predecessors; by the same logic, the procedures of Sallust must have been at least as responsible as those we know Tacitus to have applied.

Can a case, then, be made for Sallust independently of inferences from the procedure of his successor? Unfortunately we possess virtually no controlled evidence whatever. The exception is a letter embedded in *Catiline* 44. 4–5, for as it happens the letter is also "quoted" by Cicero in *Catiline* 3. 5. 12. The two versions are almost identical. The letter dispatched to Rome by Lentulus (a confederate of Catiline), according to Cicero, read as follows:

> Who I am you will know from the man I have dispatched to you. Take care that you be a man and consider into what situation you have come. See whether you now need anything and take care to attach to yourself the assistance of everyone including the dregs of the population.

Sallust has this:

> Who I am, from the man I have dispatched to you, you will learn. Be sure to reflect on the great disaster you are in, and remember that you are a man. Give careful attention to what

your plans require. Get help from everybody including the dregs of the population.[15]

Sallust has perhaps provided us with an example of modest "inversion" directly from Cicero, though that is not subject to verification. The more important observation is that the message is identical, the clauses are almost coincident and the words, but not the meanings, vary. Thus, although more attention has been paid to the differences between Sallust and Cicero in regard to the letter (cf. Tacitus and the Lyons Tablet), the noteworthy fact is that the letter in Sallust can be fully trusted as a reflection of what (he thought) was the substance of Lentulus's letter. Since his method was presumably consistent, the implications affect the *Historiae* and our judgment of how speeches and documents were reported by the Latin historians in general. For it may be taken as certain that none of these writers composed in a vacuum, but that they were governed, loosely or tightly, by their understanding of the rules of the genre.

An example of "inversion" as it perhaps was applied by Sallust can be found in the letter of Mithridates to Arsaces (69 B.C.) in *Historiae* 4. F 69 M. Formally the letter is modeled on Thucydides; the opening takes us back to the speech of the Corcyraeans in Thucydides 1. Unquestionably the epistle is an art form with pretensions rising above the mere transmission of Mithridates' plea for assistance. These, however, are the items of the letter stripped of their intellectual-rhetorical casing: (1) If you join me, as you should, you can dictate your own terms to Tigranes [1–4]; (2) the Romans are greedy of empire and riches and will not stop with me; you know this from their past actions [5–9]; (3) here is my side of the dispute with Rome [10–15]; (4) do not wait until it is too late: they will show you no gratitude [16–23]. Although reasonable judges may dispute how much of this letter is Mithridates' and how much Sallust's, no modern analytical or methodological principle suggests that Sallust invented these items any more than he invented the terms of Pompey's letter from Spain, 2 F 98 M.

---

[15] Cicero: *Quis sim scies ex eo quem ad te misi. Cura ut vir sis et cogita quem in locum sis progressus. Vide ecquid tibi iam sit necesse et cura ut omnium tibi auxilia adiungas, etiam infimorum.* Sallust: *Qui sim, ex eo, quem ad te misi, cognoscas. fac cogites, in quanta calamitate sis, et memineris te virum esse. consideres, quid tuae rationes postulent. auxilium petas ab omnibus, etiam ab infumis.*

It would, however, be as perverse to maintain that Greco-Roman writers of contemporary history were invariably the reliable reporters of the substance of speeches as to argue that "rhetoric" invariably corrupted speeches beyond recognition. The main point is that a definite convention existed, a theoretical principle approximated in practice by most writers, just as even Appian, a fervent classicizer, attempted to demonstrate his fidelity to it in much later times (BC 5. 45, 191). It is an error to accuse the ancients (as we seem tacitly to do) of the kind of schizophrenia that would lead them, almost conspiratorially, to say one thing and to do another. Naturally exceptions must have arisen since the convention was a matter of self-discipline and discretion. Polybius (perhaps incorrectly) accused Chaereas and Sosylus, the Hannibalic historians, of inserting deliberative speeches never actually delivered into their accounts of the senate at Rome after news of the fall of Saguntum (3. 20. 1), and, if he is right, it is an example of the dangerous potential for imaginative reconstruction, *ornare*, placed in the service of the presentation of issues at a traditional moment for exploration of the rationale for action (*hoi enontes logoi*).

THE REPORT OF SPEECHES PRESERVED IN OTHER HISTORIANS

How individual writers reproduced speeches found in the histories of their predecessors will undoubtedly have varied with the writer, but there is no reason to suspect the adoption of a qualitatively different approach. As we have seen, Polybius presupposes fidelity in the transmission of speeches by secondary writers in his criticism of the irresponsibility of Timaeus; his own (presumably accurate) summaries of the speeches of Pictor and Philinus point the same way. Our best evidence, however, is the practice of Livy. Since he was an orthodox or academic writer, representative of a type most frequently assailed for the subordination of history to stylistic and thematic concerns, his work can be regarded as the best of all possible gauges of standard practice in Hellenistic times and thereafter. By great good fortune, we possess a touchstone for his speeches, for we are able to compare side by side some of the speeches he adapted from Polybius with Polybius himself. If this "rhetorical" historian conveyed the gist of what actually was said (as it was reported by Polybius), then we may accord historical value to the tradition at second hand. In fact there is no doubt of Livy's reliability; the point is conceded by the many modern scholars whose more direct attention centers (we are again reminded of Tacitus and the Lyons Tablet) on Livy's special mode of rhetorical modification of the Polybian text.[16]

In fact, Livy does allow himself liberties with content and staging that indicate how easy it was to controvert the Thucydidean principle. One example occurs in 33. 33. 5 (cf. Polyb. 18. 46. 14), where Livy imputes to the Greeks of the time an observation made by Polybius *in propria persona*. Another, and scarcely more harmful, case involves the translation of Polybius's notice (21. 11. 1) to the effect that Prusias feared for his lands into a letter from Antiochus to Prusias (37. 25. 4).[17] More serious is Livy's inclusion of Hannibal in a council-of-war held by Antiochus.[18] But we may be hasty in assuming that this is Livy's own invention; *that* technique is not apparent from his work. In all, Livy's record can scarcely be regarded as seriously flawed: his delicts are minor and against them there remains the indisputable fact that he substantially reproduced the source-content of the speeches he inherited from others.

Of all writers, Pompeius Trogus, though he eschewed direct orations,[19] seems to have been among the most irresponsible. But even the most grievous sin of this first-century writer (in Latin) of a universal history—the branch of the *eidos* of history most amenable to rhetorical manipulation—proves reassuring as well as unsettling. Trogus (in Justin 29. 3) attributed to Philip V of Macedon a speech that actually was delivered by Agelaus of Naupactus on the same occasion (Polyb. 5. 103. 9–5. 104). Trogus, in short, has kidnapped a speech, preserving its main outlines, and given it to the main character—a procedure that confirms, just as it undercuts, what has been maintained here. But free fiction is avoided. The famous Mithridates speech, for example (Justin 38. 4–7), will only be regarded as a fiction by those who judge its conformity with rhetorical

---

[16] E.g., "Livy's speeches differ invariably in presentation (and occasionally in content)," says P. G. Walsh, *Livy* (Cambridge, 1961), p. 219; see p. 235 for a balanced summary. See also Walsh's discussion in *Greece and Rome*, New Surveys in the Classics, no. 8 (Oxford, 1974), pp. 26ff.

[17] Walsh, *Livy*, p. 84. A close reading of Polybius's text will reveal how easily (and legitimately) Livy could have deduced from it both the letter and its terms.

[18] See Walsh, *Livy*, p. 223.

[19] Justin 38. 3. 11. His objection to the relative preponderance of speeches in Livy and Sallust (*historiae modum excesserint*) marks, perhaps, a follower of Duris. See above, chapter 4.

precepts to be the infallible sign. The strong anti-Roman sentiments of the speech, once taken to show that Trogus (or Timagenes, his source) was no friend of the Romans, and now adjudged a mark of his skill,[20] may plausibly be credited (ultimately) to Mithridates himself.

In general, however, the only law is uncertainty. If we need not be overly skeptical about major deliberative speeches or critically important harangues, other types of less monumental importance seem by nature amenable to invention. The battle exhortation, for example, was sufficiently commonplace for any schoolboy to invent its typical substance. Could not the historian allow himself the construction of such a speech (which he knew full well had been delivered) with a clean conscience? What else, for example, could D. Brutus have urged before the second sea battle at Marseilles against Caesar's forces than that "his men should regard as already conquered those whom they had overcome when their forces were unimpaired" (Caesar *BC* 2. 5. 2)? Rhetorical precept and the exigencies of the situation converged exactly. In cases of this type, then, where both the historian and the general had recourse to the same generalities, commonplaces, and probabilities, resort to invention may have been regarded as defensible, at least in the absence of more precise information. Naturally, we must also bear in mind that speeches of this type were actually listened to by the soldiery at moments of keen anxiety and attention; if notable, they would have been remembered and, presumably, recorded by the historian. The matter is one in which we have no alternative but to suspend judgment.

THE REPORT OF SPEECHES DELIVERED BEFORE THE BIRTH OF HISTORIOGRAPHY

Thus far we have spoken of the contemporary historian and of the subsequent writers who transmitted speeches originally published by him. More difficult is the situation confronting us when we inquire into the speeches of "olden times," prior to the advent of contemporary history (*Zeitgeschichte*). Did writers invent speeches freely when it was unlikely that they would be contradicted or did they try to reconstruct actual speeches from the bare remnants of tradition? A key to the procedure followed is offered by Herodotus in 8. 83. 1–

[20] Schwartz, *RE* s.v. "Pompeius Trogus," col. 2308.

2. Before the battle of Salamis, Herodotus says the following of Themistocles:

> Dawn appeared and after they made an assembly of the marines, of them all it was Themistocles who announced that things were well. His entire speech contrasted what was better with what was worse, everything that is inherent in man's nature and constitution. Urging them to choose the better part of these and winding up his speech, he ordered them to embark in the vessels.

The alternatives could not be clearer. If Herodotus has invented this *report* of a speech, he is fundamentally mendacious not only because the false notice is gratuitous but because it is not a (mere) speech but the fabrication of a deed (*ergon*). Herodotus (on this view) has provided a false description of an event, alleging that something occurred that did not take place. Suspicion of the Greeks, and of Herodotus in particular, surely cannot reach this far. Any such extreme skepticism (for example, on the part of Fehling) is totally invalidated by the character of the historiographical tradition as we know it to have descended from Herodotus. The only conclusion possible is that Herodotus heard a report of Themistocles' words. If this is so, the full-dress speeches dating from the time of the Persian Wars may also be conceded to derive from the testimony of sources, since what applies in one instance, minor in nature, also should apply to others of far greater impact and importance.

We tend to underestimate the tenacity of oral tradition in a preliterate society and the importance of reminiscence in such a society as new events provided a basis for comparison. In an insular and close-knit community, as was Athens before the empire came, it is certain enough that individuals regarding themselves in a heroic light repeated to the next generation all of the historical circumstances they could remember about the great battles of 480–79 in which they had had a part. And what of the warriors of the previous decade who, as we know from Aristophanes, had defined themselves by the brilliance of their achievement at Marathon? That Herodotus questioned members of both generations, the warriors and their children, we know a fortiori because he tells us that he spoke to an actual participant, Epizelus (6. 117; cf. 6. 105, where the Athenians recollect the words of Philippides, 8. 65, 9. 16). The material Herodotus utilized was undoubtedly tainted by false recollection and vainglory; but not on that account are we to conclude that his speeches were not based on reports of tradition extracted by him in the course of his "researches."

The picture becomes more obscure as we proceed backward in time, when the difficulties confronting the historian proportionately increased. It is our great good fortune, however, to find Herodotus himself insisting on the actuality of the Great Debate of the Persian nobles (3. 80 with 6. 43. 3). Whatever our view of the historicity of the debate (which is hardly genuine), *he* believed that the speeches had been delivered. To what extent he contributed arguments of his own, or felt that it was allowable to do so, is a question similar to that raised by Thucydides' procedure in his speeches, and Herodotus provided no methodological discussion to guide us. Since style cannot mechanically be separated from substance, we must suppose that Herodotus freely adapted his source. But Herodotus's defense of his account of the debate assures us that the link is unbroken between what he believed had actually been spoken and his own version; there is no warrant to say of these and the other speeches, with Jacoby, that "they are of course, in substance and formally, thoroughly the property of Herodotus."[21] On the contrary, his defense of the historicity of the debate in despite of doubts raised against it and, therefore, of his account of it, points in the opposite direction. For Herodotus, the issue transcends the debate: he is defending the integrity of his work as a whole. It is certain, consequently, that he expected his speeches to be taken as true in substance and not as mere products of his own skill.

Indeed, it seems to me that consideration of the speeches of Herodotus (and Thucydides) has been marked by a distinct lack of realism, though categorical skepticism is often regarded as its most infallible sign. We are asked to believe that Herodotus could undertake to write a vast history with as much accuracy and inquiry as he could manage, and yet at crucial moments spin off one speech after another merely according to his own notions or desires. Evidently, it made no difference to him whether he obtained a report of what was said or whether he did not. In either case, the speeches are "of course" "thoroughly" "his own property" "in style and substance."

---

[21] Jacoby, *RE* s.v. "Herodotos," col. 494.

What of his readers? Did they know this secret? Was it a convention already in 420 that although both speeches and deeds were the *erga* the historian was obligated to reproduce, the speeches, though *erga*, were the inventions of the writer? The assumption imputes a state of mind and of conscience to the Greeks of the fifth century that on analysis refutes itself. The same writer cannot both be responsible in one aspect of the historical narrative and unfettered by reality and indifferent to truth in another. Only our habituation to the view that speeches in Herodotus are rhetorical or dramatic interludes blinds us to the enormity of the deception we thereby ascribe to the historiographer, who did not suggest, and could not predict, that they would be estimated so lightly. What we have done, in fact, is to endow Herodotus anachronistically with some of the most unhistorical attitudes prevalent in the Silver Age of Latin and, what is worse, to assume that he wrote his speeches in the confident expectation that his contemporaries and later generations would somehow take the condescending attitude to them developed in the nineteenth century. In this matter, scholarly discussion seems to have been greatly prejudiced.

Although Herodotus's defense of the Great Debate implies that he expected his readers to accept as historical the substance of what he told them in the speeches throughout the history, it is impossible to see how he could have managed this feat when describing still earlier times. Speeches pronounced by Solon were perhaps built around his poetry; and Croesus had become a legend in his own right. That someone told him about these "famous conversations" is not beyond the bounds of possibility. Certainly Herodotus felt no impropriety in attributing to Socles of Corinth a lengthy recollection of Periander (5. 92), and it is not for us to say how detailed remembrances of this type (distorted though they undoubtedly were) may have been. The art of storytelling goes back to Homer, and it is a part of its nature to incorporate lively and important conversations. Herodotus may well have elaborated this material along the lines dictated in the story. Even so, let us not insist on the invariability of his method. Herodotus was only the "Father of History," and his Homeric inheritance and poetic spirit make him subject to no ordinary rules. Thus it can hardly be doubted that Herodotus could be induced to depart from his ordinary method if the gain seemed to him to compensate for the violation. I have in mind, especially, that beautiful and quietly contemplative passage in 7. 44–52 where Xerxes and Artabanus (in a private conversation) discuss the forthcoming campaign in the context of universal truths and human psychology. It is one of the high points, artistically, of the entire work; and though it could be argued that Herodotus was certain that such a conversation was indeed entertained by these figures, this is a far cry from his reconstruction of speeches known to have been delivered.

In one kind of speech present in the works of Herodotus and his successors the free play of imaginative creation must at once be conceded. The dialogue of Candaules and Gyges, of Gyges and Candaules' wife, of Harpagus and Astyages, Cyrus and Solon, Themistocles and Sicinnus, to name some obvious examples, may be considered part of the art of the storyteller, not *erga*, and to have been recognized as such by the ancients. These verbalizations serve an explanatory purpose and further the action of the episode at the same time as they inject vividity and liveliness. Since such conversations develop naturally from the internal logic of the situation under description, they are not arbitrary creations but a functional element in the story. It is nevertheless a fictional device providing the writer with an opportunity to play upon a range of emotions normally the province of the epos and the drama. Ctesias was an especially skillful master of the technique, as Demetrius (*On Style* 209ff.) testifies. There can be no doubt that here the boundaries of fiction and historiography came together.

The "ancient" history of the Romans and the speeches contained therein possess a different pedigree. The cause lay in the late development of Latin historiography and in the need that was consequently felt, by Greek and Latin alike, to weave a tradition with a suitably Hellenic texture—but without the firm basis possessed by the Greeks in an oral tradition still alive in the fifth century B.C. The problem centered in the monarchy and the early republic; after the Second Punic War, historians proceeded like their Greek models, recording contemporary speeches in the orthodox way. Thus Fabius's speeches could be summarized by Polybius on the presumption that they were historically accurate, Cato included his own in his own work, and the writers from Fannius onward were steeped in the Polybian tradition. The annalists of the second and first centuries were, however, obligated by the nature of their genre, local history, to write the "ancient" as well as the contemporary annals of their city, a period admittedly shrouded in the mists of legend (Cicero *De legg.* 1. 1, 3). Abhorrence of a vacuum or the heady opportunity to fashion Roman history according to their own lights induced the annalists to bring the record of earlier times into material equality with that of the present day.[22] Hence the invention of speeches and their insertion into an already precarious tradition. Now, with this fraudulent record in place, it fell to the lot of Livy, Dionysius, and others to use it as if it were a solid foundation,[23] just as Livy relied on Polybius for later times. On ancient Roman history, therefore, Livy stands to the annalists as Ephorus to Herodotus. The method is similar; what differs is the integrity of the record. Since Livy was inherently conservative,[24] the value of his speeches depends entirely on the quality of his source, and above all whether it was a historian or an annalist.

With the exception of the rhetorical writers of the empire, therefore, the Thucydidean principle of 1. 22 seems to have governed the practice of the historians, both Greek and Latin, whether they dealt with ancient or with modern times. The rhetorical formulations, the sometimes profound and sometimes elegant analyses, belong to the historians; so does the organization of material in accordance with rhetorical principle. Everything was heightened, made precise, given point and relevance from foreknowledge of events. Always there was the admixture of the imagination and intellect of the historian, and it obviously increased in the degree that the recollection of speeches actually delivered grew dimmer, or the same speech was recast by a succession of authors to suit the best rhetorical theory. The vagaries of the historical tradition accessible to the writer also facilitated self-deception. Knowledge that a speech actually had been delivered, the conviction that a speech must have been delivered, the inference that a speech probably was delivered because it

[22] There is no reason to believe that Quadrigarius constituted an exception. Beloch, *Römische Geschichte* (Berlin, 1926), p. 104, rightly scouted the notion that he commenced in 388 B.C. Cf. M. Zimmerer, *Der Annalist Qu. Claudius Quadrigarius* (Diss., Munich, 1937), p. 9.

[23] Hence the significance of the "speech" of Menenius Agrippa (*cos.* 503), accepted as genuine not only by Livy (2. 32. 8) but by Tacitus *Dialogus* 21.

[24] It is instructive to study the continuity of the progression of Hannibal's dream first appearing in Silenus, *FGrHist* 175, taken up by Coelius F34 Peter, and polished by Livy 21. 22. 5–9, for the dream is the analogue of the speech, and its relatively conservative treatment is therefore notable.

was required, are easy gradations leading to unintentional perjury, and it would be rash to deny the occasional occurrence of such defalcations as these. Then there is the whimsical situation of writers like Livy, who will fashion a speech for the first Brutus with (probably) the same conscientiousness that he brought to his adaptation of the speeches of Polybius. But these imperfections in the practice of the historians should not detract from the basic integrity of their approach, even if that approach substantially differs from our own, and it is therefore reasonable to assume that we possess the core of the speeches as well as the record of the deeds of the Greeks from (at least) the end of the sixth to the first century B.C. The situation at Rome is, of course, more complicated, since the historical tradition was contaminated by the contributions of the annalists. Even so we may cautiously assert that the record of the speeches of the Romans and their opponents is substantially trustworthy from the time of the Second Punic War to the end of the fourth century A.D.

V

Points of Contact between Historiography and Other Genres and Modes of Thought

Of all ancient forms of high literature, history stands alone in its generic assumption of impartiality and in the writer's concomitant self-effacement. That the *Iliad* and *Odyssey* possess this property is not to be denied; but it is equally plain that the spirit of poetry as it emerged in archaic times and flourished thereafter repudiated Homer's distant stance. Vital engagement quickens the poetry of Archilochus, Alcaeus, Solon, and their successors. In a word, the poet desires to express *himself*; the historian hides behind the sentiments of his characters, or can dimly be sensed in the peculiar course taken by the events of his description. The difference is irrelevant to subject-matter, which often consists of "historical material." Archilochus described battle and criticized politicians. Alcaeus vividly pictures his political struggles and antagonisms. Solon advocated political reform, justifying it with an analysis that, except for his egocentricity, could appear in a history. But the spirit is not the same; it is illuminating to consider that what the poets wrote could at best appear *within* a history. For example, the exhortations of the seventh-century poets Callinus and Tyrtaeus are the words—at once rhetorical and personal—of a general to his troops. But although we find such speeches in the histories, the exhortation as such, obviously, was categorically improper (and irrelevant) to the business of the historian. To put it simply and in modern terms, history attempted to portray reality "objectively" and in perspective, while poetry sang without apology to the tune of individualistic and flagrantly partial perceptions of the same great world.

From this point of view, the orator falls into step with the poet and ranges himself against the historian. Here, perhaps, because of the essential correspondence of subject, the divergency seems the more striking. The orators deal with historical events, and sequences of events; a magisterial approach—like that attempted today by heads of state—might, perhaps, have been expected. But the special hopes and needs of the politician ill consort with objectivity. The differences between historiography and political oratory are intrinsic and profound, as we may judge from the use of history itself by each type of writer. Among the orators, the requisite historical background is invariably presented with stunning selectivity. The criterion is not, of course, man's "memorable deeds"; deeds unworthy of relation may better suit the case—Philip's debauches, for example, or Aspasia's house-guests. Events that help one side and hurt another are selected, manipulated, and distorted, the sole purpose dictating the arrangement and inclusion of material being the capture of a crowd on the all-important instant. Polemical purpose, in other words, dictated elaboration of detail. Moreover, it was a necessity of the situation that the material purveyed contain ethical point, and it often descended to characterization beneath the dignity of historical prose—or any prose. Demosthenes' *On the Crown* and *Philippics*, Cicero's *Verrines* and speeches against Antony are classic examples of speeches of this familiar type, though they are masterpieces and undoubtedly above the general level. In any case, it is clear that history and oratory, if anything, supplement each other because they provide a virtually antithetical perspective on events. The ecumenical point of view of the Greek historians contrasts starkly with the local patriotism and domestic antipathies of the orators. In Rome, where the city-state *was* the field of historical study, comparable differentiation was maintained, although in smaller focus. The Roman historians wrote the history of *stasis*, the orators advocated the views of their cliques. In both Greece and Rome, then, the separation of persona of the historian and the orator was maintained together with fidelity to an "objective" and "subjective" mode of description.[1]

Not surprisingly, certain important exceptions arise. The authors of epideictic orations, e.g., Gorgias in his speech at Olympia, enunciated (what they conceived to be) catholic and statesmanlike viewpoints. The genre, sadly enough, outlasted history. However, another and more significant exception centres on the Athenian drama, which in fact occupied a unique position within the world of poetic composition. In the first place, the dramatist reminds us more of Homer than of Archilochus; even Euripides is an elusive personality (if we keep to his plays). For the dramatist stands apart from his creation; he allows the play to speak for him (if it does) in a manner too subtle and indirect to allow more than a general impression of his attitudes. Such an approach naturally requires that the presentation and exploration of issues latent in the mythical subject be self-explanatory and autonomous—precisely as in a history. Not to beat about the bush, we must therefore ask directly whether history owes this tremendous debt to the drama, and the answer would seem to be affirmative. The impact of tragedy in large and in small is unmistakable among the first historians. The telling evidence, however, is of a type we may call vestigial: the first historians operated in what (from a later perspective) is a peculiar, inconvenient, and unnecessary manner: *they visualized episodes as if they formed the scenes of a play.* Since the point is crucial, it may be illustrated by one transparent example in Herodotus 1. 34ff. Here he articulates a series of events into a set of acts that result in the chastisement of Croesus because he was hybristic enough to suppose himself "to be the happiest of men." The scenes, which are devoid of comment by Herodotus, are as follows: (a) Croesus' dream, warning that his son would die from an iron spear-point; (b) the arrival at Sardes of Adrastus, son of Midas, and his purification [35]; (c) the arrival of messengers from Mysia to request assistance against a fierce boar [36]; (d) a dialogue between Croesus and his son. The son conclusively demonstrates to his father that the dream must be irrelevant to the prospective hunt (intrinsically and by length this is the central scene) [36–42]; (e) A messenger informs Croesus of the catastrophe [43. 3]; (f) Croesus

---

[1]Naturally there are exceptions, such as Sisenna, who wrote as a Sullan.

grieves, the corpse-bearers appear, followed by the unfortunate mur-
derer, Adrastus, who immolates himself [44–45. 3]. Croesus is at all
times center-stage, and events are presented to the reader only when
and how they are presented to Croesus. The development would not
have been arranged differently by a tragedian.

This manner of viewing events carries important implications.
The way a sequential pattern is conceived and consequently arranged automatically implies the adoption of some techniques and
the exclusion of others. You cannot picture a sequence as if it were
unfolding in a play and simultaneously yourself describe the meaning
of the scenes. Specifically, the historian's visualization of history in
terms of dramatic structure necessarily entailed his adoption of dramatic techniques of description as well as personal reticence. Like
the dramatist, therefore, he became the tacit observer of his own
creations, resisting the temptation of speaking in his own person—
or, rather, rising to the ideal of making his subjects speak for him.
The corollary, obviously, is that the Herodotean speech owes its inspiration to the drama.

Even were we to suppose that Herodotus contemplated the introduction of set speeches because of their ubiquity in Homer, the fact
remains that his most significant speeches are not only un-Homeric
(*Iliad* 6. 145–49 is a rudimentary anticipation) but parallel exactly
the burden of speeches in tragedy. By this means, Herodotus often
expresses a dimension of reality transcending the limited importance
and evanescence of particular events.[2] Several circumstances combine, therefore, to suggest that Herodotus formed his conception of
the "meaningful" speech because of tragedy and that he was encouraged to introduce them because he counted on the fact that his audience was habituated to the technique by way of tragedy. But perhaps
we may go further and include Thucydides within this intellectual
orbit—not merely as the successor of Herodotus but as one who was
similarly influenced by the same technique. Just as Herodotus applied the speech to make explicit the moral and metaphysical aspect
of historical occurrences, Thucydides, heir to precisely the same tradition, applied the speech (in a fashion consonant with then prevalent interests) to ventilate philosophical-political issues in "para-
tragic" fashion.

[2] See Fornara, *Herodotus, An Interpretative Essay* (Oxford, 1971), pp. 18ff.

Except for drama, the spirit of poetry continued to be anti-historical. Perhaps nothing better illustrates the point than the treatment accorded the few exceptions of which we have knowledge. One such work is the *Argonautica* of Apollonius of Rhodes. He was a student of Callimachus, writing in the third century B.C. Now what is peculiar about his epic poem of Jason and Medea is the persona of the poet. For although it has been asserted that Apollonius attempted to unite Callimachus with Homer, write an epos, love story, travel fable, and learned mythical geography all in one,[3] this is to confound definition with the enumeration of the various components of the work. Apollonius was concerned to write a mythico-historical epic. What is fascinating is that he adopted standard historiographical procedures, even to the point of posing as a sort of historian.

The tone is set in 1. 18–22:

> Poets still sing that Argos built the ship with the aid of Athena's counsels; now let me recount the race and name of the heroes, the twisting voyage through the sea, and everything they did as they wandered.

Apollonius is the epic historian informing the hearer of his special *historia*, and he is strict in applying the appropriate historiographical terminology when "relating" his "logos" (e.g., 1. 122, 196). The approach reminds us of Herodotus, even to the point of his imitation of Ionian naivety in 1. 154: Lynkeus was sharp-sighted,

> if the report is really true that this man

could pierce the very earth with his glance. One of the most revealing verses is 1. 1220, where Apollonius resists a feigned temptation to digress since

> that would drive me far from the theme of my song.

The persona is that of the Ionian storyteller.

Apollonius's interest in the places and peoples he describes seems authentic. Throughout his work, he is interested in the customs of the places touched at by the *Argo*. Like Herodotus and the Alexander-historians, his eye is set for the ethnographically spectacular. Thus in

---

[3] F. Susemihl, *Geschichte der griechischen Litteratur in der Alexandrinerzeit* (Leipzig, 1891), vol. 1, p. 387.

2. 1018–22 we meet a people who reverse the usages of marketplace and home. Similar ethnographical observations (reminiscent of Herodotus) are made about the Colchians in 3. 202ff. In short, Apollonius has assimilated the methods of historiography. The structure of the poem is that of a historical narrative, with digressions, descriptions, and speeches, precisely as if Jason and the Argonauts were "of the human generation" and this work a history in verse.

Although Apollonius's Medea scene was emulated in antiquity, the work as a whole was poorly received. The nub of the criticism was his lack of personal passion and involvement—the *Argonautica* was simply not poetic, and ran counter to the theory and praxis of Alexandrian times. Callimachus had praised another poet for *not* emulating Homer, whose distance and "objectivity" was antiquated, and Apollonius was criticized for the same reason in reverse.[4] The incompatibility of the genres of poetry and history could not be more directly shown.

Another example of similar point occurs in Roman times. Lucan was the *exceptio probans regulam*. Writing his epic, *The Civil War*, in the time of Nero, he reached with both hands into the armory of the historiographers and drew out, most notably, "the ethnographical review" (1. 396ff.) and a "historical-ethnographical digression" (4. 593ff.), ending book 4 with a superb "critical appraisal." From our point of view, these "additions" are pieces of poetic coloration on all fours with Lucan's "subjective" characterization of Caesar and the revered Cato. For our approach is dictated by Lucan's own method, which inclines us to read the work as history. More interesting is the reaction his work evoked among his peers. Lucan's contemporaries deplored his *historical* approach, considering it subversive of poetry. This is clear from a definition of the genre provided by one of the characters in Petronius's *Satyricon*, also written in the time of Nero (118. 6). We are told that the poet is not to versify deeds, *res gestae*; he must instead allow his "unconfined spirit" to summon up oracular ambiguities and provide ample opportunities for the intervention of the gods: "The [epic] work must rather appear the chant of a maddened intellect than the honest testimony, with witnesses at hand, of a solemn narration."

---

[4]See U. von Wilamowitz-Moellendorff, *Hellenistische Dichtung*[2] (Berlin, 1962), vol. 1, p. 206, vol. 2, p. 218. H. Herter provides a good characterization in *Der Kleine Pauly* s.v. "Apollonius," col. 450.

Petronius directly repudiates Lucan and his use of historical method in poetry. In addition to his use of "historical elements," on the highest level, Lucan's rejection of the gods and substitution of fate gives (or appears to give) an intellectual framework for the unfolding of events that reminds us not of "poetry" but of the idiosyncratic Athenian tragedians, Herodotus, Thucydides, and, in general, of the prosaic approach to explanation inimical to poetry.

The assumption of "objectivity" or the surrender to explicit personal involvement provides one standard for measuring history against other forms of writing. Clear differences of perspective exist, for example, between history and the memoir, the utopian "history," and other prose forms that developed shortly after the origin of historiography. But such an approach, though valid, would prove narrow. More can be gained from the devotion of closer attention to the general character of these prose forms, and it will be useful to view them as "history's competitors." Undoubtedly, some arose in response to the inherent limitations of history (as they were conceived), while others capitalized on their resemblance to historical writing in order to gain a credibility that otherwise must have been marginal at best.

Competition between prose forms began in the last period of the fifth century and shortly thereafter. It was a period of experimentation in prose that witnessed, in addition to the genesis of the five types of historical writing (see chapter 1), the development of memoir-literature, the creation of the dialogue, and the emergence of "philosophical history." The last two, the dialogue and what may also fairly be called "utopian history," unite in their intention to adumbrate, refute, or purvey theories of behavior. The dialogue, however, rapidly became stylized; the actual historicity of the scenes depicted became irrelevant to the contents of the work and was taken *cum grano salis* or as a mere formality. (It would be an interesting question, beyond our scope, to consider the possible relationship here between the idealizing speeches of history and the artistic transmutations of actual conversations in the dialogue.) The utopian novel, on the other hand, scrupulously maintained the fiction of historicity, however great its departure from it. To infer that the heavy debt of this hybrid form to history hinged on the prestige of histor-

ical writing would, however, be unfair and simplistic. Since the publication of Hecataeus's *Genealogiai*, and even before it, a historical,
especially an ethnographical, context was the proper vehicle for the
description of wonders, and history remained the inevitable medium
for their publication. In part, then, it is an instance of "new wine in
old bottles," for the ethnographer's report has insensibly been transformed into the ethnographer's own invention.

Utopian history seems to have begun in a Socratic context. The
sensational death of Cyrus the Younger, the prince Xenophon accompanied in the march of the Ten Thousand, concentrated attention upon him and his House at a time coincident with the budding
interest in ethics; a setting was provided for theoretical works distant
enough from Hellas to allow free rein to the imagination and close
enough, at the same time, to foster the illusion of reality,[5] for it still
was a literal age. In Xenophon's *Education of Cyrus*, the elder Cyrus
(the historical nucleus) is transformed into the exponent of Xenophon's views about education, the family, honor, justice.

Onesicritus (*FGrHist* 134) attempted a more serious imposition,
for Xenophon's flight could delude no one. This Alexander-historian,
however, who was a Cynic in philosophy, combined his account of
Alexander with the "discovery" in India of the prevalence of views
about the proper ordering of society that corroborated his own. The
work, according to Diogenes Laertius (6. 84), was analogous to
Xenophon's *Education of Cyrus*,[6] probably because of the manner in
which historical characters served as the mouthpiece of the philosopher's opinions, though the similarity may have been more fundamental, since the subject of each work was the education of a
prince. In the philosophically expository segments of the narrative,
Alexander seems to have been presented as the "philosopher-at-
arms" receiving instruction from the wise men of India. F 24 (Strabo
15. 1. 34) examples his method. Here Onesicritus praises the *mores*
of a people with clear relevance to the *nomoi* of the Greeks.

[5] Wilamowitz, *Aristoteles und Athen* (Berlin, 1893), vol. 2, pp. 13f. For Antisthenes' dialogue (Diog. Laert. 5. 12) see R. Hirzel, *Der Dialog* (Leipzig, 1895), vol. 1,
p. 122 n. 2.

[6] The doubts of L. Pearson, *The Lost Histories of Alexander the Great*, Philological
Monographs of the APA, no. 20 (1960), pp. 83ff., are dismissed by A. Momigliano,
The Development of Greek Biography (Cambridge, Mass., 1971), pp. 82f. See, above
all, Hermogenes in L. Spengel, *Rhet. Graec.*, vol. 2, p. 12, ll. 11–12, for the propriety
of the title, "How Alexander was Educated."

[Onesicritus] speaks at length about the land of Mousikanes, praising it. Some of its characteristics are said to be common to the rest of the Indians, such as their longevity. They reach the age of one hundred and thirty years. . . . He mentions also their frugality and health, though their country possesses an abundance of all things [which might have perverted them had they been so inclined]. A characteristic special to them is their possession of a sort of Lacedaemonian common mess [*syssitia*] where the community takes its food. Their meat comes from hunting. Also special is the fact that they do not use gold or silver, though they have mines. They also use adolescent youths in the place of slaves, as the Cretans use the Aphamiotai and the Spartans helots. They pursue no science except medicine. For extended development of the sciences sometimes is harmful as in the case of the science of war and others like it. Onesicritus says that they have no trials except for murder and hybris. [cf. F 17]

Although the utopian flavor of Onesicritus's work is strong, at least it proceeded from historical reality. The next logical step taken by the exponents of philosophical viewpoints was to fabricate historical experiences, presenting them as if they were true. Euhemerus (*FGrHist* 63), active at the turn of the fourth century, took advantage of the exotic setting rendered familiar to the public by the Alexander-historians and therefore already associated in the public mind with the fabulous. He proved (as it were) his famous anthropological explanation of the deification of humans by an inscription discovered on the island of "Panchaia" off the coast of Arabia Eudaemon (F 3). Euhemerus strove for verisimilitude, carefully following in the footsteps of the historians by writing a standard ethnography of his imaginary group of islands. The "discovery" by Iambulus, probably a third-century writer, of an island utopia in the southern ocean (Diod. 2. 55–60) also was motivated realistically (though more sensationalistically), and this island too was described with meticulous historical technique. Earlier (ca. 300), Hecataeus of Abdera or Teos (*FGrHist* 264 F 7–14) had done the impossible: he actually discovered the land of the Hyperboreans on an island, Helixoa, off Celtica! Naturally he described the utopian state of this legendary community of the just.

Thus we perceive that a rudimentary component, almost an accidental feature, of the works of actual historians had developed into a
genre in its own right, providing pleasure and instruction. A gradual
but complete inversion of proportions is apparent when we compare
Herodotus's description of the wise Ethiopians (3. 20ff.), Theopompus's account of the land of Merops (*FGrHist* 115 F 75) and pass
therefrom to Onesicritus, Hecataeus of Abdera, Euhemerus, and
Iambulus. The Alexander-historians, by habituating the public to
the notion of miraculous possibilities, and by instilling a thirst for
such exotics, opened the floodgates.[7]

The comparative "objectivity" of history certainly assisted the
utopian writers. Their tales were not essentially about themselves,
but told what they wished their readers to believe about imaginary
societies. This authorial distance worked as a constraint, however,
to those who wished to write about themselves and describe their
adventures or policies, whether pridefully or defensively. It also may
have been regarded with mixed feelings by an audience for whom
history was rather more impersonal and rigorous than suited its literary cravings or need for political instruction. Hence, perhaps, the
proliferation of a number of works at once disparate and similar,
such as Xenophon's *Anabasis*, *On the Ten Years* by Demetrius of Phalerum, and Aratus's *Commentaries*. All are facets of the same phenomenon, i.e. autobiographical literature presenting historical data
in a form alternative to history and therefore freed from its rules and
constraints.

The idea was given expression in a work issuing from the pen of
the gifted and prolific fifth-century writer, Ion of Chios (*FGrHist*
392). He has been called the "founder of memoir literature" by
Hirzel, the author of a splendid study of the dialogue in antiquity,
because of his work, the *Epidemiai*, or "Visits," Ion's recollections of
his meetings with famous people both at home and abroad. These
men belonged to the literary world (Aeschylus, Sophocles), to politics (Cimon, Pericles) and to philosophy (Socrates). (Such catholicity is unusual; later writers tended to write about individuals falling
into a single category—poets, philosophers, and so on.) Ion sketched
with care the settings of these conversations; Hirzel shrewdly notes

---

[7] For a late (and whimsical) example, see Lucian's *True History*. For the relation of
travel literature and the Greek "novel," see E. Rohde, *Der griechische Roman und seine
Vorläufer*[5] (Hildesheim, 1974), pp. 178ff.

this significant parallel with the format of the Socratic dialogue,[8] though a connection also exists with the conversational technique applied by Xenophon in his *Memorabilia*, or "Conversations with Socrates."[9] It is worth noting (for the intellectual picture is complex) that at about the time Ion wrote the *Epidemiai*, Stesimbrotus of Thasus (*FGrHist* 107), also an established literary figure and so-called "sophist" (T 3–5), published his work *On Themistocles, Thucydides* [son of Melesias] *and Pericles*. The work is usually described as a "political pamphlet," but the designation is inadequate and somewhat misleading. Although it seems to have been a tendentious product (F 5, 10, 11) containing outright misinformation (F 1, if the text is sound), the more important point is that Stesimbrotus purported to give a view of Athenian political leaders as observed by himself, a non-Athenian residing inside the city. He obtruded his personality to the extent (at least) of affirming his personal observation (F 10), as well as his use of hearsay (F 4). The work partly falls into the category of reminiscence literature; political animus may inform the tendency of the work, not its genre.

A prose form was therefore established legitimizing the expression of literary and political commentary and reminiscence, something generically out of place in history, but an imperious necessity to a people that had expressed its individualism in poetry as early as the seventh century, and to whom history was an unsatisfactory vehicle. In this sense, Ion's influence extends beyond the *Memorabilia* of Xenophon to his *Anabasis*, the famous march of the "Ten Thousand" who sought to place Cyrus the Younger on the throne and were compelled to fight their way out of Asia after his death in battle. It is a work of organized reminiscence, proceeding historically but containing character sketches and conversational elements native to this literary genre. It is obvious, at the same time, that the *Anabasis* is hybrid, proximate to history as well, like Caesar's *Commentaries*. One chief difference from history is the very narrow linear development of the *Anabasis*; we miss the establishment of a broader context, the study of the political dimensions of the phenomenon, ante-

---

[8] *Der Dialog* (Leipzig, 1895), vol. 1, pp. 36, 37 n. 3, 38.

[9] A. Momigliano, *The Development of Greek Biography*, p. 53, fairly stresses the originality of the work. But of the two elements of which it is comprised—the recollections of conversations and the defense of Socrates—Ion was a clear precursor of the former.

cedents included, the geography and ethnography of the region, and, perhaps as important as anything else, sedulous investigation of detail. If we ask, however, why Xenophon invented this literary form instead of attempting a history, the answer probably extends beyond any disinclination he may have had to supply these desiderata. History, even the monograph, required a subject more extensive and epochal than a mere campaign, however noteworthy. War and politics, specifically Greek politics, were essential components, and these were lacking in the march of the Ten Thousand.

The memoir serving as a personal apologia also acquired an independent existence in the fourth century, though here the connection with Ion is very tenuous and that with Stesimbrotus only a little less so. Personal reminiscence about political figures has progressed to political reminiscence by the figures themselves. One such work was apparently written by Demades (*FGrHist* 227), an Athenian politician of the last half of the fourth century. Something more is known of the tract, *On the Ten Years* (*FGrHist* 228), written by Demetrius of Phalerum. The work was apologetic in nature, for Demetrius had ruled Athens for a decade (317–7) under the auspices of Macedon. It is possible that a major influence or inspiration were the Socratic writings exculpatory of Socrates, such as Plato's *Apology*. On the other hand, just as a law-court proceeding served as the model for Isocrates' *Antidosis*, a written speech that pretended to be an actual defence of his life and character, so the *Antidosis* can be viewed as a precursor of Demetrius's *On the Ten Years Rule.*

One last thread of the skein is the genre represented for us by Aratus of Sicyon (271–213), who wrote memoirs—*hypomnemata*—that were closely autobiographical and essentially limited to the events in which he himself took part (Polyb. 2. 40. 4, 47. 11, Plut. *Arat*. 3. 3 = *FGrHist* 231 T 3, 5, 6). This work is a political memoir as we use the term today: a reasoned account of one's political career intended to explain and justify one's actions.

When we turn to the Latins, if we regard genre instead of nomenclature, it is apparent at once that the memoir of Aratus's type was the form preferred by statesmen in a milieu infused with Hellenistic culture by the radiant influence of the Scipionic circle.[10] The works

---

[10]G. Misch, *Geschichte der Autobiographie* (Leipzig, 1931), vol. 1, p. 137. The Greeks supplied the form, not the predilection, which was inherently Roman. See Momigliano, *The Development of Greek Biography*, p. 93.

of M. Aemilius Scaurus, P. Rutilius Rufus, Q. Lutatius Catulus, and Sulla unite in their autobiographical character[11] and in their exposition of a subject thematic only in that it concerned themselves. Catulus is exceptional in this respect, for it appears that he limited his account to the events of his consulship.

Now it is important to observe that in none of these cases (except, perhaps, Catulus's) does the word "commentary" as used in Latin match the kind of work that was written. *Commentarii* properly denoted something written for personal use, to refresh the memory or to establish a functional record to subserve the composition of a more finished work.[12] It was not a title applied to their works by the above mentioned authors, who regarded their writings not as memoranda but as ends in themselves and as part of the genre long practiced by Hellenistic Greek politicians. These accounts can therefore appropriately be described as *hypomnemata*, the title taken by Aratus. However, *hypomnemata* is a Greek word with a variety of meanings, and one of them is, in fact, equivalent to the Latin term *commentarius*. Hence the source of confusion in nomenclature, which has led to the identification of memoirs and historical commentaries as if they were the same. Although a sub-category of Greek *hypomnemata* includes works equivalent to what in Latin would be called *commentarii*, the category of *hypomnemata* known to us from Aratus, and which unquestionably applies to the works of Scaurus et al., is in fact not covered by the Latin term.

The generic differences separating Caesar's work[13] from the political autobiographies (*hypomnemata*) of his predecessors leap to the eye. The *Gallic Wars* is obviously not a running account of Caesar's political career offering analysis, explanation, or overt justification. The subject is not Caesar (formally) but the conquest of Gaul; it is the stuff of a potential full-dress war monograph—a correlation that brings us closer to Xenophon (though the differences are many) than

[11] Scaurus (F 3, 6 Peter) and Rutilius (F 9 Peter) described themselves in the first person—unlike Xenophon and Caesar. The difference is significant. It is possible that Rutilius, Catulus, and Sulla wrote in Greek: see Peter, vol. 1, CCLXVI, CCLXXII, CCLXXIII.

[12] See, e.g., Cicero *Ad Att.* 2. 1. 2, and Lucian, *How to Write History* 16, 48. The material is collected by G. Avenarius, *Lukians Schrift zur Geschichtsschreibung* (Meisenheim am Glan, 1956), pp. 85ff.

[13] I ignore here the *Civil Wars*, which represents a more complex literary problem since it presupposes the *Gallic Wars* and is, in addition, concerned with immeasurably more sensitive issues.

to Aratus and his imitators. Finally, we know that Caesar himself considered his work a "commentary" (in the Latin sense), since it is so described by his follower and continuator Aulus Hirtius in a passage (*Gallic Wars* 8. *Praef.* 4) that also emphasizes the extemporary nature of the work:

> All agree that nothing has been done by others with the expenditure of great effort that is not surpassed by the grace of these commentaries. They have been published so that the knowledge of such tremendous affairs will be available to writers, and they have been so warmly approved by everyone's judgment that the possibility of writing [the history of the conquest of Gaul] seems to have been snatched away from the writers, not offered to them. Nevertheless, my admiration of this achievement is greater than that of everyone else. For others know how well and faultlessly he wrote them; I know how easily and speedily he completed the work.

With this passage we may compare Cicero's assessment of the *Commentarii*:

> But although he wanted others who wished to write a history to have material ready from which to draw, he perhaps pleased the pedants who want to put the work in curlers but he scared off men of sense from writing; for nothing is sweeter in history than clean and shining brevity. [*Brutus* 262]

The double use of the word *historia* is noticeable: "a history" and "history" have been juxtaposed, the former denoting a finished work of the genre, the latter a quality of narrative properly found in historical works. Both Hirtius and Cicero, therefore, unite in viewing the work as a "commentary" in the strict sense of the word, *generically* a utilitarian sketch intended as an aid for historical writers. Whatever Caesar's private purpose, however he visualized the propagandistic value of the *Gallic Wars*, in form it was no more a history than it was a memoir. But there is equally no denying that it broke the mold. In the hands of a man of brilliance and taste, this preliminary sketch became an art form in its own right.

Signs distinguishing the work from history are abundant and informative. First, there is no preface. Caesar's superb sense of incisive brevity enabled him to dispense with an element as inappropriate to the commentary as it was necessary to history, where jolting abruptness needed to be avoided. (Compare the opening of Xenophon's *Anabasis.*) Another similar sign is the absence of background information, for example, the simplicity of Caesar's plain reference to himself in 1. 7. 1. Curiously enough, from our perspective the complete absence of rhetoric and self-description magnifies his person by suggesting that description is superfluous. It is as if we should know who he is, what the scope of his command was. (But this is to read the work without a sense of genre, with the prior knowledge of what Caesar will become, and with the prejudgment that the commentary is an established masterpiece.) The lack of elaborative rhetoric in 1. 25. 1, the avoidance of any description of battle carnage at the Rhine especially (a commonplace in historical writing, in which rivers run with blood, and the corpses block the current) in 1. 53. 3, tell the same story. So does his plain and repetitive style: *pugnatum est* (*sit*) "the battle was fought", occurs four times in the brief space of 1. 26. 1–4. In this context, Caesar's account of the bridging of the Rhine in 4. 17 becomes the more interesting. On the one hand, this is truly a "deed worthy of narration"; on the other, it is described tersely, without fanfare. Clearly the description is (or is intended to seem as if it were) provided for "others who wished to write history," as Cicero inferred. Something similar will be found in 7. 72. Caesar avoided the obviously appropriate rhetoric, but carefully provided a technically accurate report of the means by which the bridging (and his fortifications) were accomplished.

Nevertheless, the work undoubtedly altered its character as the years progressed; Caesar became more ambitious. A characterizing speech (as unwonted to Caesar as appropriate to history) of the Usipetes and Tencteri appears in 4. 7. Caesar permits himself the luxury of an extended description, with "historical" coloration, of Roman deliberations in which he had no part in 5. 27–31. In books 6 and 7, the canvas has been stretched noticeably wider. Not all is seen through Caesar's own eyes: some is seen, for example, through the medium of Labienus in 7. 58f. "Fortune" enters, along with ethnography in 6. 42 (cf. 6. 30). The sketches of the Suebi (4. 1–3) and of the British (5. 12–14), though graceful, are different in character from the splendid ethnography of 6. 11–28. Even the "memorable," that standard rubric of historiography, occurs in 7. 25. 1, and a full-dress speech is now for the first time inserted because of its "unusual and dreadful cruelty" (7. 77).

The work was carried by a momentum of its own as the years

passed, Caesar perhaps coming to realize that the record could not be improved by an inflated version and being induced in consequence to embellish it modestly himself.[14] Still, it is far from a history. Apart from the limited ethnographical treatment, geography is provided only for what is strategically necessary. The one-sided treatment of the enemy is a similar deficiency: no description of the opposition is provided except in actual conflicts. Above all, there is lacking that sense of teleological goal or higher mission that Roman history required. In a word, this is a skeleton of a history, at least as the Latins of the time of Cicero conceived of it. But although there will always be an uncertainty about Caesar's more precise political purpose in writing this work, no valid reason exists to deny its generic nature as a commentary. It seems almost paradoxical, therefore, to observe that of all the forms of memoir-literature we have reviewed, this, the commentary, stands closest (in theory, at least) to history in point of its objectivity or, better, pose of neutrality. At the same time, as we may infer from fragments preserved from various memoirs, where subjectivity was unconcealed, the memoir and not the commentary unabashedly applied the varied principles of historical description. Thus the commentary is closer to substance and the memoir closer to form: these are complex and fascinating interrelationships.

The commentary was by its nature a preliminary draft and could therefore hardly emerge as a competitor of history, as did the utopias and (presumably to a much lesser extent) the memoirs. The most serious challenge posed to history, and one which not only altered the character of historical writing but eventually replaced it as the dominant form, came from biography. It is a phenomenon that will not surprise us; indeed, it seems a virtually universal predilection: people tend to be more fascinated by the character of singular individuals than by the grand flow of monumental historical events.

It is indicative of the different purposes of history and ancient biography that each is directed to mutually exclusive ends. Ancient biography[15] developed outside the orbit of history, and its *physis*, or

[14] For a totally different and, in my opinion, fantastic view, see H. Gärtner, *Beobachtungen zu Bauelementen in der antiken Historiographie besonders bei Livius und Caesar*. Historia Einzelschrift no. 25 (Wiesbaden, 1975), p. 62.

[15] The most important study remains that of F. Leo, *Die griechisch-römische Biographie nach ihrer literarischen Form* (Leipzig, 1901); Momigliano, *The Development of Greek Biography*, pp. 10ff., presents a lucid account of the major work on the subject in recent times.

nature, cannot be understood except with reference to its origin in ethical preoccupations. At first (in Aristotle's school) the life of an individual was studied in order to shed light on his poetry, politics, or philosophy (though it also followed that the works of a poet, for example, were studied to provide information about his life). Alexandrian biographers continued the discipline, making it, in principle, more scientific. The traditions about the activities of an individual were assembled, with variants included, and these were studied in order to shed light on his life. As this suggests, history, the record of man's memorable deeds, was irrelevant to biography except when deeds illuminated character. Conversely, subjects for illustration suitable to biography—for example, a sense of humor indicated by characterizing anecdotes—were unsuitable to history. The difference of perspective and selection is made clear by Nepos (the earliest writer of an extant biographical work, though he wrote in the last half of the first century B.C.):

> Pelopidas of Thebes is better known to historians than to the general public. How I am to set forth his virtues is a matter of uncertainty because I fear that if I begin to relate his actions I will seem not to be writing his life but to be writing history. [16. 1]

History portrays the deeds of a man (or men). Lives delineate character. So Plutarch asserted that

> We are not writing history but lives. Revelation of virtue and vice is not always manifest in the most famous actions. A small thing, a word or a jest, frequently has made a greater indication of character than casualty-filled battles, the greatest armed confrontations and the besieging of cities. [*Alexander* 1. 2; cf. *Nicias* 1. 5]

The influence of *biography* (i.e., the genre) is best kept separate from the frequent expression of "biographical interest" in historiography generally. Natural interest of this type, transcending genre, is evinced by writers as early as Herodotus and Thucydides; it appears also in Aristophanic comedy, in Stesimbrotus and Ion, in stories about the Seven Wise Men, and elsewhere. Theopompus, who incorporated a biographical approach reminiscent of Stesimbrotus when he excoriated the Athenian demagogues in the tenth book of the *Philippica*, was clearly fascinated by Philip; so was Duris by

Agathocles, Phylarchus by Cleomenes, Tacitus by Tiberius. Polybius's treatment of the two Scipios is overtly biographical and appears, in fact, to reflect the peculiarly Roman conviction that individual life and conduct (*vita moresque*) were valid historical topics.[16] But character analysis entered historiography by way of the categories of praise and blame in demonstrative oratory. Naturally, since some of the components of biography also derive from rhetorical practice, fundamental similarities are detectable; thus the "obituary notice" used by Polybius as an occasion for the "critical appraisal" is equally a unit of formal biography.[17] But the fact that the same elements are found in both vessels does not alter the fact that the mixture was qualitatively different and that the generic separation was scrupulously maintained,[18] the chief link between them being the historical nature of the material.

A drastic alteration in the balance between historiography and biography was effected when Suetonius published the *Lives of the Twelve Caesars* in the reign of Hadrian. The work appeared at the perfect time, when Roman political history was becoming the record of absolutistic monarchs. The tension between emperor and senate inducing Tacitus to organize his histories along the lines of their irreconcilable enmity was sapped; what now was interesting and relevant were the life, character, and habits of the ruler of the world. After Suetonius, a line of Latin biographers from Marius Maximus, still much read in the time of Ammianus (who deplored the fact in 28. 4. 14) to the so-called Scriptores Historiae Augustae, writers of the lives of the "thirty emperors" from Hadrian to Numerian (died A.D. 284), separate Tacitus from Ammianus Marcellinus, who began his history, in fact, where Tacitus left off. The new mode, in which the life of the *princeps* was treated by category (a scheme apparently borrowed from the biographical school of Callimachus) throve on the presentation of (often spurious) documentary material.[19] Its in-

---

[16] See chapter 3.

[17] See Leo, *Biographie*, pp. 234f.

[18] Tacitus's *Agricola* is, however, an interesting example of the way in which the formal limitations of genre can be overstepped. Though the work is a eulogistic biography, it is much more. The ethnography of Britain, account of seven campaigns, and speeches of generals before battle add a historical dimension. As a whole, it is impossible to classify (without very special pleading).

[19] An extraordinary example is provided by Marius Maximus (F 16 Peter); cf. Dio Cassius 74. 2.

clusion is, no less than its fraudulent character, one of the best in-dications we could wish of the antipodal distance of this type of liter-ature from historiography. Everything was pursued "as if one should know how often [the emperor] took a walk, how many times he var-ied his diet, when he changed his clothes, and whom he favored with promotion, and when it occurred."[20] Ammianus states his con-viction of the unsuitability of such trivia to history in 26. 1.

The main question is how this movement, to which Plutarch added the weight of his own considerable prestige, affected the his-torians, and it would appear that the answer lies chiefly in their adoption of a certain shift in emphasis. Character is studied in its own right, almost independently of the political framework of his-toriography in which it had served a functional purpose. This per-spective appears in the Greek historian Dio Cassius, who wrote his massive history of Rome in the early third century. For example, he commenced his account of the reign of Commodus with these words:

> This man was not naturally wicked, but, on the contrary, as guileless as any man that ever lived. His great simplicity, how-ever, together with his cowardice, made him the slave of his companions, and it was through them that he at first, out of ignorance, missed the better life and then was led on into lust-ful and cruel habits, which soon became second nature. [73. *ad. init.*, trans. E. Cary]

Psychological analysis of this kind can, of course, be found in earlier writers. It is notable, however, that this piece from Dio reflects the ethical typology most familiar from Plutarch; analysis proceeds from the character to the event. Dio propels his account by the char-acterizing anecdote (4. 2–3); even Commodus's beautification of Rome is presented (in reversal of history and biography) as an exam-ple of his love of the beautiful (7. 4). The emperor's love of soft liv-ing (and inexperience) are similarly promoted to explain his inatten-tion to public affairs (10. 2). However, Dio's assimilation of standard biographic technique could not be better illustrated than in the de-

---

[20] Junius Cordus (F 1 Peter). In F 8 we learn how many pounds of meat Maximinus ate habitually, while from Julius Capitolinus (*The Two Maximini* 4. 2–3) we are informed not only that he avoided vegetables, but that he collected his sweat in small jars.

scription he provides of Victorinus, erstwhile prefect of the city, in an obituary notice:

> [Victorinus] in point of moral excellence and forensic elo-
> quence stood second to none of his contemporaries. Indeed,
> two incidents that I shall now relate will reveal his whole char-
> acter. When he was governor of Germany at one time, he at
> first attempted by private persuasion at home to induce his lieu-
> tenant not to accept bribes; but when the latter would not lis-
> ten to him, he mounted the tribunal, and after bidding the her-
> ald proclaim silence, took oath that he had never accepted
> bribes and never would. Then he bade the lieutenant take the
> same oath, and when the other refused to perjure himself, he
> ordered him to resign his office. . . . Such, then, was the char-
> acter of Victorinus. [73. 11. 2–4, trans. E. Cary]

Ammianus, that extraordinary combination of historian, rhetorician, and biographer, was also prone to view the emperors from the
perspective of the biographer seeking to use "the word or jest" "to
see the signs of the soul." Unforgettable is his description of the en-
try of Constantius into Rome, a passage that pins him to the board:

> For he bent down low his short body when passing through the
> high gates, and as if his neck was embraced by fortifications he
> kept the direction of his eyes straight and did not turn his face
> to the right or the left, as if he were the mere statue of a man.
> Nor did he let his head shake when the carriage-wheel jolted
> nor was he ever seen to spit or to wipe his face or nose, or
> scratch it, or move his hands. [16. 10. 10; cf. Suet. *Tib.* 68]

Ammianus also made frequent use of the characterizing anecdote—
for example, in 22. 7. 2, where Julian fines himself for having com-
mitted a technical misdemeanor. Interesting for the same reason is
7. 3:

> One day, when he [Julian] was supervising the suits [being held
> in the senate], the philosopher Maximus was announced to
> have arrived from Asia. He jumped up without decorum and,
> forgetting who he was, he advanced on the run a good distance
> from the vestibule. After having kissed [Maximus] and treated

him with reverence, he brought him back with him to the accompaniment of inappropriate ostentation.[21]

Plutarch would have appreciated the story. A comparable reversal of the historical and biographical priorities is indicated in 22. 9. 10, 10. 5, where Julian's patience and clemency are extolled by single examples selected for their ethical point without regard to the intrinsic significance of the occasion.

It would be misleading, however, to imply that Ammianus was affected by biographical techniques and procedures only insofar as they guided his delineation of character. It is interesting to see that even this magisterial writer cannot resist interpolating irrelevant documents into his work; it is as if he were drawn on involuntarily by the example of the imperial biographers. A grotesque example is his rendering (in Greek) of a text inscribed on an obelisk, which (as he admits) he owes to the scholarship of Hermapion (17. 4. 18–23). Though 18. 3 too shows obvious affinities to the Scriptores Historiae Augustae, it belongs in another category. Here we have the unedifying saga of Barbatio and his jealous wife. In 16. 8, on the other hand, we are given a description of court life and its attendant paranoia, which betrays the same influence. As a final example one may consider Ammianus's depiction of the cruelty of Valentinian in 27. 7. We must accept the fact that Ammianus was contaminated by the times. What is extraordinary is his usual elevation above them. Since Ammianus possessed dignity and a sense of the majesty of history, he took the high road, and is never vulgar, even when he slips.

The degeneration of history is signified by the diatribe of Lucian against contemporary historians in *How to Write History* and by the accompanying popularity of a genre, biography, dominated by alien interests and predisposed to gross characterization and fraudulent exposition. It is less surprising that three hundred years separate Tacitus from his continuator, Ammianus Marcellinus, than that such a continuator arose. Curiously enough, the public fell away en masse from the greatest of prose genres at that very point in time charac-

---

[21] Probably we should accuse Ammianus here of the suppression of relevant background, for Maximus was not just any philosopher but stood in close personal relation to Julian, having in fact been instrumental in his conversion. See Libanius *Orat.* 12. 34, 13. 12.

terized by Gibbon as idyllic (*Decline and Fall, ad init.*). We observe the intellectual debasement of even the "elite" of the empire. The inference that historiography suffered this impoverishment (in writer and reader alike) can be supported, and the stages of the decline can be observed, if we follow the progressive course of the digest or "compilation" together with the "epitome." The tastes of the reading public progressively turned soft, self-indulgent, and superficial.

Oddly enough, "compilations" began proudly. It was a genre catering to the insatiable appetite of philosophy and poesy for historical and ethnographical data. On the one hand, the Peripatetics (following the lead of Hellanicus and Damastes [*FGrHist* 4 F 66–70, 5 T 1]) amassed comparative material on barbarian customs, constitutions and other matters. The Alexandrians, moreover, aided immeasurably by their great library, not only continued this tradition (it is exemplified in Callimachus) but also produced works of which one guiding principle was to collect all variants relating to a given subject. This was the procedure followed by Callimachus's student Istrus (*FGrHist* 334) in the field of history (just as another student, Hermippus, followed it in biography). Among Istrus's numerous works (seventeen are certain), which were antiquarian in focus, two are about early Athens. These collections, or rather digests, are works of severe scholarship. Variant material was collected and organized with a view to the elimination of problems and discrepancies. When they were poets (not historical writers), Istrus named his sources. The reason, as Jacoby observed, is that genealogists and historians were regarded "merely as transmitting poetic or epichoric [local] tradition, not as independent witnesses, whereas the poets are the creators of tradition or at least the first and original witnesses to it."[22] The point, in any case, is that Istrus named the authorities in pursuance of scientific method.

Compilations of this type soon became popular, though in a vulgarized form. The citation of authors for purposes of comparison on the minutiae of history yields to the citation of well-known authors (for their own sake) in a broad, and often exotic, geographical-

---

[22] Jacoby, *FGrHist* 3b (text), p. 623. Citation of the poets may thus be compared with the standard practice of the citation of philosophers in expository as well as critical literature. Historians are never cited in analogous situations, on the assumption that the *res gestae* (whatever their more precise formulation by one writer or another) are common property.

historical context. The point is illustrated by this use of their predecessors by two well-known first-century writers, Alexander Polyhistor (*FGrHist* 273) and Juba, king of the Mauretanians in the time of
Augustus (*FGrHist* 275). Alexander wrote in Rome in the middle of
the century, and he acquired his sobriquet "Polyhistor" ("the writer
of a lot of history") by publishing compilations on Egypt, Bithynia,
the Black Sea, India, the Jews, Chaldea, Caria, Cilicia, Cyprus, and
Rome. So also Juba, though he descended a step lower. He wrote
similar but less ambitious works on Arabia, Syria, Libya, and even on
the origins of Rome (perhaps as a compliment to Augustus). Alexander's emphasis on the East may correspond with a surge of public interest aroused by the prospective campaigns of Pompey, but the range
and type of material provided by both writers is self-explanatory. Popular writing of this sort tells its own tale, and it is suggestive of parallels in modern times. People began to like history in abridged form [23]
or by way of "famous passages," and it evidently became preferable to
read a little about a lot than a lot about a little.

It is appropriate in this context to dwell briefly on the epitome. If
the custom of composing books out of various sources had begun as a
scientific method of bringing all relevant material to bear on disputed points, and ended by becoming a popular genre in its own
right, [24] the epitome, though it ended similarly, originated more
humbly. Theopompus (*FGrHist* 115 T 1) had epitomized Herodotus
(in two books) and was epitomized in turn (T 31) by Philip V of
Macedon. Agatharchides (86 T 2) had compiled a general historical
epitome, apparently for his own personal use. The practice became
fashionable in the first century. Brutus made epitomes of Fannius,
Coelius Antipater, and Polybius, presumably for the sake of *exempla*,
since he was a serious student of philosophy. By this time, however,
the epitome was becoming something more than a writer's aid, and
claimed a measure of literary respectability. Jason of Cyrene (*FGrHist*
182 T 1), for example, praised the enterprise by emphasizing the mass

[23] It is worth noting that Strabo's history (*FGrHist* 91), entitled "Historical Memoranda," was apparently modeled on this type of work. Unlike regular histories,
Strabo's included the citation of specific writers (e.g., Timagenes, Hypsicrates, Asinius Pollio). Though there is no reason to insist that his work was a "mere" compilation, it seems clear that it represents a step taken towards popularization.

[24] The same thing happened with collections of *exempla* (see the preface of Valerius
Maximus), and of love stories, originally collected as the raw material for the poet
(e.g., by Parthenius for Gallus). See Rohde, *Griechische Roman*, pp. 99–102, 121ff.

of material the reader had to plow through in order to "make the circuit" of history; he had the temerity to assert that his epitome would bring pleasure (*psychagogia*) to some, refresh the memory of others, and bring profit to all. These of course, were the virtues once claimed for their works by actual historians. The trend later resulted in the epitomizing of Livy by the highly placed litterateur C. Vibius Maximus (first century A.D.). Finally, it could induce someone like Florus, who wrote in the second century A.D., blandly to assume the value of such works:

> So, as the history of Rome is especially worthy of study, yet be-cause the very vastness of the subject is a hindrance to the knowledge of it [cf. Jason of Cyrene], and the diversity of its topics distracts the keenness of the attention, I intend to follow the example of those who describe the geography of the earth, and include a complete representation of my subject as it were in a small picture. I shall thus, I hope, contribute something to the admiration in which this illustrious people is held by dis-playing their greatness all at once in a single view. [*Praef.* 3, trans. J. C. Rolfe]

After this, the epitome became a standard literary form, published without apology and sometimes (for example, by Aurelius Victor and Eutropius) written with care. Thus what had begun as a conve-nient abridgment ended by driving out the original works that had originally been its inspiration. The epitome became not only accept-able but actually preferred (cf. Ammian. 15. 1. 1).

It is a saddening story, especially when taken in conjunction with the numerous other signs of social collapse, anarchy, despotic rule, and the fading away of intellectual liberty. Tacitus had argued that it was impossible to practice oratory except under conditions of politi-cal liberty. It was impossible also to write history or to expect it to be read. Ammianus, who, in fact, wondered about the risk of continu-ing his history into "modern times" (26. *ad. init.*), is in this sense an exception to the rule. We should keep in mind, however, that he was part of an extraordinary group of intellectuals, pagans all, who at the end of the fourth century brimmed with devotion to the past, to ancient Rome, and to the intellectual and moral greatness it represented. These men concentrated their energies and sought to re-establish the republic of letters, of taste, and of patriotism, if only existentially. The poetry of Ausonius, Symmachus's letters, Claudian's epics, the scholarship on the text of Livy and others, and innumerable other undertakings, categorically differentiate this splendid period from the preceding age. But the general public read nothing but Juvenal and Marius Maximus; if they were curious about "the memorable" they read the *Collectanea* of Solinus, a compendium of compendia. As for Ammianus himself, his great work received a predictable response: it is never cited. Even so, the work *was* written, and the renaissance of which Ammianus was a part *did* in fact occur; it was as real as the span of nine hundred years in which the Greeks and the Latins demonstrated for all time their incomparable vitality and genius in the field of historical writing.

VI

Modern Historiography: An Epilogue

Even were I possessed of the requisite erudition, an attempt to provide a systematic discussion of post-classical developments could yield nothing more, in this brief epilogue, than a list of names and simplistic labels. Instead, however, we may usefully inspect the milestones studding the road from ancient to present times, noting when the ancients predominated, when their extraordinary prestige dissipated, when new methods came to be employed and when doubts about these methods arose in their own turn. Some of these steps are of great interest, not only because of the intellectual presuppositions underlying them, but because they help to mark the distance in theory and practice between ancient and modern historiography.

The first milestone stands in need of no elaboration. It was the rediscovery of the ancient world that enabled the classical influence residual in the historiography of medieval times to reassert its authority in the Renaissance.[1] The link connecting Machiavelli with Livy is well known. An equally fascinating, and perhaps more instructive, example of the hegemony ancient authors came to hold is

---

[1] For history written in Latin and in the vernacular, see M. Phillips, "Machiavelli, Guicciardini, and the Tradition of Vernacular Historiography in Florence," *AHR* 84 (1979): 86.

supplied by Polybius's emergence as a repository of wisdom: by A.D. 1600 he had become the military historian par excellence.[2]

To say that criticism worthy of the name was now applied to the authoritative figures of the past would be an overstatement. Men were, of course, uncomfortable about the frequent intrusion of the fabulous; indeed, it has been alleged that even the uncritical repetition of ancient material involved the real beginning of historical criticism, since it was accompanied by a "very critical awareness that the ancient authorities were conditioned by their own source."[3] Awareness such as this, however, is shared by Herodotus and Livy; what constitutes actual criticism is the methodical confrontation of the problem, not the observation that a difficulty exists. Historical criticism would remain dormant until awakened by a combination of new and epochal developments in other fields, specifically science; with time their larger significance would eventually become apparent for history as well.[4]

It was needful, first, that the comparative exaltation of ancient works be reduced to its proper proportions. The conviction in the sixteenth and seventeenth centuries that man lived in a degenerate age, wholly incomparable with the ancients in point of learning, knowledge, and culture (an obvious impediment to criticism) was gradually undercut in that period by a series of great achievements, of which Copernicus's is a potent example. More directly relevant (though intimately related) were the works of historical theorists like Jean Bodin (1530–96),[5] who elevated the arts and sciences of modern times above those of the ancients. It was inevitable that ancient writers would come to be regarded with a critical eye and ultimately be corrected in accordance with the best principles.

It lay in the nature of the case, however, that these "best principles" needed to be sought in some sphere other than history itself. As is well known, they actually emanated from a revolution of science. Francis Bacon (1561–1626) was a major figure here. By insist-

---

[2] See A. Momigliano, *Essays in Ancient and Modern Historiography* (Oxford, 1977), p. 93.

[3] Ibid., p. 85.

[4] The process of absorption was slow. Even Gibbon's criticism, at a much later time, trenchant though it was, remained the criticism of the sceptic, the writer of sound sense, still writing in accordance with the methods of the ancients themselves.

[5] See J. B. Bury, *The Idea of Progress* (New York, 1955), pp. 37ff.

ing on the necessity of experimentation, Bacon incidentally under-
mined the ancient histories. For the antipode of experiment is the
acceptance of that which is handed down. In the new order of ideas,
theory existed to be tested. It was not only permissible, but mandatory, to be methodically critical, which in historiography is the
equivalent of experimentation. Thus history, too, by the late eigh-
teenth and early nineteenth centuries, gravitated into the orbit of
science, and it was with the greatest optimism that historians considered the possibility of setting down a truly historical record both
of past and recent times.

The transformation alluded to may be said to have commenced
with the work of earlier scholars such as Jean Mabillon (1632–
1707), who proved the value of critical method for the exposure of
false and the verification of authentic medieval documents, while
Friedrich Wolf's *Prolegomena to Homer* (1794) provided historians
with a sense of the possibilities of minute source criticism. The principle of *systematic* source criticism was born, and tremendous developments unquestionably ensued. In classical history, Barthold Niebuhr (1776–1831) tore down the great façade of the early Roman
Republic erected by Livy; and it is symptomatic of the movement
that Niebuhr could speak of his *History of Rome* as a book of science
in which spelling and presentation were secondary considerations.
But this came in the first flush of enthusiasm; as Eduard Meyer observed, modern writers, however scientific their expressed methodology, pay more attention to style and arrangement than they
would like to admit.[6] It is plain, nevertheless, that an elemental redefinition of historiography has been made. Niebuhr and others
came for the first time to regard the historical works of the Greeks
and Romans (for example) as just so many pieces of data, the anterior sources of which were capable of being tracked down. The old
histories were to be dismantled and put together again (in combination with other data) in order to provide a more critical history.

The radical alteration in the nature of history effected in the nineteenth century transcended the systematic application of method:
the concept developed that history was a science in the strict sense
of the word. The new science required not only a rigorous and sys-

[6] *Kleine Schriften*[2] (Halle, 1924), vol. 1, p. 367, n. 1.

tematic analysis of the data, but also regarded the inclusion of *all* data as an essential condition of realizing "actual history."

The new scientific view is well indicated by the assertion of Leopold von Ranke (1795–1886) that history must be written "the way it actually was." The context is important:

> To history has been assigned the office of judging the past, of instructing the present for the benefit of future ages. To such high offices [Ranke's *History of the Latin and Teutonic Nations 1494–1535*] does not aspire: it wants only to show what actually happened [*wie es eigentlich gewesen*].[7]

Thus are the judgmental and beneficial features of history jettisoned; Ranke aimed for scientific neutrality and strove at all costs for objectivity.[8] It is consonant with this that Ranke denies to his work any significance transcending the actual history described, thus parting company with almost all other historians, ancient and modern. The ideal of dispassionate objectivity was shared by Thucydides, whose belief that his history was intrinsically valuable for the knowledge it contained is also close to Ranke's (though Thucydides claimed more than this). In any event, the premise of objectivity, so necessary to the illusion of history as a true science, and to the idea of writing history as it actually happened, soon fell under devastating attack. By insisting that men's ideas were determined by their economic condition, Karl Marx denied the possibility of dispassionate higher analysis.[9] The subjectivity of individuals within the societal matrix was a perception further enforced by the development of analytic psychology. The degree to which our perception of "objective reality" is hostage to our infinitely complicated social and personal identities was soon grasped. Charles Beard observed in 1935 that the theoretical possibility of obtaining objective truth is clouded by

> questions, which run deeply into the human mind, the substance of history as actuality, and the power of scholarship to grasp history objectively. Beyond doubt, scholars of compe-

[7] The text is reproduced in the anthology of F. Stern, *The Varieties of History from Voltaire to the Present* (New York, 1956), p. 57.

[8] See H. Butterfield, *Man on his Past* (Cambridge, 1969), pp. 92ff.

[9] See, for example, Charles Collingwood, *The Idea of History* (New York, 1956), p. 123.

tence can agree on many particular truths and on large bodies of established facts. But is it possible for men to divest themselves of all race, sex, class, political, social and regional predilections and tell the truth of history as it actually was?[10]

Subjectivity and its accompaniment selectivity thus came to the fore. The Rankean view that it is the task of history simply to discover the facts—i.e., that history is the total aggregation of fact—was speedily seen to be assailable not only because of the "subjective" manner in which we perceive "the facts," but because the retrieval and reproduction of the totality of true facts is self-evidently an unattainable ideal. More than this, it is inimical to the (subjective) concept of relevance. Some historians came to believe, therefore, that the comprehensiveness prized by Ranke actually contravenes the true function of the historian. As Sir Lewis Namier wrote in 1952:

> But as no human mind can master more than a fraction of what would be required for a wide and balanced understanding of human affairs, limitation and selection are essential in the historian's craft. . . . The function of the historian is akin to that of the painter and not of the photographic camera; to discover and set forth, to single out and stress that which is of the nature of the thing, and not to reproduce indiscriminately all that meets the eye.[11]

From here it was but a short step in logic to the extreme position taken by E. H. Carr.[12] To Carr, the subjectivity of the historian and the indeterminate importance of past events (until, that is, they have been selected by the historian) combine to make the historian

---

[10] From the essay, "That Noble Dream" (1935), quoted from Stern, *Varieties*, p. 317.

[11] *Avenues of History* (London, 1952), p. 8. The implications of this view are intriguing in respect to ancient speeches, for a case can be made that the speech of the ancient historian—if he is perceptive—may cut closer to the reality of the historical moment than the actual words of the orator. In this connection, it is appropriate to emphasize once more that the ancients regarded speeches as "events," not as "documentary evidence."

[12] *What Is History?* (New York, 1962), p. 14.

not only the writer but the maker of history (cf. Callisthenes).[13] "His is the dual task," wrote Carr, "of discovering the few [sic] significant facts and turning them into facts of history." The historian is perceived as the supremely autonomous intelligence, whose ultimate subjectivity has paradoxically been transmuted into the quintessential feature of his craft.

Because of these and other developments, Ranke's movement of *Historismus* exerted a less sweeping influence even in first flush than the prestige of some of its adherents might lead one to believe. A variety of types of history came to be written, which in direction and purpose remind us, in fact, of the prevalence (or universality or generic essentiality) of ancient patterns of thought. Time and again, a chord is struck recalling echoes from the past. Cato and Livy would have been fascinated to learn that Jules Michelet made the people of France the "hero" of his work. To be sure, Michelet did not intend the equivalent of Livy's *populus Romanus*, but regarded "the people" as a social entity. We do not seek to set forth parallels, however, but rather to illustrate certain categorical similarities between the ancients and moderns. Thus Thomas Carlyle took the position that universal history was the history of great men, while Fustel de Coulanges, supreme advocate of "scientific history" though he was, opposed Carlyle's view in a passage that, for all its differences, reads like Livy:

> Political institutions are never the creation of one man's will; even the will of an entire people would not suffice to create them. The human elements which bring them about are not of the kind which the caprice of one generation can change. Peoples are governed not by what they fancy but by what the totality of their interests and the essence of their beliefs prescribe. That is undoubtedly the reason why it takes many generations to establish a political regime and many other generations to tear it down.
>
> Hence also the necessity for the historian to extend his investigations to a wide span of time. . . . The age in which an institution appears at its height, glittering, powerful, dominating, is hardly ever the time when it was established or when it

---

[13] See chapter 2.

gathered strength. The causes of its birth, the circumstances from which it drew strength and vigor often belong to a far earlier time.[14]

Recurrence of theme or coincidence of subject can, of course, be regarded as accidental similarities, vastly overshadowed by the very substantial differences separating the historical writings of the ancients from those of the moderns. Fustel was "scientific," Livy was not; Macaulay was an "artist" on a plane utterly removed from that occupied by Tacitus, and so on. It is, therefore, all the more illuminating to observe that in one vital respect ancients and moderns are united in purpose, representatives of each age maintaining that the function of the genre is to instruct. The ancients applied the concept of history's utility to ethics or politics or both. If their conviction that historical knowledge could be utilized in this fashion seems shallow to us ("mere rhetoric"), we might recollect that political knowledge and ethical direction are values also promoted by modern writers. Historians of the nineteenth and twentieth centuries (Ranke aside) are no less constrained to urge the utility of their works, though the formulation is less simplistic, at least superficially, and the relation of history to its intended effect is proportionately more remote. This difference can be explained by the nature of the audience contemplated by ancient and modern historians respectively. The Greco-Romans addressed the ruling elite, instructing them on how to act well and to avoid pitfalls when in some fashion or other they emulated the careers of one or another of the historical characters set before them. Moderns have "the general public" in view, and the "value of history" becomes correspondingly vague.

Sub specie aeternitatis, history has altered but little. The value of history has been perceived in both ancient and modern times as connected with its educational function. In one way or another, it has come to be regarded as a beneficial guide to conduct. For all of this, most historians, certainly most academic historians, in practice, work along the lines laid down by Ranke: we try to write thorough histories, while suppressing our prejudices. Thus, in the long view, the most radical changes in historiography in modern times, the development of a scientific method and the corresponding drive

---

[14] Introduction, *History of the Political Institutions of Ancient France*, quoted from Stern, *Varieties*, p. 189.

to reassemble as many pieces of history as possible into a "true," "significant," or merely "intelligible" pattern, arose from the movement associated with Ranke's name. To speak of a transmutation of the craft would, however, be to invert the relative importance of manner (method) and substance.

If method has undeniably been altered and improved, the substance of history has rather been augmented than changed. History continues to march with politics and war, the "memorable deeds of man" as the ancients defined them. The chief difference is focus. The modern historian no longer invariably studies "great deeds" in themselves, but examines their preconditions or contributary elements, and he does so without regard to whether they are "ignoble" or not. But if the ancients and the moderns part company on this score, agreement holds on a fundamental level: major historical writing (as opposed to doctoral dissertations and the research published in learned periodicals) is artfully arranged, well-written and, above all, intrinsically concerned with the exposition of memorable events. That our definition of "memorable" is more comprehensive than the ancient scarcely affects the issue: the Clio of old is with us still, though in modern dress.

Index of Important
Names and Subjects

Index of Important Passages

Index of Important Names and Subjects

Hermapion, 189
Hermippus, of Smyrna, 190
Herod, the Great, 46
Herodotus, of Halicarnassus: on mythical times, 7; indebted to ethnography, 16; antedated local history, 17; major innovation of, 30–32; relations to Hecataeus, 30; relation to Thucydides, 30, 32; influenced by Homer, 31–32, 62, 77, 96–97; narrative technique of, 31–32, 171–72; preface of, 54; portrayal of individuals by, 63; main subject of, 63–64; insistence on supernatural omnipotence, 77–79; environmental theory of, 82; selective historical approach of, 92, 97; anachronistic technique of, 105; purpose, 77–79, 105; amplification of detail in, 134; introduces speeches in historiography, 143; speeches in, 162–66; the Great Debate in, 164–65; on Periander, 165; on Solon, 165; dialogue in, 166; indebted to drama, 171–72; mentioned, 8, 12, 14, 18, 20, 36, 47–49, 51, 64, 79, 83–84, 99–100, 107, 137, 157, 173, 178, 185, 195
Hesiod, of Ascra, 4, 110
Hieronymus, of Cardia, 50–51, 66
Hippias, of Elis, 22
Hirtius, A., 182
Hirzel, Rudolf, 178
Historia (research): history's defining characteristic, 47; in Greece and Rome, 47–61; alters character, 56–57; mentioned, 30–31, 63, 99, 173
History: ancient definition of, 1, 3, 30, 37–38, 91, 98, 115–17; not a science, 2, 95, 137; patriotic, 20; contrasted with annals, 26–27; defining element of, 29–30; as war-monograph, 32; as *Hellenika*, 32–36; encomiastic, 35–36, 102–4; the first Roman writers of, 38–42; universal, 42–46; different orientation of Greeks and Romans in, 50–61; not disinterested, 52, 103–4; partisanship eschewed by Greeks and Romans in, 63, 68–70, 72, 99–100; subject of defined by Herodotus, 63; owes causal nature to Herodotus, 76–77; expla-

nation in, 76–90; use of environmental theory in, 82; objectivity of, 99–104; purposes of, 104–34; moral examples in, 106–8, 117–20; critical appraisals in, 108–9; paradigmatical, 109–20; rhetorical-artistic, 117–18; retributive, 118–19; pleasure of, 120–30; surprise in, 127–29; verisimilitude in, 134–37; theoretic of, 137–41; compared with poetry, 169–70; compared with oratory, 170–71; debt to drama, 171–72; utopian, 176–78; in the Renaissance, 194; in the sixteenth century, 194–95; transformed by modern science, 195–96; enhanced by modern methods, 196–97; scientific, 197, 199; subjectivity of, 197–99; utility of for moderns, 200
History, Latin: indebted to *Sikelika*, 38–40; ethnocentricity of, 41–42; distinguished from Greek history, 52–55; narrow historical viewpoint of, 53; facilitated by easy access to information, 56–57; disappearance of major works of, 67; monothematic, 67–68; primary concern of, 84–89
Homer, 8, 13, 31–32, 62–63, 76–77, 110–11, 165, 169, 171–72, 174
Horography. *See* Local history
Hypomnemata, 180–81

Iambulus, 177
Ion, of Chios, 178–80, 185
Isocrates, of Athens: supposed influence on Ephorus, 42, 109–10; rhetorical aims of, 110; on pleasure, 123; mentioned, 5, 21, 34, 112–14, 130, 148
Istrus, the Callimacheian, 190

Jacoby, Felix, 2–3, 7, 16–17, 20–21, 29, 36–38, 52, 111, 132, 164, 190
Jason, of Cyrene, 191
Jason, of Pherae, 34, 83
Josephus, of Judaea, 4
Juba, king of Mauretania, 191
Julian, emp. of Rome, 188–89
Julius Caesar, C., 57, 59, 179, 181–84
Junius Brutus, M., 191
Juvenal (D. Junius Juvenalis), 193

Ktiseis, 43n.

Index of Important Passages

Compositor:	G & S Typesetters, Inc.
Text:	Linotron 202 Goudy Old Style
Display:	Phototypositor Goudy Old Style
Printer:	Thomson-Shore, Inc.
Binder:	John H. Dekker & Sons